THE WORLD'S PRESS ON
THE ETERNAL MASQUERADE

ABERDEEN FREE PRESS.—This sprightly and vigorous book . . . the wit at times is mordant and bites deep, and a cynical touch is not awanting, but withal the book is very entertaining, as it reviews modes and materials, manners and morals.

ABERDEEN JOURNAL.— . . . Mr. Bradley is clever, decidedly, and not seldom original. There are no smooth, solemn platitudes about his writing. He says what he thinks, whether he be talking about Eve and her fig leaves or Queen Victoria and her bustle. . . . Others before him, and particularly his despised predecessor Carlyle, have traced the progress of fashion throughout history, but none so wittily and flippantly as does Mr. Bradley. . . . In flapper parlance, his sentiments on womankind are " priceless." . . . The unco guid may be shocked by sections of his book, and the dull and humourless bored, but the average reader will be consumedly amused.

ARTS GAZETTE.—Carlyle wrote history, and also a philosophy of clothes in " Sartor Resartus." Mr. Dennis Bradley, who has more inside knowledge of the latter subject than Carlyle ever possessed, has also written a book in which dress and history are profitably mingled. Mr. Bradley is perfectly fearless in expressing opinions whether of the past or the present, and that is the salient

iii

merit of his book. . . . Whichever way we look upon it, this is a most original and entertaining book.—J. T. GREIN.

BART'S BROADSHEET.—H. Dennis Bradley posssesses the gift of phrase. He writes with ease and brilliance. In fact, he is a man of genius. . . . He is a literary artist. . . . He is a man of letters. There can be no mistake about it. He possesses the genuine gift.—BART KENNEDY.

BIRMINGHAM POST.—Mr. Dennis Bradley is a bold man. He first depreciates Carlyle by saying that his philosophy was " sexless, drab, and sterile," and then, having as it were turned him out, audaciously proceeds to sit in the chair of the master, and to hold forth ostentatiously a sex-distinguishing discourse on clothes, or, as he calls it, a philosophy on a clothes-peg—perhaps, we might add, sometimes in the front garden and sometimes in the backyard.

THE BYSTANDER.—He succeeds in maintaining a continual fire of epigrammatic persiflage that ranges from the flimsy clothing of Eve to the costumed philosophy of the moderns. . . . A book full of the *mousse* of life and none of its mustiness.

CAMBRIDGE REVIEW.—An amazing cynical scamper through history, with many amusing excursions by the way.

THE CATHOLIC HERALD.—In his own scintillating style, Mr. Bradley has given us a refreshing record of the centuries.

THE CHERWELL (Oxford University).—His treatment of the Victorian age would make Dean Inge profane. . . . Mr. Bradley's epigrams are as pointed and the aphorisms as witty as his previous literary work would have led us to expect.

DAILY GRAPHIC.—Mr. Bradley is not nearly so dull as Carlyle. He has a way of explaining history through clothes which is entertaining, if only because of his heterodox opinions. Boadicea and Bonaparte come under his lash, while he

thinks a lot of King Charles, the so-called
"Martyr" Walpole, and Queen Victoria.—MR.
LONDON.

THE DAILY NEWS.—I have always been a sincere
admirer of the works of Mr. Dennis Bradley. . . .
I know very well, of course, what his critics
say. . . . They say that there is a good deal
of nonsense in Mr. Bradley's writings ; they say
that his roses are altogether too pink and his
raptures far, far too warm. . . . There is plenty
of good plain nonsense in other eminent writers—
in Shakespeare and in Rabelais and in Sterne,
for example. There is nothing more difficult to
write than good nonsense ; and Mr. Bradley's
nonsense seems to me to be both good and well
written. . . . It [" The Eternal Masquerade "] is
very impudent : but it is very clever. . . . A
dull person may be bored with it, and a good
many persons will be shocked at it : but on
the whole it is genuine post-war, and of a certain
value, like nearly all Mr. Bradley's work, because
it is genuine.—STUART HODGSON.

DORSET DAILY PRESS.—The book is packed from cover
to cover with epigram and aphorism, kept up by
unflagging verve until the last word. . . Few
writers hit folly as it flies with such accuracy of
aim, few books so echo with mocking laughter
before which dullness disappears and fools fly in
terror. The little historical vignettes with which
the book is scattered here and there are brilliant
pieces of work written with a pen dipped in
colour. . . . I cannot imagine a more amusing
companion for an empty hour, though for all
its brilliant lightness of touch, some profound
truths are enshrined within it, and it will often
prove the *point d'appui* of serious thought.—GUY
THORNE.

DUNDEE ADVERTISER.—The imprint of T. Werner
Laurie Ltd. has been associated with many
remarkable books, but with none so remarkable
in a new and bewilderingly brilliant way as " The
Eternal Masquerade." . . . Its singularity of
phrase, caustic wit, and extraordinary knowledge
. . . its analytical process applied to probing
human nature under its trappings, achieves as
much, if not more, than the titanic and reverberant
method of Carlyle.

THE ENGLISH REVIEW.—Clearly Mr. Dennis Bradley is an Irishman—which accounts for his disdain of Carlyle, a Scot, and of Cromwell, the Puritan, for Mr. Bradley's philosophy is joy, and in his pose of *Sartor redivivus* his *codpiece* is a strange arquebus. The book is divided into three portions : (1) Sartor sardonic, (2) historic, (3) modern, and in clothes Mr. Bradley knows some. But clothes are merely his cloak or wimple. His *motif* is life, the liberty of man, peace, a new order, and thus equipped he lashes out at history and historians, and pleads for a new order.

To say that his assertions are controversial is too mild ; they are futurist. He knocks down all the " pets " of tradition from " fat " Boadicea to Bonaparte, reviews the whole gamut of English history with a dictionary of generalisations. Then there are the epigrams. They literally " wind " one, and some of them are very good. He stumbles about, loves the word " beastly " ; he venerates King Charles, Walpole, and even Queen Victoria ; but he is a wise man about women. The book leaves one hot, gasping. Is it serious ? What does he mean ? Yes ! doubtless Mr. Bradley is serious, almost a missionary. The last chapter shows that (see what he says about finance). He feels, and, possessing great moral courage, he turns his wit and fury upon mankind, the herd, and the knaves who rule them, without stint.

There are some brilliant bits in this astonishingly dogmatic, emotional, unkempt historical review, and not a few deeply penetrating *apercus*. It is jolly good fun, anyway, unless one is an historian ; but, fortunately for Mr. Bradley, historians have no trade union. Here and there white passages of truth fascinate. Sometimes he hits the bull's eye with such a bang that the reader must fain smile. One can only say, " Go it, Mr. Bradley. Do it again."

We need this kind of mental shock. And many of his points are true enough, that about L.G.'s Bradburies being worth a Henry VIII debased sovereign, and that on Cromwell's Belfast Eton collars. What will Oxford and Cambridge say ?

THE EVENING STANDARD.—Mr. Dennis Bradley's " The Eternal Masquerade " is salted with his own philosophy. Sometimes one cannot help feeling that there is too much salt; some of his comments on fashions of the past and present are perhaps a little too tasty. . . . The trouble with Mr. Bradley's literary lingerie is that it has too many frills; it rather reminds us of the front row of a second-rate ballet. . . . What should Mr. Bradley know of the moral effect of baggy knees ?

GENTLEWOMAN.—The book is chiefly interesting for its flippant good sense, and the ironical cocksureness of an iconoclast who conceals the fury of a real reformer beneath a cloak of wit. . . . A clever and amusing contribution to a subject of perpetual interest.

GLASGOW BULLETIN.— . . . an enormous mass of epigrams and aphorisms treating on all subjects under the sun.

GLASGOW HERALD.—Carlyle stripped the clothes and trappings off society, but Mr. Bradley tears them off and does not seem to mind greatly whether he removes portions of the skin or not. . . . On every page are found epigrams and aphorisms, some very shrewd, some very funny, many very forced, and not a few merely fatuous. Mr. Bradley is the cynic and iconoclast *in excelsis*.

GLOUCESTER CHRONICLE.—Mr. Bradley demonstrates in no uncertain manner his skill as an apophthegmatist. . . . It is a book which grips one's interest throughout the gamut of its pages. . . . To those who have not made too deep a study of the historical past Mr. Bradley presents a new view point, and some of our most cherished ideals of dead monarchs are ruthlessly smashed. With each chapter a masterly survey of the period is given.

GRAPHIC.—Mr. H. Dennis Bradley has much facility in word-spinning and phrase-making and his new book, entitled " The Eternal Masquerade," is distinctly entertaining.

ILLUSTRATED SPORTING AND DRAMATIC.—I would advise you, to complete your enjoyment, a copy of that most original and entertaining book, " The Eternal Masquerade." . . . And in addition to the enjoyment of all its originality and wit, you will find this book a valuable history of dress throughout the ages.

IRISH TIMES.—Partly philosophical and partly historical, this great pageant at times assumes epic proportions. . . . Mr. Bradley's humour is sardonic, and his views on history are in opposition to those held by the majority ; but he has a clever way of emphasising his theories in such a way as to make it difficult to argue with him. He is a man of very distinct personality, which stamps every page of his book.

JOHN O' LONDON'S WEEKLY.—Mr. H. Dennis Bradley . . . is a philosopher and wit. In his new book the reflections on clothes are interspersed with well-pointed gibes at the rulers of men.

LADY.—Mr. Dennis Bradley has a keen eye for the world's foibles, and expresses his opinions courageously and with so much epigram that every page of his book is interesting. If ever an author deserved to be called original, Mr. Bradley does, for his thoughts are never clouded by other people's opinions.

LIGHT.—Mr. H. Dennis Bradley is a writer and thinker of great power and originality. Lately, while " dipping " into his best known book, " The Eternal Masquerade," we came on a number of passages characteristic of his thought. They are sufficiently vigorous and incisive. Fear, hypocrisy, dullness, illusion, formalism are amongst the things which he hates, and in dealing with these he uses his pen like a scalpel.

LIVERPOOL COURIER.—It is a flood of literary epigram poured over the clothes of men like the gentle rain from heaven. It is the history of fashion through the ages, adorned by quibble, quip, and quiddity. It is Carlyle rewritten by one who concentrates in himself the essence of the nineties and the quintessence of the Georgians. It is the cynic as satirist, finding in the art of dress food for his satire and excuse for his cynicism . . . to utter a panegyric on his prose or to frame an appreciation of its content would be simple. To select from his glittering pages a few phrases for quotation as a sample of his quality is difficult. It is to suffer the embarrassment of riches.

LLOYD'S WEEKLY NEWS.— . . . a survey of costume from the fig leaf down to Paquin gown is vastly entertaining and full of information. Mr. Bradley knows his subject, has a nice, sharp sense of humour, and interlards his discourse with shrewd comments on the Courts and Commons of several epochs. Mr. Bradley has a lofty purpose of his own, not unconcerned with the setting right of the world !

LONDON MAIL.—Mr. Bradley is a philosopher who does not know how to be dull, and he has many things to say about clothes—mental and material . . . He takes us back to the days before the Romans came over to stay, and he whisks us through the centuries very pleasantly, giving us countless epigrams for entertainment during the journey. . . . This is a book you must read.

NEWCASTLE CHRONICLE.—Mr. Bradley is a thinker. He entertains little respect for conventions, and handles them roughly. He often smashes them to pieces and smiles sardonically at his destruction.

NOTTINGHAM GUARDIAN.—This daring book carries us through the centuries at break-neck speed on a flood of literary epigram and sardonic humour. It is a brilliant summary of English history. He has a dashing, picturesque way with him, and is highly diverting in his unexpectedness of expression, to say nothing of his originality of idea. He enjoys his own humour too, and throws his flamboyant phrases at his reader with evident anticipation of being rewarded with a smile. It is an iconoclastic book, and shatters the treasured traditions of the past.

PENARTH NEWS.— . . . a book that will help any man to find himself. Mr. Dennis Bradley knows how to bare the souls of man, and to make most of us feel that our own plans of existence can be improved upon in most cases very considerably. . . . If everybody could read this book the strength of our Empire would be trebled.

PLAY PICTORIAL.—Carlyle wrote " Sartor Resartus," and Mr. Dennis Bradley, with a wider and more intimate knowledge of clothes, treats of clothes and the man from the days of the Druids to the post-war apology for the " dressy " man. Reign by reign, from William I, he moralises on the fashions of the time, and their bearing on the morals of the period, and his deductions are as humorously pungent as they are historically correct.

ROCHDALE OBSERVER.—He is full of wit and mockery. . . . " The Eternal Masquerade " is astonishing, overwhelming. . . . His style is brisk and brilliant ; his work is full of epigrams. He leaves us breathless.

THE SCOTSMAN.—There is in " The Eternal Masquerade " a brilliant summary of English history, illustrated and enforced by a study of the costume of each period, remarkable alike for the evidence it gives of a careful study of the development of dress from the earliest times to the present day, and a knowledge of history which is both extensive and peculiar. Though his estimates of personal values may be erratic, he is generally humorous and entertaining. . . . His appreciation of modern female costume is both appropriate and reasonable and may be heartily commended to some of those critics who regard it as a device of the Evil One.

SKETCH.—Mr. Dennis Bradley is well known as a witty and trenchant writer. His first book, " Not for Fools," made a considerable stir, and his new volume, " The Eternal Masquerade," is a brilliantly written, epigrammatic book, as full of entertainment as of information.

SOUTHPORT GUARDIAN.—Mr. Bradley has a puckish wit, independence of thought and judgment, and frankness of expression. . . . It is all very frank, very unhistorical, and very clever ; sometimes naughtily clever, but never boring.

SPORTING TIMES.— . . . a remarkable achievement of that thoughtful writer, Mr. H. Dennis Bradley. The work is intensely provocative, as the writer is utterly fearless in his estimate of kings and queens, stately beauties, alluring courtesans, Crichtons and clowns.

THE SUNDAY TIMES.— . . . a pungent, individual, go-as-you-please criticism on human life and human problems. . . . Mr. Bradley is one of those writers who, as Charles Reade puts it, " write in red ink and with the biceps muscle." . . . One may dissent from his views—a good many people will dissent very strongly on many points—but nobody can be for one moment in doubt as to what Mr. Bradley means to say, or as to his own belief in the justice of his views.

SURREY COMET.—We have not seen a book recently which contains so many daring challenges of the conventional in thought and habit. It is a volume one might read paragraph by paragraph to a friendly circle or a large crowd, and every sentence would lead to endless debate.

SUSSEX DAILY NEWS.—This is a book of wholesome plainness of speech. It is almost always wise, and almost always cleverly entertaining.

TATLER.—The success of " The Eternal Masquerade " is assured by reason of its scholarly treatment of the subject of clothes and the man. . . . Mr. Bradley is no mean master of literature. . . . There is not a dull page from cover to cover.

THE TIMES.— . . . he calls a bustle a bustle, and other things by their names, with embarrassing frankness. All we can say is that he praises woman's dress, as worn at the moment, with the generosity of understanding. *Tout comprendre c'est tout pardonner ;* and Mr. Bradley comprehends so much that there is nothing left to pardon.

THE TIMES LITERARY SUPPLEMENT.—It is the Latin who knows woman supremely well and admires her the more for it, but Mr. Bradley knows what she wears and why, and discusses the subject with a Latin grace. Every woman should read this gay review of modes, materials, and morals. Mr. Bradley has theories of his own on questions other than clothes, of course ; he writes of love and socialism, government and art, war and liberty, and fires off epigrams and jokes and paradoxes in the generous spirit of the showman who is determined to keep things lively, or of the chef who knows that he can throw almost anything into the stock-pot, even scraps off the plate. It is all very entertaining and sprightly.

TRUTH.— . . . sententiously amusing book. . . . There is a good deal in Mr. Bradley's idea that one of the main objects of wearing clothes is the concealment of ugliness, especially in later life, and one cannot but agree with him that a company of elderly business men in *puris naturalibus* would be a far from beautiful spectacle. . . . There are many . . . interesting things in this suggestive and entertaining book.

WESTERN MAIL.—Mordant wit and complete freedom from conventional restraint give rare spice to Mr. Bradley's analysis of the motives and tendencies of modern civilisation. Tradition for its own sake is laughed at, and politicians and their methods are made the subject of the most caustic comments to be found in all the brilliant pages ; but indignation can hardly fail to be assuaged by the sheer cleverness of the author's display of intellectual gymnastics. . . . In just the same way does the author's delicate but piercing style stimulate thought in his readers. Not wantonly, however, does Mr. Bradley tear off the mask in his attempt to find the truth, for the earnestness of his endeavour is expressed in such lines as these : " Power is a curse ; the most evil weapon that man can annex." . . . It is the method and literary appeal of " The Eternal Masquerade " that will attract most readers. . . . Truly, it is the virile expression of a deeply thoughtful mind.

FOREIGN AND COLONIAL PRESS

THE AGE (Melbourne).—The writing is vivacious . . . a book in many respects clever and worth reading for the sake of its historical annotations.

ANOKA HERALD.—It is somewhat difficult to determine exactly the nature of the task which Mr. Dennis Bradley has set himself. . . . As one proceeds from page to page one guesses that the book is a vehicle for a weird and impudent philosophy, a book of idly spun aphorisms, a critique on human morals, a melting pot of strange ideas. . . .

ATLANTA GA-JOURNAL. . . . Though written in an attractively flippant style, it is, nevertheless, a serious work. . . . An ardent foe to all shams and artificiality, Mr. Bradley's keen satire lays bare the hypocrisies of the Cromwellian era when the Puritan influence abolished all laces, ruffles and vivid colours and sponsored drab, ugly clothes and manners to match. . . . The characters of the various reigning monarchs of England and of their courts are vividly drawn and with a satiric and epigrammatic touch that is very effective.

BALTIMORE NEWS.— . . . a delightful literary surprise . . . the work is indeed a complete historical sketch of England from the Conqueror down. . . . Mr. Bradley handles his subject with a charmingly light touch. He is never tiresome nor " heavy " in the slightest degree. On the other hand, he has a keen sense of humour and if he philosophises, it is not in the dull manner of the platitudinarian.

BALTIMORE SUN.— . . . an unusual and uncommon book.

BOOKMAN (New York).—A unique volume. . . . The author writes with more than modern frankness and a daring sense of humour, so that considerable excitement might be derived from reading certain chapters aloud to a maiden aunt.

BOOKSELLER (New York City).—This remarkable book . . . a "Sartor Resartus" in a lighter vein— with a satiric and amazing history of England. The author is blessed with a knowledge of the lively personal details that make history readable, and with a fine sense of humour.

BOSTON EVENING TRANSCRIPT.—Mr. Bradley strips society of its conventional attire and exposes its nude instincts, impulses, and politics.

BOSTON TRANSCRIPT.— . . . All scolds are privileged when they are fanciful and witty, and Mr. Bradley's whimsicality is all his own.

BRISBANE COURIER (Queensland).—Mr. Dennis Bradley has proved himself to be a man full of epigrams and mocking elfin laughter. In "The Eternal Masquerade" he tears with devastating effect through the show and hypocrisy of the different ages. In a very remarkable manner he shows that the character of an age is mirrored in its clothes ; and so he gives us a review of English history by parading before us in all their trappings as miscellaneous a company as ever marched together in the pages of a book. . . . Mr. Bradley hits off the character of the time with epigram, sometimes caustic in its sting and sometimes illuminating in its sweep. It is a very clever book.

CHICAGO POST.—There are few readers of Carlyle's "Sartor Restarus" who haven't suspected that the clothes philosophy should not have been allowed to drop just there. . . . In "The Eternal Masquerade" the author has done no less than go back to the moment when Julius Cæsar stood on the cliffs of Gaul looking toward England, and from that moment down to our own has traced the philosophy of clothes as affecting the rule of each and every English king. . . . The book is diverting. . . . That it is a capital way to hit off English history and make it stick in the slipperiest memory is also evident. For pure information on the subject of costume so described that pictures would be *de trop*, it leaves nothing to be desired.

CLEVELAND PLAIN DEALER.— . . . It is satire . . . it is humour ; it is a brilliant and pungent commentary on the foibles of mankind. The author is not without his prejudices, political and artistic ; and this fact is responsible for much of his impudent cleverness. It is a delightful book and worth anybody's attention.

CLEVELAND PRESS.— . . . The book is written with a claim on liberty, an ache for truth, a hatred of oppression and a resentment of bunk that is characteristic of much post-war writing in England, which seems likely to upset most readers in the United States. . . . The book is written with a degree of emotion that commonly is associated with the feminine manner of speaking one's mind. Is is indignant, occasionally brilliant. . . . But certainly it is stimulating, whether the author is raging against politicians or sticking to his main subject.

DETROIT NEWS.— . . . an epigrammatic history of England . . . the whole gaily besprinkled with philosophic dicta on statesmanship, manners and morals. Regarded as an historian Bradley is always the ironist who delights in reversing conventional doctrines about which of the English monarchs were good and why. . . . The author's style is graphic though occasionally forced, his opinions are glittering if not always profound, and he is full of a puckery Carlylean humour. The oddity and picturesqueness of all he says make a book that, once read, the reader will take care forever after to keep close at hand.

EL PASO TIMES (Texas).—A review of British history in the light of ironic truth—exceedingly brilliant, savagely critical and sometimes wandering from the point. Mr. Bradley is confessedly interested in the creation of a world " fit for an artist to live in." From this he quite naturally arrives at a devout, almost slavish, worship of woman . . . he dilates brilliantly upon religion, militarism, politics, world comities and the future of irony. . . . The best of the book is in its aphorisms. Who gives a hang whether a man's philosophy at all points hooks together (like a Victorian frock) when he can thus dispose of Thomas Carlyle ?

JOHANNESBURG STAR.— . . . It is a dazzling compilation of epigrammatic persiflage, illuminating philosophy, brilliant historical vignettes, iconoclastic daring, facile word spinning, rude gibes and pungent moralisings.

JOHANNESBURG STAR.—Mr. Bradley writes his way through a barbed-wire enclosure of epigrams, witticisms, aphorisms, anachronisms, farthingales, acrimony, panniers, bravado, wigs, silk waistcoats, and all the other trappings of beaux and belles to the goal of his hopes, which is summed up in the making of a world " fit for artists to breathe in."

THE MORNING TELEGRAPH (New York).—He revels in the foibles of our powder and patches, our wigs and hats, our panniers and hoops and bustles, our tight-laced waists, our pushed out busts, and, finally, our up-and-down figures to-day. He writes of our frivolities with an ecstasy I am sure he does not quite realise. His humour is pungent, but we know he adores us in " The Eternal Masquerade," which is his " Sartor Sardonicus."—MARION RYAN.

NATAL ADVERTISER (Durban).—London's newest literary discovery. . . . The success of " The Eternal Masquerade " will come as no great surprise to the many who have known its author as raconteur and wit.

NATAL MERCURY.—Mr. Bradley gives full vent to his satiric humour. . . . Altogether it is a fascinating book.

NEWARK EVENING NEWS:— . . . unlike Carlyle, this newer author is impudent and cynical ; his thought is at all times clear. . . . He is as full of epigrams as a plum pudding of raisins. . . . He saunters down the pageant of English history, he makes many pungent remarks and presents his own reconstruction of well-known figures, not always in conventional fashion.

NEW YORK EVENING POST.— . . . his introduction of matter utterly extraneous to his text cannot but come with a shock to his readers. His book, except for its pacifist propaganda, is a saucy, delightful, and, assumedly, authoritative account of the development of the fig leaf into the habiliments of to-day. . . . Epigrammatic, impudent and instructive, despite its anti-war explosion.

NEW YORK HERALD.— . . . penetrate the external mantle of things, and you will find a truth vastly different from the truth that seems to be—such is the fundamental thesis that Mr. Bradley undertakes to expound. . . . Obviously such a theme lends itself readily to satire ; and satire, as it happens, is of the very fibre of Mr. Bradley's work. His style is crisp and tart ; his sentences are highly seasoned for one who prefers truth to cleverness. For while at times the author is passionately serious, he is more than once guilty of that wit which defeats its own purpose because of its manifest self-consciousness. On the whole, however, he contrives to interest if not to amuse the reader ; he successfully employs satire as a transparent drapery for his thoughts.

NEW YORK TELEGRAPH.— . . . Mr. Bradley has written a book which contains a great deal of information and interest. His attention is principally devoted to woman. And though he turns rather materialistic eyes towards her, with his thoughts directed towards her clothes and body rather than her mind, he voices ideas which are decidedly worth reading. With it he has given us a survey of history—largely sartorial of course—which will inspire those who have rather forgotten the lessons of their youth with a new interest in the subject. Mr. Bradley is a clever writer, and if you do not insist on agreeing with all the sentiments expressed by an author you should enjoy his latest book.

NEW YORK TIMES.— . . . is always sprightly and epigrammatic in style, always satiric in tendency, philosophic in outlook, crisp and pleasing in manner. In many places he has recourse to witty paradoxes, and one doubts the seriousness of his purpose ; yet when he launches into a discussion of a subject such as militarism he is bitterly and ironically serious. . . . The book abounds in sparkling passages calculated either to dazzle or to annoy the reader. " The Eternal Masquerade " is both interesting and original.

NEW YORK WORLD.— . . . we are vastly entertained by his erotic, pungent wit and his satirical erudition. . . . Mr. Bradley never discusses the ladies without a preliminary snicker or two before arriving at the crux of the anecdote ; and yet he knows them so well that one becomes as eager as a sophomore to hear more about this entertaining sex. . . . He lets fall upon the reader's ear the sort of epigrammatic lore which studs the pages of Mr. Mencken's " Smart Set." . . . This avidly written book catches our fancy as a piece of entertaining popycock, written by a Petronius so vastly pleased with his own conceptions that he charms us into believing himself to be a first-class sartorial wit.

OKLAHOMA CITY NEWS.—It is " Sartor Resartus " brought down to date, for here we find some of the same irony, sarcasm, prophetic insight and great teaching purpose of Carlyle. . . . For the people who get the point that this human world with all its masks, are just so much clothing in which we either hide or reveal the mind, soul or spirit within will find this a very suggestive and helpful book.

OTAGO DAILY TIMES.—Mr. Bradley has acquired the habit of the epigram—it was admirably displayed in a previous volume from his pen. . . and the present book exhibits both the strength and weakness of the epigrammatic style. Not once but many times Mr. Bradley overstates his case for the sake of achieving an epigram, and occasionally he sacrifices sense to smartness. . . . He paints a fascinating picture of the women of to-day.

QUEENSLANDER (Brisbane).— . . . It impresses one at once because of its scintillating wit, its cynical brilliance, and its merciless exposure of human instincts and impulses . . . a clever criticism of human life during the different ages . . . a remarkable summary of English history, not of its social and industrial progress, but of its intellect. He is fearless in his criticism, just as fearless as was Carlyle in his " Sartor Resartus," and he has the advantage over Carlyle inasmuch as he knows more about that particular subject than did the great sage of Chelsea.

RICHMOND DISPATCH.— . . . In the elaboration of his thesis, Mr. Bradley has prepared a volume which displays a varying philosophy, a keen vein of humour and a marked brilliancy of style. . . . This work is a real little gem of writing. . . . It will undoubtedly have a permanent value.

RICHMOND NEWS LEADER.— . . . A history of England told in an impudently personal style. The first section is an introductory string of aphorisms designed to tear away the philosophy embraced in " Sartor Resartus " by Thomas Carlyle. . . . The second section is a meteoric history of England. . . . The third is a collection of conclusions similar to those of Norman Angel, Bertrand Russell, Bernard Shaw and other modern philosophers. . . . The pageant is a beautiful one, even though it may shock some of its beholders. A close-up view of modes and morals may be shocking but very true.

SALTLAKE CITY TELEGRAM.— . . . clever but impudent . . . is at one and the same time shocking, entertaining, and informative. . . . Whether you read for pleasure or profit, you'll find " The Eternal Masquerade " to your liking. It is a book that is charmingly and distinctly different.

SAN FRANCISCO BULLETIN.— . . . There is no masquerade about H. Dennis Bradley. He begins as La Farge would have suggested, at the beginning, walks down the avenue of the centuries and with his bit of blackthorn cracks heads right and left.

. . . He's an impudent, imprudent iconoclast. He smashes idols right and left. He even whacks Christianity, declaring that it toppled like a house of cards in the World War when the God of the Churches took a vacation, contemptuous of the wreck of civilisation. . . . This is a valuable book. It is a contribution to history. . . . It is fine reading and amusing, even in its sharpest criticisms.

SAN FRANCISCO CHRONICLE.— . . it is a view of history, politics, war economics, æsthetics and sex, as reflected or symbolised in the idea that one is no more likely to find the naked truth walking abroad in the world than unclad bodies. . . . If ever there was a book which contained a little bit of everything, this is it . . . it is diverting to dip here and there for anecdote or aphorism or forgotten scrap of social history.

SATURDAY NIGHT (Toronto).—Wit as pungent as this excuses all the author's prejudices. As a follower of William Congreve, Mr. Bradley has evolved a style, and dares to voice a philosophy, which definitely proclaims the arrival of the Georgian. " The Eternal Masquerade " is one long, studied insult to the cherished traditions of the past generation. Not only is his work Georgian in thought, but it takes form naturally in a quality of satire which has been absent from the world since the virile days of Rabelais and of Voltaire.

The nineteenth century fed on Lamb—tender Lamb. Gentle and urbane its writers were, and if they must speak of unpleasant things they made them appear pleasant. The century ended in the deification of Robert Louis Stevenson, who never uttered a resonant oath or a sincere prayer. The unleashing of the tongue is quite the mark of our time. If the new men are all going to be as hilariously funny as Mr. Bradley, we can well put up with their brusqueness. With its terse and vigorous diction and an irony that attains at times a Voltairian pointedness, " The Eternal Masquerade " is the treat of the summer. . . .

After the first shock of astonishment, the reader notes the pithiness of phrase, the subtlety of innuendo, and the unerring aim. The skill and audacity of the performance can, at the last, elicit but one response—torrential laughter.

The young iconoclast will take the book to his heart ; the reactionary will spew it out. All parties should bear in mind that this is a great opportunity to test their sense of humour. Let its cleverness and brilliancy cloak what philosophy it will, " The Eternal Masquerade " has achieved a triumph of the kind that we most need to-day —a riot of boisterous laughter with its assurance of man's eternal resiliency.

SPRINGFIELD REPUBLICAN.— . . . Dennis Bradley is anything but a rubber stamp. His views of history are his own, sometimes orthodox according to accepted traditions, but quite as often not. Lese-majesty does not trouble him a little bit, since all the rulers are dead whose reigns and characters he epitomises. . . . One gets much entertainment from the display under the jesting talk of the showman who is a philosopher as well, albeit a member of the school in which Diogenes flourished.

THE SPUR (New York).—Mr. Bradley has a Puckish wit as well as a keenly observant mind which is capable of clear perspective. Always wittily, and always instructively, the reader is led through the maze of history . . . where Carlyle was heavy, he is light and graceful. He has a rare gift of witty epigram, and even an impudence which earns its own forgiveness. Perhaps that explains why he has not needed an Emerson to introduce him to an American audience.

ST. LOUIS GLOBE.—Like many other writers of the present day Mr. Bradley has a firm aversion to all trite and platitudinous thinking. He is iconoclastic in his treatment of the vagaries and caprices of the English people throughout the ages, and very few illusions escape unshattered —especially those which have tended to make life drab and colourless. . . . Undoubtedly this book will fall into the hands of some who will be shocked at it, and call it immoral. But it is nothing of the sort, and may be read with perfect impunity by the most ethical of readers. In fact, the more dogmatic element could derive a good deal of good from it.

ST. LOUIS POST DISPATCH.—Like Cæsar's, so this writer's (even more colossal) Gaul is divided into three parts . . . a fetching and impudent book on the manners, morals and dress of society. . . . The main strain of this book is neither satiric nor historical, but ethical; the newest "Sartor Restarus" pleads against war on the conviction that war in its design means the loss of all freedom for both victor and vanquished, and that the call for "a war for freedom" is the transparent lie of a call to accept new bonds of slavery.

SYRACUSE POST STANDARD.— . . . What an admirable title it is. . . . He sees character in clothes, and sardonic humour and historical humour; and he recites what he finds with the acid contempt of a historian disillusioned and disgusted. . . . He traces history and clothes in their mutual influences throughout the reigns of English monarchs with a sprightly and biting wit, which is never dull, often sparkling, and always impudent.

TRENTON TIMES.—Mr. Dennis Bradley presents a unique study of raiment from Eve's fig leaf down to the period when woman has pretty nearly returned to her original nakedness. Mr. Bradley dwells like an artist upon each era's development . . . a fetching and impudent book. . . . Still, Mr. Bradley is clever enough not to violate the conventions of polite speech.

VANCOUVER SUN.—Mr. Dennis Bradley has written a book which I shall place on my bookshelf with Carlyle's "Sartor Resartus," Planches' "History of Costume" and Mrs. Palliser's "Old Lace."

I have read many histories of England—including Gilbert A. Beckett's "Comic History of England"—a delightful book, but not half so comic as this "History of England" as told by costume.

The words of Puck, "What fools these mortals be," is the comment which embraces a complete review.

VOGUE (New York).—To the Sage of Chelsea he pays the scantest courtesy, and he is the gayer if not the profounder philosopher. His method is not to strip humanity of its bright raiment and find inanity beneath. . . . With a light hand he reviews the pageant of history, reign by reign, synthesing political action with sartorial art.

First Published . . . June 1922
Second Printing . . . October 1922
Third Printing . . . November 1922
Fourth Printing . . . December 1922
Fifth Printing . . . February 1923
Sixth Printing . . . April 1923
Seventh Printing . . . September 1923
Eighth Printing . . . October 1923
Ninth Printing . . . November 1923

THE ETERNAL MASQUERADE

BY
H. DENNIS BRADLEY

AUTHOR OF
" NOT FOR FOOLS "

FIFTY-FIRST THOUSAND

LONDON
T. WERNER LAURIE, LTD.
30 NEW BRIDGE STREET, E.C.4
1923

This book is dedicated to my great and greater grandsons

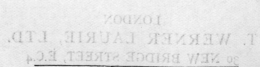

Made and Printed in Great Britain. Wyman & Sons Ltd., London, Reading and Fakenham

THE ETERNAL MASQUERADE

THE ETERNAL MASQUERADE

CONTENTS

BOOK I.—SARTOR SARDONICUS

CHAPTER V

AFFILIATED APHORISMS

CHAPTER VI

THE DECORATED PILGRIMAGE

BOOK II.—SARTOR HISTORICUS

CHAPTER I

CLIO IN COSTUME

CHAPTER II

THE FRENCH KINGS

CHAPTER III

WILLIAM I (1066-1087)

CHAPTER IV

WILLIAM II (1087-1100)

CHAPTER V

HENRY I (1100-1135)

CHAPTER VI

STEPHEN (1135-1154)

CHAPTER VII

HENRY II (1154-1189)

CHAPTER VIII

RICHARD I (1189-1199)

CONTENTS

CHAPTER IX

JOHN (1199-1216)

CHAPTER X

HENRY III (1216-1272)

CHAPTER XI

EDWARD I (1272-1307)

CHAPTER XII

EDWARD II (1307-1327)

CHAPTER XIII

EDWARD III (1327-1377)

CHAPTER XIV

RICHARD II. (1377-1399)

CHAPTER XV

HENRY IV (1399-1413)

CHAPTER XVI

HENRY V (1413-1422)

CHAPTER XVII

HENRY VI (1422-1461)

CHAPTER XVIII

EDWARD IV (1461-1483)

B

CHAPTER XIX

EDWARD V (1483)

CHAPTER XX

RICHARD III (1483-1485)

CHAPTER XXI

HENRY VII (1485-1509)

CHAPTER XXII

HENRY VIII (1509-1547)

CHAPTER XXIII

EDWARD VI (1547-1553)

CHAPTER XXIX
CHARLES II (1660-1685)

CHAPTER XXX
JAMES II (1685-1689)

CHAPTER XXXI
WILLIAM III AND MARY (1689-1702)

CHAPTER XXXII
ANNE (1702-1714)

CHAPTER XXXIII
GEORGE I (1714-1727)

CONTENTS

CONTENTS

CHAPTER XLII

THE VICTORIAN WOMAN

CHAPTER XLIII

EDWARD VII (1901-1910)

BOOK III.—SARTOR MODERNUS

CHAPTER I

THE MODERN LOOKING-GLASS

CHAPTER II

WHITHER MEN MAY WANDER

CHAPTER III

HAIL! WOMAN FULL OF GRACE

CONTENTS

CHAPTER IV

THE FUTURISTIC VISION

AN APPRECIATION

By Caradoc Evans

AM staggered and amazed at "The Eternal Masquerade." Nor am I alone in my amazement, for no recent work has been noticed so widely or at such length by the Press.

Newspapers of divers opinions have discussed it, each discoursing upon this or that text. Dealing with the quality of Mr. Dennis Bradley's humour, Mr. Stuart Hodgson, the editor of *The Daily News*, speaks of "other eminent writers—Shakespeare, Rabelais, and Sterne." *The Times* finds this book embarrassingly frank, and Marion Ryan in the New York *Morning Telegraph* rejoices that her sex is adorned in it. A Toronto critic admires its Voltairian pointedness and Mr. Guy Thorne its brilliant lightness of touch; it leaves *The English Review* hot and gasping, and Mr. London of *The Daily Graphic* finds that Mr. Bradley is not nearly as dull as Carlyle. And so on. To say the truth "The Eternal Masquerade" is like the Bible—full of texts; and because of that—though it is the most daring book I have read—I would like to place it in the hands of every man and woman between the ages of sixteen and thirty.

What impresses me chiefly about it is the author's knowledge of woman. Mr. Bradley knows her more completely than any living writer. He discovers the reason for each of her garments, her powder puff and perfume, and what not, and then strips her of her external decencies and probes her motives. I fancy I understand what meant the woman who said of " The Eternal Masquerade " : "It is so impudently intimate that I have made it my bed book."

I have now a puzzling question to ask ; it is this : Why does not anyone stand up for Carlyle, whose observations in " Sartor Resartus " to Mr. Bradley are as funny as the bustles and bell-bottom trousers of the Victorians ? Is Carlyle indeed dead ? The author of " The Eternal Masquerade " deals with him jocosely and brutally, and yet not a tear has been shed for the Chelsea Scotsman.

There is no food here for the squeamish or for fools, nor for the literary censors of our country : policemen, watch committees, preachers. I would no more expect to see it in a policeman's office or a preacher's study than I would on the antique table under Cromwell's picture in 10, Downing Street. If our politicians were capable of studying anything other than the arts of cheating and swindling, I would ask them to study the last chapter in " The Eternal Masquerade." But if they did they might put Mr. Bradley in prison. Beyond saying that it is therefore well they remain in the niches in which it pleased God to put them, I shall very wisely not enter farther into this matter.

June, 1922.

I am very glad that I wrote the above, for newspapers in our Dominions, the United States of America, and in other parts of the world have justified my opinion of " The Eternal Masquerade." To speak all in a few words, it seems to me that this much may be said of it : " It took the world by storm."

CARADOC EVANS.

July 27, 1923.

BOOK I
SARTOR SARDONICUS

CHAPTER I

ORNAMENTAL PHILOSOPHY

Why this philosophy is hung on a clothes-peg—Delicate Garden
of Eden myth—Unashamed Eve and blushing Adam—
Fig-leaf symbol of rediscovery—Woman's clothes as means
of repairing man shortage.

THE philosopher can hang his discourse, or himself,
on any chosen peg. But in his economy of effort he
is likely to choose the nearest at hand. Which is
why this philosophy is hung on a clothes-peg.

Before you, therefore, is a new vision of the
perennial masquerade. A philosophy wrapped in
subtle humour and decorated here and there with
ironic laughter. A review of the fantasy of life and
the farce of history—an appreciation of the force of
attraction and a condemnation of the force of
destruction.

It is no acceptance of the inevitable, or surrender
to obvious suggestion thrust upon one by literary
critics. It is no resignation to fate.

All of us are placed in some miserably prescribed
niche in life, and the world endeavours to keep us
there. And the world, which means the majority of
fools, is resentful if we endeavour to escape from it or
even decorate or enlarge it. The world regards that
niche as all-sufficing if the stomach is filled and if it
provides warmth and shelter. Any excursion from
it is rebellion.

But the artist has divine discontent. He tears
down the walls of his niche and makes a cavern, and
in his restlessness creates an abyss, on the edge of
which he scents adventure.

May be that the literary niche in which the
philosophy of *The Eternal Masquerade* is confined
appears narrow. But the revelry and devilry
eternally associated with clothes have cut such

freakish capers throughout the ages that on occasions one has been driven to rest nakedly in one's intellectual bath.

After a refreshing pause, one has again become allured. Our civilisation is too crude to remain undraped.

If our eyes were really opened, if the scales of blindness with which we are all afflicted were removed, if the mask of clothes was a transparent one, if all things were as translucent as they are transient : what should we see ? We should only see to the extent of our imagination ! The artist would see beauty ; others merely the crude reflection of their own eyes. The philosopher sees beyond— into the cavity of mind and the recess of purpose.

All things are clothed. Clothes should be the beautiful mask. The language of a poet must be decked with beauty. The words of the philosopher must be clothed in wisdom. The canvas of the artist must be coloured with illusion. The designs of woman must be wrapped in allurement. The principles of politicians must be disguised in lying metaphor.

Life stripped of its illusions would be a sexless existence, but the exposure of false ideals would lead to a new virility.

Let us take two sweeping glances at to-day and at the long-forgotten past. To-day the most popular mantle of man—voluminous, enveloping almost the whole world of mankind—is the cloak of hypocrisy. In the dim days of his origin man was a primitive beast clad in honest hair, and physically as ugly as the majority are mentally ugly to-day. In neither type could art exist.

Savagery is still the primitive force of all things, even in literature ; in which criticism a personal laughter is contained.

Every custom has its beginning. Take the beginning of clothes.

There is the delicate Garden of Eden myth, which at least inspires scenic effect, with the unashamed

Eve and the blushing Adam. Adam with his adolescent mind carelessly gambolling, and Eve with her subtle purpose deliberately gambling. And after their tasting of the fruit of life and suffering from the inevitable satiety of inexperience, is it not logical to assume that Eve, with the inventiveness of woman, sought disguise as a fresh allurement ?

Hence the fig leaf, the symbol of rediscovery.

The myth is more pleasing than the reality. A beautiful lie is more attractive than a troublesome truth.

But in philosophy ugliness demands its innings. Through the ages there has been hostility between the scientist and the artist, which is a lack of understanding, thwarted by the duenna of tradition. Now the era of the chaperon is ended, and the eventual union of these two antithetical forces will result in the begetting of a new world.

Consider man in his origin—the primitive man as scientists have revealed him.

One would prefer to accept the illusion of the Garden of Eden to the truth of the earliest known human remains, the Piltdown skull. That again is mere evasion, due to artistic conceit.

The scientists have reconstructed the primitive man for us. He was something like a gorilla. He possessed a low forehead, from which we have developed our modern high-brows. He had huge jaws and was hairy.

This is significant. Darwin, living in the whiskered age of Victoria, gazed at his fellow-men and ruminated, and then conceived his " Origin of Species." The thought was father to work. Looking about him he must have wondered whence came these men ! And studying their tendencies and modes and manners, his deduction was simplified.

And Darwin's theory found a considerable acceptance. For each man, studying his hairy neighbour, could not fail to be ocularly convinced of the argument, even though he regarded himself as a supernatural exception.

Despite our lonely conceit, we moderns who will be ancients to-morrow, must accept the scientists, though they offend our imagination with their materialism and asphyxiate us with their poison-gas on the battlefield.

Whether we have improved mentally since our origin is a moot point. Anyway, man in his primitive state was, at least in physical appearance, devilishly ugly.

His artistic senses only began to live when he realised his ugliness.

So he clothed himself ; perhaps not for warmth, since he had fur, but to hide his ugliness. Hence, we are entitled to assume that the covering of his body was man's first attempt at art.

Woman, being essentially the artistic adapter where self and physical attraction are concerned, immediately became alive to the lure of garments in the development of her natural profession.

Having explored the possibilities of her body, she clothed herself and tempted man to provide for her. Then she annexed and wore his skins, but cultivated the art of wearing them in a different way.

Even before the process of evolution had succeeded in producing beauty, clothing as a concealment of ugliness had become a habit ; and later arose a tradition by which the bare idea of a bare body was assumed to offend man's religious and imperfectly developed æsthetic sense.

Therefore the Nonconformist's primitive view of decency, which is atavistic ; while the artist's eyes, seeking always the cultivation of beauty, are futuristic.

After man had emerged from his first crude attempts at art, aided by woman's artistry, together they eventually produced a new being.

The artist was born. His birth was delayed until the human form was fit for his acceptance. Untroubled by tradition and scornful of common habits, he saw that the nude, in certain instances, was beautiful. Hence the Greek sculptures.

He realised also that it was necessary for the great

majority of the wearers of the human body to hide their bodies. Fat old man and thick ankled women do not decorate the universe. So the artist was easily persuaded to appreciate the artistic value of clothes.

From the moment of her awakening, woman gripped the artistic ideal and understood the sex lure of clothes. Intuitively she adopted the principle of attraction, which is life and necessary to her mission as reproducer.

Man blundered on and hid himself in armour, being obsessed by the principle of fear, which is Death.

Despite the changes of time and the phases of fashion, these rules have obtained among men and women.

Understanding has not yet arrived, though it is nearer now than ever before. Woman subtly challenges with her assumption of right and produces life. Man, with his inverted sense, organises death for his own sex because he can conceive only imaginary wrong.

It is so that life exists only in the woman and in the artist, by which is meant not the painter of pictures or words, but a vague, incomprehensible, indefinite, unconfined protoplasm of thought, that is the extent of man's creative power. And in this union only are things worth while.

Yet even in a material sense clothes fill as big a part in the civilisation of the world as food.

It was never mere so-called decency that drove man to clothe himself any more than it was a mere desire to appease hunger that evolved *paté de foie gras*.

Again the touch of the artist—and the desire to please the opposite sex.

Woman's longing for prepared truffles may possibly have lifted us from the state of the pig who rooted for raw truffles.

Clothes and food are complementary—gorgeous raiment and delicate feasts. If not, why do we dress for the banquet?

Properly understood, the philosophy of clothes may compromise the whole philosophy of material existence ; beautiful raiment, woman, food and wine.

When man, tired of beauty, seeks a fresh emotion in destruction, woman strips herself to lure him back to creation.

That is no observation of a dreamer, but a fundamental fact based on history. In times of war, woman instinctively strips herself and adapts her fashions as a means to repair man shortage.

In this year of nineteen hundred and twenty-two both sexes are just recovering from the excess of their emotions. For man it is the mood of drabness. In colour he emulates the tentacled lobster, and only achieves his scarlet passion in the economic boiling pot.

Politically, he has not the faintest idea as to how he should dress himself up. Of mental clothes he is practically destitute, and his nakedness exhibits an alarming impotence.

But woman smiles. For if the good god Pan has for the moment lost his reeds, she can always amuse herself by dancing to the pipings of Poiret.

CHAPTER II

THE MASK OF ALLUREMENT

*Observations on Carlyle's gospel of eternal gloom—Carlyle
and the hat chaser—Woman dresses neither for decency
nor warmth ; she decks herself out in readiness for love
—Effect of her dress on a love-sick man.*

THE titillation of every emotion lies in the philosophy of
clothes. Woman knows this, and Thomas Carlyle did not.

Carlyle in his " Sartor Resartus " does not once
deal with woman. Which suggests that he was dealt
with once—and no more. His Teufelsdröckh once
hankered for a maiden, but she quickly passed him by ;
and he was debarred from exercising his philosophy.

Carlyle's sexless, drab, and sterile philosophy
(published in 1838) suited the mood of the early
Victorians. It heralded the age of ugliness. It is
an acceptance of the gospel of eternal gloom. Its
philosophy is adolescent and meekly evasive,
meandering on indefinitely and shrieking timidity.
The atmosphere is that of the sick-room, where the
end is approaching of one from whom there are no
expectations.

" Sartor Resartus " reeks of the religion of subjection. Carlyle is so frightened of God that every
moment one expects God to eat him up. The book
takes at least a fortnight to read if one is diligent,
and after two long weeks of Carlyle's fear of eternity
the only fear one is left with in life is another fortnight of Carlyle. How his God must have laughed
at him ; laughed in generosity, or otherwise to save
Himself from feeling insulted at His fear-stricken image.

It is pretty obvious why Carlyle dared not write
the philosophy of woman's disguise. Early in life
he was probably a " finished " man. One is left
with the impression, based on the sartorial history of
his generation, that chilly as was his mind his body

was chillier still ; and wearing the grey, woolly underclothes of the period he was naturally irritated by them. Moreover, living at the time he did, if he ever conceived an idea of woman's clothes or underclothes, he thought red—and then thought better of it.

An illuminating instance of Carlyle's generosity of spirit may be related. When walking over Chelsea Bridge one gusty morning in March, he happened to be wearing a hat that was a fraction too small for his head. An impudent wind suddenly caused his headgear to blow off, and a passing urchin started an exciting chase to retrieve it. Triumphantly handing it back, he was rewarded by Carlyle, not with base coin, but with the following priceless words : " Well done, my lad. Now you may say that you have held the hat of the great Thomas Carlyle." And the urchin, overcome by the honour, but painfully alive to the more grim necessities of existence, probably thenceforward abandoned the unremunerative career of hat-chasing as a means to sustenance.

Leap from Carlyle to woman, who possesses the superior subtlety of her own philosophy.

Men, as a rule, have no conscious philosophy of clothes and so are self-conscious in wearing them. Women possess a completely conscious philosophy of clothes and so possess the art of appearing to wear them unconsciously.

It is absurd to imagine that the clothes we wear or the clothes other people wear when in contact with us have no effect on our moods. Their effect is colossal and sometimes devastating. Women know this. Men know nothing, but are subconsciously affected. Man accepts destiny, woman accepts design.

Woman has no appreciation for her beauty when undraped. She knows too that beauty is seldom understood and that men soon become blind. Therefore she refines satiety and encourages variety.

She dresses neither for warmth nor decency. Decency, in its prostituted modern sense, does not appeal to her ; but ornament and decoration, which are her decoys, at all times find acceptance.

Men and women are created with legs set in the same place, but women are clever enough to realise the importance of clothing them differently.

In physical form there is very little difference between the sexes. Both are bi-sexual. Man is popularly supposed to be the physical sex hunter. But when one analyses modern dress it is obvious that woman employs every artificial means to stimulate and accentuate whatever differences there are.

It is well that it should be so, for stimulation is necessary to man. It is sex culture.

Not only do men and women have legs, but most of their anatomy is alike. Their mental and physical out-look are alike and they have appetites in common. The enormous artificial difference in dress is woman's subtlety. Its sole object is to attract. There is wisdom in her philosophy, for if she ceases to captivate man, humanity will end and art will perish.

Man does possess the instinct to decorate his body, but it is a self-conscious instinct. To woman, decoration has become her art. Yet the blushing nymph in her diaphanous georgette and the sober male in his funeral black are both descendant from the Aborignal Anthropophagus.

If with the fig leaf shame was born, has not shame, or its stimulation, added another emotion to mankind? For which shame must be accepted as a virtue, since without emotion man degenerates to the vegetable.

But shame in its prescribed acceptance is a sense, the meaning of which intelligent men and women do not deign to acknowledge. Shame, as popularly conceived, is in reality the label attached to emotion by the eternal negativists.

To attack the iniquities of parasitical governments, to question the virtue of imposed patriotism,—that is politically labelled shame. The ushering into the world of a beautiful and an innocent new life, and to cast it upon the world without the preliminary mumbling of a parish clerk, is called a woman's shame. The last is an amusing illustration of bureaucracy's attempted beggary of beauty.

It is hardly realised by the slothful that a mental revolution is at hand. The old dictates contain only a farcical value. Woman with her skirts cut to the knee is equipped to leap. She is realising ascendancy in new directions. Before this century none of us had flown. Man has conquered the air ; a significant achievement. Woman will exhibit her eternal response ; she will develop new mental flights and lure man back to earth. There is fortunately no escape until the centre of gravitation is altered.

This is woman's century. Only a few of us will have the power to control her. To imagine that she will be concerned because she omitted to pay the fees of legality to an unsanitary registrar would be sheer stupidity. Love does not celebrate under the presidency of a third party clothed in dirty linen.

Woman laughs at labels and discards Victorianism for victory. Confident in herself she would rather accept a bust than a bustle. She has watched a ghastly mass organised by man's shamefulness, and when men talk of woman's shame, she will retort by birth control.

Her position is beyond anything thought of in history. She is acknowledging her virility and strength, and without realising it she has the cards of the universe in her hands. Man's structure of civilisation has reached the breaking point. He has decayed from his aristocracy and sunk to a universal vulgarity of government. But there is always a saviour, and women are the mothers of men. If men do not see the folly of the ruthless destruction of their sex, women may take up the weapons of sex-war and cease to produce. They have the power, for are they not the producers of mankind ?

Why should they submit to the pains of labour for the splendid fruits thereof to be left as manure on battlefields ? It is a man speaking. If he were a woman he would refuse to bear another child until men had arrived at a new orientation.

The twentieth century will see an amazing readjustment of the balance of power between the sexes.

In the historical section of this book the student will observe that throughout the ages woman has accepted man-made dictates and was content just to display her marvellous capacity for adaptation. Beyond her eternal mission to allure man to produce, she played an insignificant part in the world's material scheme.

To-day she has annexed her freedom in all things. She is the world's free agent.

Her clothes are indicative of her mood. She expresses her individuality and revels in her self-confidence. She has ceased to adapt and commenced to originate. She is no longer controlled, even by fashion. Herd-like uniformity is anathema to her. She has a splendid disregard for the past and a healthy contempt for tradition. She has leapt from the anæmic pose of the Victorian era to an attitude of torrential proclamation. Her clothes are the symbolic decoration of her centrifugal force.

In the exhibition of her forcefulness, she has had the subtlety to add to her allurements. She has developed the art of the transparent mask, and is confident in her challenge.

In her dress she realises that the clothing of the body is a culture as important as the culture of the body itself. Romance and beauty depend upon it. She has learnt to shed the coarse layers of fat which came with maturity to the indolent woman of previous generations.

She is as virile at fifty as the nineteenth century Victorian was at thirty. Her physical energy is trained in every direction, and by her variations of sport she retains her youthfulness and defeats obesity of mind and figure. Her adornment is a compliment to sex, regarding which she retains no stultifying ideals or negative principles. Her concern is for an artistic draping to illusion. Her design is to deck herself out in readiness for love. Her garb is studied, consciously and subconsciously, to provoke man's emotions.

Love is the visualisation of one's own image of loveliness, whether physical or mental. But the imagination must be inspired to go on creating and re-creating. It must be decorated in a thousand different forms. If the being with whom one is in love is not moulded to the image one has conceived then the illusion is dispelled and love stagnates. Therefore woman's instinct to re-dress herself perpetually.

Consider the effect of woman's dress on a man in love. Unconsciously he is enormously affected by it. To him, the woman is adorned in angel's plumes. At her smile his mind becomes a volcanic eruption. But the beautiful apparition of the air, with eyes peering through the vista of centuries of knowledge and intuition, will mentally photogragh every detail of him, yea from the lace of his shoe to his butterfly bow.

Bring the man down from the ethereal clouds and translate him in the words of earth, what are his emotions ? The greater the love the more volcanic the passion. What is his most cherished desire ? Is it a dreamland of spirituality he thirsts for ? Is it a heaven of beautiful thought and coloured visions he would exist in ? The man is honest and will admit that it is physical possession he is gasping for.

That determination for possession is also the purpose of the woman. But her purpose is clothed in an alluring disguise, whilst man stands nakedly avowed.

So we must accept man and woman standing together on the rock of fundamental passion, with the freedom to create and re-create their world as they will. If they are wise they will clothe their world in fantasy, joy, mirth and laughter ; if they are foolish, their pall will be pain, strife and tears. According to their dreams shall be the strength of their structure of love.

CHAPTER III

THE SYMBOLS OF FEAR

*Death as man's fashion artist—All uniforms are contemptible
—War is the survival of the unfittest—Church and State
combine with a double illusion—Church vestments
employed to dominate the herd—Better to possess the art
to create a transitory fashion than to organise a decade
of disaster.*

WOMAN in the fearlessness of her dress expresses her faith
in the attraction of life ; man, the more timid animal,
accepts a garb imposed upon him by the fear of Death.

Man has accepted the false doctrine of fear. Fear
rules the world, and until mankind can banish fear
from its heart, there will be no peace.

Woman proclaims her individuality ; man submits
to his uniformity. See man in his millions in the
peace armies, decked in ridiculous colours which he
is told symbolise glory ; see him camouflaged in drab
to hide the bloodiness of truth in the battlefield, when
the rattling of the sabre is heard only in the security
of the Council Chambers, and the romance of the
fighting patriot is asphyxiated by the ghastly contri-
vances of the scientist.

In their lust for power, uniforms are the symbols
used by those in authority to intimidate the stupid
herd. The purpose is not only intimidation, but also
exaction, for the herd is held in subjection by the
impoverishing burden of providing for their upkeep.

The garb of militarism is the false emblem of
ephemeral power ; a class symbol imposed by those
who dominate. Thus all uniforms are contemptible,
and only individual expression in clothes is truly
emblematic. We must accord to woman the
compliment of personality, and admire her hatred of
uniformity ; we must place man in the category of
the fear-stricken herd, enchained to convention, and

donning whatever slave-garb the small minority of dictators subtly choose to ordain.

Man is the creature of the drill-sergeant ; perpetually forming fours and disciplined out of his individuality ; a puppet dancing to a dirge of Death.

Woman scorns to drill. She knows no discipline, and revels in a sphere that is under her own control.

Fear drives cowardly governments to arm ignorant serfs under the frightened pretext of defence. And man, with his talent for gullibility, claps on his tinpot helmet, fixes his gas-mask, dons his dusty lice-harbouring garments and sallies forth unquestioning to the fray.

He has been cunningly discouraged from any attempt to think intelligently for himself. Throughout his life he has been educated in a false religion. He has been trained to accept subjection as a virtue ; to worship abjectly at the altar of fear and offer himself to vain sacrifice under the guise of bravery.

His awakening comes too late. In the darkness of the night, entrapped in his foul trench, his mind is for the first time stripped of all illusions, and the nakedness of his false ideals is exposed. With the shock of reality comes the annihilation of his faith in all things. He sees the whole of his virile generation gripped in the machine of war ; he sees the whole of the boyhood of the world being blasted into eternity by the aged and rotten doctrine of the rule by fear.

He realises the romance of war, when, after weeks of endurance in soul-crushing filth, an attempted " advance " is commanded, and tens of thousands of men of all nations are sent " over the top," cursing the God they had been taught to believe in.

For the symbol of a flag millions of killed and maimed are left on the battlefield as food for vermin and carrion crows, or to survive as human remnants, limbless, sightless, and with lacerated entrails. Of such are the penalties attached to the symbol of a crudely coloured piece of rag.

And whether the flag be one of many emblems, or whether it be simply red, the same dastardly policy of destruction is attached.

All these military banners, standards, heraldic coats-of-arms, appearing as symbols of glory, are lying masks covering the hideousness of human ambitions.

Did the millions of young Britishers want to fly at the throats of the Germans, or even dream of doing so, in July of 1914? Did the millions of young Germans know aught of what was coming, or have any voice in a declaration of war or policy? Only the few rulers knew, the rest of mankind was regarded as cannon fodder. The cowards quarrelled with their diplomatic pens and hid miles behind the fighting line to watch their bloody sport. And the God-invoking Kaiser was the first to flee his country when defeat was in sight. They are magnificently generous, these fear-inspiring leaders, in their expenditure of other men's lives, but astoundingly crafty in the saving of their own.

The tragedy of war is that not only are the best and finest generations exterminated, but that the old and decadent survive.

War is the survival of the unfittest.

To the modern intellect war is a ghastly and an illogical crudity. The individual who accepts the inevitablity of war classes himself as a fear-stricken serf. Why should a man be ordered by a government to kill his fellow-men with whom he has had no quarrel, and yet be denied the right to fight a duel when he is personally aggrieved? Why should it be right in war to kill an innocent man whom one has never met or seen, whilst it is wrong to kill a guilty man who has done one some dastardly injury?

The sacrifice of human life can seldom be justified individually. It can never be justified internationally. War is merely the usage of the power of the few, by which they impose their will on the foolish many.

The majority, possessing no intelligence, are first cajoled, then goaded, then intimidated. In effect, the rulers shape their own designs, then drape them in a common disguise, and turning contemptuously to the herd, merely enquire : " Does this cap fit you ? " And the herd, finding the cap is of an average size, does not realise that it is wearing the fool's cap.

Later in this twentieth century it is logical to assume that wisdom will come by the pressure of economic necessity ; then the foolishness of rule by fear will be exposed. Even a cursory study of history should prove that war is a temporary transference of the ugly mantle of power.

Yet in our public schools militarism is preached and practised more than ever before, and our boys are educated on lies. Under the guise of discipline and the excuse of defence they are inspired with fear from the earliest days of their youth.

What religion stood the test of Armageddon ? The doctrine of Christianity fell like a pack of cards ; its principles, scorned and unpractised, were savagely set aside. The God of our churches isolated Himself and took holiday, contemptuous of the wreckage of our civilisation. The few who are left with any belief can only accept the God whose Kingdom is within.

What noble purpose did the church achieve or attempt during the ghastly years of the Grear War—a war beside which all other wars were back-yard scraps ?

Did any religious sect raise its voice in protest ? Did any seek solution or offer consolation ? They all joined forces, as they always have done, with their various States, and their ministers expounded their sickly doctrines that war was God's visitation on the world for its wickedness. Clergymen sat on Military Tribunals, and, unctuously rubbing their hands, gained a rejuvenating thrill by ordering young lads to the trenches. In their pulpits they revelled in the orgy of sacrifice, and gained the dictator's thanks for the efficiency of their intimidation.

Christ's apostles in Europe conveniently discarded all the teachings of Christ, and were in complete political agreement with the rule of fear.

Christianity so-called is a miserable mockery of its original conception, and the Church and State have become a material combine. The State demands the lives of its subjects in time of war and the Church inspires the sacrifice by the promise of a roseate hereafter. It is a powerful combine with a double illusion.

Both forces appeal to the senses through the medium of clothes. The pomp and circumstance of Church and State are adequately upheld. In the Church clothes and the accessories of clothes play on the emotions and reduce the average human being to a proper state of awe, and affect him temperamentally. This effect has been equally well studied by the dictators of the Free Churches. In each case, the appeal is got by " dressing the parts."

In the Church it is easy for the artist to appreciate the magnificent vestments as symbols of ecclesiastical power, but it is difficult to accept them as symbolic of Christ. If the Church used her power for good only, there would be no criticism of the adornment of herself or of her ministers. When we know that the garments of the Church are employed to govern, dominate, and to intimidate the herd, that the politics of the Church are interlaced with those of the State, that from the pulpits of the world men are urged, exhorted, persuaded, and driven to kill their fellow-men, one sees through the vestments of sanctity the awful masks of death and destruction.

It is time that religious sects cast aside their hypocrisies and their negative doctrines and placed on the altar a God of love instead of a fearsome tyrant.

Intelligence discards the transparent falsity of appearances. Nothing is in reality what it seems, and no one is in reality what he appears. The clergyman whose whole life has been wrapped up, enveloped, enmeshed, and warped by the narrow social atmosphere surrounding him, is no more a minister of Christ than William Hohenzollern, whose aspect of life was cramped and corrupted by the tin-pot manœuvring of his puppet soldiers, could ever justly be described as a warrior. The clergyman weakly deserts his mission, and the ex-Kaiser cravenly deserts his men and runs away to Holland.

The world in its apathy is always prone to accept imposed values, and is only awakened to their spuriousness when it is too late. The ignorant tiller of the soil is of infinitely more value to mankind than any emperor brandishing his instruments of death and fostering a culture of destructive arrogance.

The ex-Kaiser created his great illusion by clothes, by the lying symbolism of his own gorgeous military adornments, by the damnable greyness of the uniforms of his disciplined army, and the deadly sterility of the uniformity he imposed on his subjects.

His mind was that of all pseudo-conquerors. Analysed it was that of the frightened serf. He ruled by the doctrine of fear and revealed himself by fearing the annexation of his own puny power.

His inevitable failure proved his foolishness and his cowardice.

His type of mind is an indication of the average governing mind throughout the world. No governments are wise, and most are corrupt. With whatever conceptions a man may enter politics, he becomes infected with the foulest of all diseases, the lust of power; a victim, large or small, to the curse of megalomania, to the emotion of imposing on his fellow-men his own significant will. Once he gains power, little or great, be he Prime Minister or Bumble Bureaucrat, he has as much consideration for those whose destinies are in his hands as a rat has for a louse or an elephant for the wriggling worm beneath his clumsy feet.

The label under which he strives to rule is of no account, whether his label be monarchist or anarchist. Look at the bestial level of Bolshevism in its tyrannical vulgarity and consider its preliminary idealistic lies. Offer the Communist power and watch the chaos he will create. Give the so-called intellectuals the opportunity to expound their adolescent theories and watch the arm-chair arrogance with which they will expose not only their lack of knowledge of economics but the same desire to impose their own miserably confined views on all mankind.

Power is a curse; the most evil weapon that man can annex. It has no equilibrium, either in war or in love.

Only the sage can be trusted with the weapon of power, and he is content to smile at its rust.

When the emotions of the Great War were being experienced to their fullest, and one's fellow-countrymen were grappling with the foul mud and industrious insects of Flanders, the writer of this historical philosophy happened to be staying at the Savoy Hotel in London on the night of one of the German air-raids, when the Savoy buildings and part of Covent Garden was demolished.

It was an amazing scene watching the gaily-dressed crowd overcome by their first realisation of the realities of war. Analysing the impressions of that time, one must acknowledge an illogical but incited cruelty in one's personal war-philosophy. There was no fierce patriotic resentment against the German air-raiders, who had been commanded to attack and would have been shot had they refused. This fashionable assembly had accepted the principle of war, had generously " given " their relatives to it and had vowed to give their last shilling to support it, so surely they should not be disturbed by the risk of a stray bomb to herald them to a more wonderful hereafter. After all, one's friends were in the trenches enduring far worse than this hour by hour, and under far fouler conditions.

The jazz band continued to play, spasmodically mixing its sentiments between the National Anthem and rag-time. Many bombs fell around and the glass roof in the vestibule crashed in. There was much excitement but no casualty in the hotel, though in a near-by building people were killed.

At that moment adornment was forgotten, and men and women became unconscious of their clothes. Masks and modesty were thrown aside in the common feeling of fear.

But when the din had ceased, and the people had timidly dispersed to their rooms, one experienced in true perspective a sense of the blind stupidity and futility of the world-madness.

It is better to possess the art to create a transitory fashion than to organise a decade of disaster.

CHAPTER IV

THE ETERNAL NEGATIVE

*The critic condemns the victims of vicious virtues—The
philosophy of super-cynicism—Strong, silent men are
impostors—Denial of love is evidence of defeat—Wedded
immorality—Children conscripted in birth should be freed
in life.*

THE unimaginative are prone to designate as vices all
those emotions they cannot feel, and to describe as
virtues the few negative feelings they are capable of
experiencing.

So their stupid conceptions find acceptance with the
majority, and the false doctrine of the eternal negative
is applied to most things.

Negation is fear and the acceptance of defeat.
Affirmation is courage, and triumph in oneself.

What is virtue ? Who dares honestly to describe
it ? Are not the majority the victims of vicious virtues
and rendered impotent by their subservience to rules
imposed by satiric fiends or anæmic defeatists for the
negation of Life ?

If one desires to live it is necessary to cast off these
bonds of shoddy denial, and realising the corruptness
of the so-called virtues preached so fearfully and for
so long, to proceed to create new codes of virtue for
oneself.

We should leave the accepted virtues to the fools,
and in generosity pray to the gods to endow them with
good stomachs for endurance.

The negative principles of life which are labelled
" virtues " are preached from most pulpits and
imposed by all Governments. By both, love is
regarded in the negative.

When the world grows up and becomes educated
enough to accept the basis of affirmative principles, it

will find existence less chaotic and considerably more joyful.

The chaos of to-day is no new phase, it is more or less perennial. A century ago our philosophers were writing of the chaos of their time, just as the philosophers of to-day are reviewing the chaos of the twentieth century. Their hope was a science of affirmation and reconstruction in place of the existing doctrines of denial and destruction. Their dreams have not approached realisation. So viewing the world we are justified in the philosophy of super-cynicism. Which philosophy is all to the good since it is the affirmation of oneself.

The thinker having energetically applied himself to every phase of political thought, studied each political party, and looked into the character of each politician, is nauseated and revolted by the discovery that beneath the cloak of fair promises the under-garments consist of disgusting greed, dishonest motives, and ruthless usage of office. He recognises that each government by reason of its own infamies mistrusts all other governments. He realises that the underlying principle of every government is to treat the subject as a slave and the individual mind as offal. He appreciates that all laws are made either for the subjection of the herd, or for exaction from the herd.

Recovering from his nausea, the thinker finds a wonderful solace in embracing his own individualism. He realises the necessity for a religion and welcomes the inspiration of a belief. But he makes his own religion, and his belief is in himself. He is a law unto himself, acts upon his own principles and accepts his own loves. In his exclusive circle the precepts are simple, but comprehensive. They embrace fearlessness, truth, love, and beauty.

Fear is negative. The world has been ruled by fear throughout the ages. The surviving virile who live in this early twentieth century have seen such fearful times and deeds and consequences that they despise fear.

The old who ruled so long by fear mutilated our generation and despoiled our earth by their politics of fear. But soon their greatest fear of all, Death, will have consumed them and all their generation. When they and all their kind are gone, when their carcasses manure the earth they coveted, it is possible we may acclaim the end of the æon of rule by fear.

The effects of fear are devastating, and that is the reason why speech with the majority of people is merely a muscular exercise of the throat, the audible form of which is a tissue of platitudes, inanities, and lies. That is because the conventional clothing of speech is hypocrisy. If truth were spoken by all, we should live in an amazingly interesting new world. And in a day the whole fabric of government and society would fall. We should be recompensed by the discovery that the strong, silent man was a drivelling imbecile. Silent men are impostors. Thought labours in the silence of pregnancy, but unless it exhibits itself it is still-born.

Love and beauty one would conceive to be the easiest doctrine in the world to accept. It is not so.

The love between man and woman is confined to a ridiculous and hypocritical limitation of insular immorality by the prescription of religions and the dictates of politics.

But in addition and with considerable force the doctrine of the negative of love is propounded by all those who are defeated in love. In their anger they not only endeavour to besmirch and vitriolise love ; they endeavour to put it in chains.

They support and even influence the law, and in their religion seek a consolation for their thwarted sensual emotions.

It is amazing how moral people become when they are denied the joy of possession. In their disappointment they naturally accept a negative philosophy. They denounce love as false, when love does not accept them. Thus they show their stupidity in not understanding that love is displaying a higher morality in its dignity of selection.

The denial of love is the evidence of defeat. And bred of defeat is the false doctrine of sacrifice.

Sacrifice is the horrid negation of life. Nor is it truly labelled, for there is no sacrifice in abandoning what one cannot achieve. Making a virtue of necessity is a concession to a lying conscience. The denunciations of the so-called virtuous are the irritated outcries of jealous maniacs.

We must dismiss the doleful song of the " divine depth of sorrow " as a decadent dirge. We must compose new poems of the " wild surging of joy." In all things, if we aspire to heights, we must be singularly " Sinn Fein," or the golden hours of Youth will fade before we discover the secret of life, and our energies will be weakened before we learn how to live.

Prejudice in all forms is negative. The world is peopled by fools whose imagination is sterile, and because of their weakness they seek refuge in negation. They do not realise that with determination, self-confidence, and absolute freedom of thought one can achieve all one's desires.

For centuries the myth of freedom has been offered as a political bait. Material freedom is an illusive millennium which cannot be acquired. But at least we can demand to be left free to love at will. This may appear a desire for the earth, but it is preferable to the aspiration of an anæmic mysticism. The freedom to love, which must not be confused with promiscuous animalism, must be beyond indelicate interference by Church or State.

This is not an advocacy of what is called free-love with its attendant coarse usage and low regard for the temperamental effects which inevitably lead to chaotic consequences. It is the recognition of love as an emotion beyond the material arm of the law, and beyond the negative precepts of the Church. Marriage and protracted divorce laws are degrading to anyone with a sense of morality. There is no defence for a system which regards as moral two persons living together in marriage when there exists between them an actual physical aversion. Such cases are multitudinous and are an insult to Nature. There is far more immorality in the marriage circle than outside it.

If man and woman love each other, that is their personal right, and to endeavour to thwart their love is the negation of life. That their child should be smirched with the label of " shame " is an iniquity. Under any circumstance to place a stigma on an innocent being is grossly cruel and logically unjust.

The future of the world lies in the hands of our children, whether born in wedlock or not. And if we enjoy love and its fruits we must discharge our debt of gratitude with generosity. It is sheer hypocrisy to accept the principle of the child's obligation to the parents. Such an acceptance denotes a cowardly evasion of responsibility. The child is not asked if it desires to enter the world. Had some of us been consulted on the subject before we made our debut, we should have made all sorts of stipulations before consenting to make our first appearance. We must discard the traditional theory of the child's duty to the parent. The child is no volunteer, but is conscripted to the world by its parents' passion. Therefore, it is the parents' duty to the child that is infinite. The parents' duty should be the first principle of our religion ; since through us the child is conscripted in birth we should free it in life. Its development should not be stunted by the eternal doctrine of " thou shalt not." If our children are spared the deliberately imposed, devitalising, and devastating old teaching they will be free to evolve the new thought and new principles of which the world stands in dire need.

It is in the new generation, which is already beginning to think for itself and display a virile criticism of old methods, that the hope of the future lies for the regeneration of a greater spirit.

Thought must be free or progress stagnates. The greatest handicap of education is that it takes one too long to discard so much of what one has been taught. It is more secure to build upon the foundation of one's own opinions and then explore every channel for the discovery of the things of value.

If we abandon all negative politics of destruction we may welcome the revelation of a joyful wisdom.

CHAPTER V

AFFILIATED APHORISMS

*A vision of nakedness—Kings and politicians stripped of
their garments would make poor spectacles—Decorative
untruths—Intriguing career of old clothes—Starch a satiric
symbol—Philosophy adorned in literary lingerie.*

Good and Evil.—It is amusing to conjecture whether
clothes make for good or evil. But the more intricate
problem is to define what is good and what is evil.
If good is conceived as the "laws and orders of
government" and the acceptance of the conventional
dictates of society, then evil is to be preferred. If
good is the denial of love and the negation of beauty,
then again evil is to be preferred. On this argument it is apparent that women's clothes, by their
daintiness, delicacy and allurement, make for good,
which is considered evil ; that men's clothes, by the
uniformity of their drabness, or by the blazon
symbol of military uniformity, make for evil, which
is accepted as good.

On the foolish acceptance of terms, one is inclined
to the opinion that we must cultivate evil and cease
to be good.

Nakedness.—We are compelled to accept clothes,
for without them most people would present poor
spectacles. Without their aid could dignity exist ?
In their decorative untruth they can transform vice so
that to the world it appears in the shimmering garb of
virtue. If one seeks beneath the masks, one finds
hypocrisy unrobed and cant stripped bare. Truth then
becomes not a fetish, but a philosophy.

Our world is ruled by clothes. Without his
physical trappings where is man's power ? Could a
naked King rule ? Could a nude Prime Minister
inspire anything but ribald laughter ? Picture the

treaty-makers of Europe with their Hôtel Majestic gestures, settling the destinies of posterity, not only destitute of mental vision, but visibly destitute of physical covering. One can conceive the grotesque effect of this dual exposition of their nakedness. But such a revolting exhibition is unnecessary, for the politician is sufficiently transparent : a carcass cased in a bundle of rags, a face trained to the varying expressions of deceit, a nose keen to scent all possibilities of vicious usage, and a tongue disciplined to the dressing of specious lies.

The vision of nakedness, if gazed upon too deeply, would strip us of all accepted illusions, and we should be compelled to create afresh. The theatres would be forced to a new standard of drama ; without the aid of frills dramatic characterisation would demand a more polished subtlety. We should require to find a new set of matinée idols, and many leading ladies would find themselves deposed by understudies. Revue productions would be simplified and their cost a pleasantly irreducible minimum. The stage censors would have the time of their lynx-eyed lives.

On balance, perhaps, humanity is better clothed, so long as the beautiful untruths outweigh the vicious lies.

Running to Seed.—There is no atom that is materially wasted. All things go on smouldering and creating, rotting and re-creating from the very rottenness. Even our cast-off clothes become pulp and make the paper fodder for our newspapers. It is saddening to realise that our very dress trousers which have danced in beauteous company, may represent the material foundation on which is printed a vulgar leading article.

On the remains of our worn-out nether garments may be stamped the political opinions of a pinchbeck Press Napoleon. And a million children may be misled by a childish and childless leader on paper pulped from the cast-off coat of a village poacher.

But we have no sentimental regard for our discarded remnants, and pay no attention to their usage by the stunted and the undeveloped, who in their impotence are merely a natural excrescence of a barren era.

If we could follow the downward career of all old clothes it would be intriguing. Some of these have played an intimate part in the scenes of our splendid joys, and may now be appearing in an atmosphere of soulless squalor. They may have played their part in a wonderful passion, and now merely cover a miserable past.

The clothes of notorious murderers are more fortunate and are conceded respectful consideration. They acquire with age an added value and are sheltered from decline by kindly Madame Tussaud ; in which perhaps a wisdom is displayed, for of what value would naked waxworks be accounted ?

Then consider the garments of the woman of fashion. Their descent is refined and gradual ; passing through the shallow channel of the reduced circumstanced, and consequently virtuous, poor relative. Then a little lower still, until the garments are dismembered and each bit of trimming finds a separate body to adorn, until the once gay gown may appear in ten, more or less, passionate scenes at the same time. Which again displays woman's comprehensiveness of usage.

Adversely, we might reflect on the ephemeral life of the Prime Minister's trousers, which, after a short life and not necessarily a gay one, are doomed, perhaps on the atavistic principle, to cover the seat of a Mile End " tub-thumper."

If one is tired of fantasy it is so simple to find reality by strolling through Petticoat Lane. There one may see the seats of the mighty hiding the hides of their serfs.

Odd Symbols.—Without the symbols of clothes man's professions would find sceptical acceptance. The judge's wig and robes foster the assumption of his wisdom, the triple-tiara of the Pope proclaims his jewelled holiness, the King's crown and ermine demand obeisance and tribute. The politician's uniform, the mechanic's overalls, and the clerk's black coat, all are rigid class and caste distinctions.

But the joke is that the cap and tweeds of labour are infinitely more *de rigueur* in their circles than the top-hat in society. A typical football crowd is a revelation of the hide-bound caste symbolism expressed in clothes.

Starch, the hard and unbending use of which for men's wear has existed for centuries, is evidently a satiric symbol. It is a material exhibition of a condition men apparently aspire to attain both mentally and physically.

Man's tendencies are towards stiffness, in order that he may withstand the forces opposed to him. In this he displays sagacity, for being often an animal of wind, controlled and blown hither and thither by the wind, it is necessary for him to cultivate resistance.

The Stronger Sex.—The symbol of women's clothes is single in purpose and plural in action.

The first of the Quakers, George Fox, a shoe-maker, made himself an ugly suit of leather as a symbolic exhibition of his escape from the world of vanity. Women to-day wear leather in multiple forms of attractive but unessential trimmings, as a symbolic illustration of their unfearing hardiness.

Only one woman in history succeeded in making a name for herself without the aid of clothes. But for becoming bare, Lady Godiva would never have become famous. Had the fashion existed in those days for bobbed hair she might possibly have become infamous.

.   .   .   .

The days of gallantry are passed. There is no modern Raleigh willing to fling his mantle in the mud for a virgin to walk on. But there is many a modern maid who would literally take a man's coat from his back in order to pay for her furbelows.

It would not be delicate in the analysis of woman to depreciate her motives. It would be niggardly not to show appreciation. If in addition to the accomplishment of all desires one has gleaned from the experience further knowledge, one is fortunate. But if the knowledge is captivated to the extent of accomplished desires, one is unfortunately finished.

To allure in literature, thoughts should be daintily clad and subtly disguised, but they should be sufficiently transparent to lure one on to fresh discoveries before satiety sets in.

Even fundamental philosophy should be adorned in literary lingerie.

Man can only conceive in thought-birth. Which is, on occasions, a painful process, when the mind is impregnated with a litter of thoughts not quite ready to be born. Thought-birth requires a delicate nursing in an inspiring atmosphere. A surrounding of horsehair with thick-ankled women in woollen combinations would annihilate a sonnet. But the dainty form in concealed embroideries might foster an epic—or at least an episode.

The exuberance of youth and the decorum of age are out of sympathy in the dance of life. When a woman dances she dons her choicest garments. There is no inspiration to dance amidst the ruins, or before them or with them.

Life is full of interesting irritations and responsibilities.

Women are necessary, alluring irritations, and, as a consequence, children become the absorbing responsibility. But if we egoists cannot restrain our ego and in our conceit—or curiosity—desire to reproduce further editions of ourselves, surely we owe the new life a debt, which we should pay gracefully and with generous consideration.

In the eighteenth century society adopted a pose of cultured snobbery, which developed in the nineteenth century to a stupid snobbishness.

At the present time snobbery in England is almost unfashionable. It is now only practised in the suburbs of the cities and towns, and in society by a few fortunate chorus ladies, who, by strategic virtue, have managed to climb from the footlights into the upper circle.

. . . . . .

Intellect of itself, without physical attraction, has no appeal to woman. Her philosophy may be summed up thus : " What care I how clever he be, if he be not clever with me."

. . . .

The most charming illustration of woman's illogic occurred to the writer at a dinner party, when an attractive young American lady said that " she found the freedom of his ideas exhilarated her, but she was afraid they would contaminate her—husband."

Promiscuous Fragments.—It is necessary to escape from the captivity of custom before the vista of mental freedom is seen.

It is only the timid who cling to time-worn illusions and sickly ideals. They are obsessed by the fear that by dispelling those illusions they will be left destitute. But the fearless who strip these fripperies from the mind find before their eyes a new and boundless vision.

. . . .

The majority are unable to evolve any world of thought, and are compelled to live the narrow, conventional existence of the unintelligent and uncreative. Their conversations consist in taking in each other's mental washing, and the virility of their emotions is as effervescent as soap-suds.

. . . . .

The fetish of " What people might think " is the stupid chain the majority forge for themselves in their bondage. It is a complimentary surrender for most people are incapable of thinking.

Man-made laws and orders and prescribed codes of convention are intolerable to intellect. Laws are made for the slaves, orders for the herd, and conventions for the fools. Intellect is a rebel contemptuous of captivity.

Truth is for the isolated few. Lies are for the communion of the crowd.

The majority are afraid of truth in almost every phase, because according to their conception, truth is unpalatable. To the few it is an acquired taste, with a provocative sensation. Like all strong stimulants and pungent delicacies it is not a diet for ordinary and regular consumption. One does not breakfast on champagne and caviare.

The dawn of knowledge is the sunrise on the sea. The road to knowledge is the knowledge of one's self.

The majority neither know nor acknowledge themselves. They lie to themselves, disdain their own intimate thoughts, and even their actions they ascribe to an influence apart from themselves. They are fools, and they are the unhappy majority.

Reserve is a miserly virtue. It is the niggardly doling out of emotion because the store is so small.

A dull mind indicates the deadly vice of stagnation. A strong and vivid imagination represents the force which may determine the circumstance of life.

To attract attention, either physically or mentally, is a natural ambition. Its achievement is complementary. The discounting of this by unattractive people is easily understood, for they rightly fear they would only attract the attention of derision.

To be serious perpetually is a form of living death.

Only dull people enjoy seriousness, that is their limitation. They have not the capacity to enjoy life, which is laughter, beauty, exuberance, unstinted emotion, and the animal spirit of the race-horse—ungelded.

Sentimentalism is the antithesis of the joy of life.

To be respected sends an icy shiver down the spine ; to be appreciated warms the blood.

If a religion is necessary it should be limited to a simple phrase : " Take care of the few within your circle and inspire them to feel the better for knowing you, and not the worse."

Why are we inflicted with names ? We are labelled with a name and then imposed with the task of making or losing it. The State demands that its subjects be registered with a name at birth, so that the possessor may be conscripted for death. Surely men might choose the note by which they answer the call.

The only value of a reputation is the privilege to smash it.

The cruelty of life is the necessity of work. Man's natural instinct is to gratify all the senses with which he is blessed or cursed. He is born without the instinct to work, and usually dies without the ability to.

Yet with work he is always bound to struggle. Compared with this the struggle with folly and sin is merely the lifting of a feather. Man can enjoy his folly and easily endure any sin. But the burden of work is the purgatory meriting a wonderful hereafter.

The millennium is to be free and fearless. Then one will discover jewels on earth, which fools in their blindness passed by.

CHAPTER VI

THE DECORATED PILGRIMAGE

" Sartor Historicus "—Decoration an artful disguise—Historical pomp—The purpose of this philosophy—Man in his gloom and merriness.

THE philosophy of clothes is the philosophy of all things, for clothes are a perennial symbol.

To arrive at knowledge one is compelled to study the past, which is the only concession of value one can concede to it, for tradition is negative to progress. A study of history is valueless unless we use it for the sole purpose of advancement in thought.

In the " Sartor Historicus " (the second section of this book), we shall make a pilgrimage through the centuries of English history. But, in the modern spirit, the journey will be taken in an aeroplane, and though the pace may seem excessive for the study of an Empire, it must be remembered that the vision from the air is infinitely more comprehensive than the perspective gained from a stage-coach.

We shall look down from aloft on the conquerors and the great men of the past and discourse upon their labours. We shall judge them coldly, not by what they appeared to be, or thought themselves to be, but what they were, and sentence or acquit their memories by what they achieved, that being the only equitable judgment.

Though it is necessary in the survey to expose, in its nakedness, their mentality, it is essential in delicacy to illustrate the decoration of their bodies. This, therefore, is a decorated pilgrimage.

Decoration is an art, or at least an artful disguise.

Even the dead are clothed, and the decayed flesh of kings and cardinals is wrapped in robes of ceremony when they lie in state.

The inhabitants of Zipangu, with a material fore-thought, place rose-coloured pearls in the mouth of the dead that they may have the wherewithal to purchase a peaceful hereafter.

Pomp has played a considerable part in history. When the Duke of Valentinois, son of Alexander VI., visited Louis XII. of France, his horse was loaded with gold leaves, and his cup had a double row of rubies that threw out a great light. Charles of England rode in stirrups which were hung with four hundred and twenty-one diamonds. Richard II. had a coat valued at thirty thousand marks, which was covered with balas rubies. Henry VIII., on his way to the Tower of London, previous to his corona-tion, wore a jacket of raised gold, the placard embroidered with diamonds and other rich stones, and a great banderike about his neck of large balasses. Edward II. gave to Piers Gaveston a suit of red-gold armour, studded with jacinths, a collar of gold roses set with turquoise stones, and a skull-cap *parsemè* with pearls. Henry II. wore jewelled gloves reaching to the elbow, and had a hawk-glove sewn with twelve rubies and fifty-two orients. The ducal hat of Charles the Rash, the last Duke of Burgundy of his race, was hung with pear-shaped pearls and studded with sapphires. Charles of Orleans wore a coat, on the sleeves of which were embroidered the verses of a song beginning " *Madame, je suis tout joyeux,*" the musical accompaniment of the words being wrought in gold threads, and each note—of square shape in those days—was formed with four pearls.

On our journey we will look at man in his magnificence and simplicity ; in his gloom and merri-ness. Observe him from the days when the dandy took a pride in his woad. Smile at the gorgeous masks of James the Ugly and sense the intoxicating atmosphere of his drunken court. Frown at the deadly dreariness of Cromwell and become merry again in the revelry of Charles. Despair at the fanaticism of the second James and be nauseated by the influence of the ignorant and sickly personality of William of Orange. Revive ourselves with the glorious fashions of the Georgian era, become exuberant during the reign of the eighteenth century dandies, and almost in relief laugh at the comic protuberances of the Victorians.

Then with eyes which have visualised all that has passed we shall gaze critically on to-day, and wonder, not only how we may decorate our bodies, but how to find a new refinement with which to clothe our minds.

the influence of the ignorant and sickly personality
of William of Orange. Revive ourselves with the
glorious fashions of the Georgian era, become
exuberant during the reign of the eighteenth-century
dandies, and almost in relief laugh at the comic
protuberances of the Victorians.

Then with eyes which have visualised all that has
passed we shall gaze critically on to-day, and wonder,
not only how we may decorate our bodies, but how
to find a new refinement with which to clothe our
minds.

BOOK II

SARTOR HISTORICUS

CHAPTER I

CLIO IN COSTUME

The historian looks at decorated primitive dandies and woad-stained Picts—Vogue of hides of brindled cows—Cloth, linen, and dyeing stuffs—Painted nudity—The Boadicea illusion exposed—The Anglo-Saxon aristocrat—Gunna—Christianity and clothes—Chaucer's seven-shilling outfit.

I

In the history of any civilised nation, the story of its development in art, dress, and manners forms a truer record of its progress than a dreary catalogue of its wars, pestilences, and famines.

Great warriors, great financiers, great criminals, great politicians, appear and depart. They have their places in the pages of history, and it is essential that they are kept in their places if a picture of the progress of civilisation is to be given in true perspective.

The discovery of the use of wool was a far bigger step in the progress of the world than the invasion of Britain by Romans, the life and influence of Charles Peace, or the frivolous memoirs of mediocrities.

Dull records of battles and sieges, of political intrigue, of the lives and loves of sovereigns and subjects are non-vital incidents in the path of progress. Charles Lamb's mythical Chinaman, who discovered the merits of roast pork by the happy incident of burning down his house, conferred a greater and more permanent benefit on mankind than did Tilly when he sacked and burnt Magdeburg.

Macaulay exploded the myth of the " dignity of history " when he insisted that a revolution in dress had an equal claim to record with a palace intrigue or a parliamentary debate.

II

For certain obvious reasons the dress of the people of these islands before the Roman invasion is a matter of more or less intelligent speculation.

The inhabitant of those days was a busy man ; he had little or no time for the arts, and it is safe to assume that the breakfast-table problem occupied the chief place in his thoughts, and after that the midday dinner-table problem ; and then, if he were of a sanguine disposition, the high-tea problem attracted his attention.

So fully occupied was he that his artistic abilities were shamefully neglected ; so it comes about that unlike the peoples of ancient Egypt, of Greece, even of Mexico, his dress and appearance are not to be traced in painting and sculpture.

In fact it is from Roman statues of ancient Gauls that we get some notion of the characteristic dress of the Celtic nations.

It was, as might be expected, severely practical, and its chief features were the braccae (or close trousers), the tunic, and the sagum (or short cloak). For the gratification of his sense of colour the dandy of the period probably relied on the woad, which he also used to decorate his skin when he stripped for battle, for with a knowledge of hygiene, which was probably the fruit of experience, he disliked bits of fur and cloth in his wounds.

There were, of course, certain disadvantages in the possession of a highly decorated skin ; it was liable to make one's enemies envious, or so one gathers from Boswell's defence of Blackmore's lines—

> " A painted vest Prince Vortigerm had on,
> Which from a naked Pict his grandsire won."

" I maintained it to be a poetical conceit," states Bozzy. " A Pict being painted, if he is slain in battle, and a vest is made of his skin, it is a painted vest won from him, although he was naked."

In any case, a vest which descends from grandsire to grandson can claim the merit of durability. In stripping for the fray, the naked, woad-stained Pict merely anticipated the fashionable undress of the emancipated and beautifully made-up young woman of to-day.

Furs were obviously primitive man's first practical coverings ; fig-leaves could never have been wholly satisfactory even to confirmed vegetarians, and the Bernard Shaw of the period probably abandoned vegetable wrappings for the hides of carnivoræ as soon as the winter blasts set in in earnest.

Let the advanced, emancipated woman, as she ostentatiously wraps her thousand-guinea sables about her, hug to herself the thought that she has reached the stage of civilisation attained by primitive man before he appreciated the clothing value of woollens.

It is difficult, if not impossible, to assign an exact period for the use of cloth in this island in preference to skins, and it is equally difficult to determine the date of the relics which have been found in various places, and which exhibit, in many cases, a taste, a symmetry, and a nice workmanship that were obviously intended to please, if not dazzle, the beholder.

The gold breast-plate, for example, remains of which were found at Mold, in Flintshire, could have been of little real use as defensive armour. Anyone with a knowledge of human nature would feel confident in assuming that it was meant to tempt the eyes of some fair inhabitant, just as were the torques, and the gold and bronze necklace composed of flexible links.

III

When Julius Cæsar stood on the cliffs of Gaul and contemplated the first important Channel passage, the natives of Britain were a self-supporting race of shepherds, to whom luxuries were indifferent because unknown.

But the commerce of Britain had already struggled into existence, and the merchants of Phœnicia had discovered the importance of the tin of Cornwall, and the value of the hides of the vast herds of cattle maintained by our agricultural people.

Tin, lead, copper, lime, chalk, salt, corn, cattle, skins, horses, slaves, native dogs and pearls were the exports which made Britain known to Greece, Rome, and Gaul.

That the early commerce of Britain was by no means negligible may be inferred from the fact that the very commercial minded Roman conquerors thought it well worth while to impose export and import duties.

The art of working in metals was known to the Britons ; tin was probably the first ore to be refined, but lead and iron were also used, the last being employed for personal adornment and made into tallies for money. At the time of Cæsar's invasion the principal British treasure consisted of iron rings and brass ; the introduction of coins is attributed to the merchants of Gaul, after Cæsar's departure.

If we except the allegorical fig-leaf, the skins of animals were the earliest habits worn by the inland Britons ; and when made from the fashionable hide of a brindled cow were called " brych," but when made from the inferior skin of some vulgar wild beast they were called " isgyn."

These skins were sewn together by the softer sex with bone needles threaded with leathern thongs or vegetable fibres. The smart-set female appeared in the skin of the brindled ox, fastened together with thorns—even then roses had thorns—with a necklace of beads round her sunburnt throat and wild flowers in her wilder hair.

The inhabitants of the south coast, however, by reason of their proximity to what passed for civilisation, had learnt the arts of spinning and weaving wool and flax from the Gauls before the arrival of the Romans.

The Scilly Islanders, for example, are described as wearing long black tunics, reaching to the ankles, with a girdle about the waist, and long beards, " hanging down like wings at the corners of the

mouth." The soup course at a Scilly Island dinner
party was full of thrills.

The Gauls introduced the manufacture of several
kinds of cloth, woven of fine wools in different
tinctures. Some of it, spun with yarn, was woven
in checks, forming squares of different colours—the
possible origin of the Scottish tartan.

Linen was also an early manufacture, and being
sold for sail-making purposes, constituted a considerable part of trade. Before being woven, the flax was
soaked in water and pounded in mortars, and when
whitened was placed on the loom.

To their eternal credit, the invention of soap has
been attributed to the Britons.

They also possessed the art of dyeing stuffs, and the
Tyrian purple, scarlet, violet, and the fashionable
hues of the brindle ox were closely imitated by woad,
hyacinth, and other juices of herbs.

The most ancient garment in England was the
mantle, covering the whole body, and fastened with
a clasp, or even a thorn. This mantle is supposed
to have been of one colour only, smooth on the inside,
and hairy on the outside, and was long considered
a luxury only fit for kings and nobles.

The Southern Briton took his fashions largely from
Belgic Gaul, and Strabe describes the fashionable
suit as consisting of a tunic, ornamented with
flowers ; the loose trousers, called " braccae,"
were tied close to the shoes, the shoes being of skin
with the hair on the outside. There was also in
vogue a check patterned cassock, or cloak, united by
laces on the inside, " so as to form the appearance of
flowers "—which sounds a sufficiently airy costume—
and sometimes a short woollen jacket was worn.

So much for the South Briton.

IV

The North Briton, for long uncontaminated by
Roman or Gaul, was a much more primitive person-
age, and at the period of the expedition of the
Emperor Severus in A.D. 297, he still revelled in his

painted nudity, which was embellished with rings and chains of iron. He also further embellished himself with tattoo markings, after the fashion of the South Sea Islanders of a later day. The dandy who was held in highest esteem was he who best supported the painful " fitting on " process of tattooing, received the deepest punctures, and had the most enormous figures painted on him with the maximum amount of cosmetic.

Roman dress was not adopted in Britain until about the time of Julius Agricola.

V

Unhappily few particulars survive of the early British female ; the time was yet to come when a full page display of the latest devices in the British female's undergarments would rank in a newspaper proprietor's estimation far above sordid matters of politics or peace. She, however, emulated the male of her species in wearing gold chains, rings and bracelets, and wore her hair loose on her shoulders, turned back, and falling behind.

She frequently dyed it yellow. The first prominent peroxide blonde is in all probability Boadicea, who, on the authority of Dion Cassius, had hair of a deep yellow, reaching down to the middle of her back. The historian shatters other illusions about the British Queen by describing her as a large, well-made woman of a severe presence, with a loud, shrill voice. She had a gold chain round her neck, and wore a tunic of various colours, with a robe over it bound by a girdle fastened with buckles.

VI

In Anglo-Saxon times, the garments of both male and female were linen as well as woollen, but in such a country as Britain was then—a land of vast forests and dreary marshes—wool, the warmer material, would naturally be of the first importance. So it came about that the fleeces the shepherds brought home in the warm summer months were spun in the long winter

evenings by females of every class. With a severe
utilitarianism which cannot be too highly commended, Edward the Elder commanded that his
daughter should be instructed in the use of the distaff.
Edward had no notion of going without his winter
" woollies." Alfred the Great, of baking and other
fame, with equal directness in his will bluntly called
the female part of his family " the distaff side."
Curious as it may seem, quite respectable Anglo-
Saxon families gloried in their spinsters, while at this
day the truculent female, enthusiastically refusing to
spin her winter clothing, let alone that of her male,
indignantly rejects the appellation. At times one
wonders if the world has advanced at all.

The art of making woollen cloth known to the
Britons was brought to great perfection by the
Anglo-Saxons, and the work of the English weavers
was held in high regard on the Continent, the value
of a sheep's fleece being quaintly estimated at two-
fifths the value of the animal. The arts of spinning
and dyeing made great strides at the hands of the
Anglo-Saxons, whose women of high rank became
famous for their embroideries in gold and colours.
There are descriptions extant of a wonderful robe of
purple embroidered with large peacocks and of a
golden veil worked with the Siege of Troy, which
was a king's bequest to Croyland Abbey. The best
and finest work in embroidery, however, was performed by men, especially in Abbeys—an early
instance of man's superiority to woman with the
needle.

A high proficiency in all ornamental work belong-
ing to clothing was attained, and the Norman conquerors condescendingly record the Anglo-Saxon's
excellence with the needle and his skill in embroidery.

The Anglo-Saxon aristocrat wore a cloak embroidered or plain, and loose and flowing garments
of great beauty.

Says Sir Walter Scott :

" His long yellow hair was equally divided on the
top of his head, and upon his brow, and combed

down on each side to the length of his shoulders.
. . . His dress was a tunic of forest green, trimmed
at the throat and cuffs with what was called minever,
a kind of fur, inferior to ermine, and formed, it is
believed, of the skins of the grey squirrel. This
doublet hung unbuttoned over a close dress of scarlet
which set tight to his body ; he had breeches of the
same, but they did not reach below the lower part of
his thigh, leaving the knee exposed. His feet had
sandals of the same fashion as the peasants, but of
finer materials, and secured in the front with gold
clasps. He had bracelets of gold upon his arms, and
a broad collar of the same precious metal about his
neck. . . . Behind his seat was hung a scarlet cloth
cloak lined with fur, and a cap of the same material
richly embroidered, which completed the dress of
the opulent landowner when he chose to go forth."

All of which sounds extremely graceful and
extremely practical.

The womenfolk of such a personage wore a long
and ample garment with loose sleeves, the gunna
—hence the word " gown "—over a closely fitting
one which had tight sleeves to the wrist ; over these
again a mantle was worn, and a sort of veil or hood
over the head.

Again, hear Scott on such a dame :

" Her locks were braided with gems, and being
worn at full length, intimated the noble and free-born
condition of the maiden. A golden chain, to which
was attached a small reliquary, hung round her neck.
She wore a bracelet on her arms, which were bare.
Her dress was an under-gown and kirtle of pale sea
green silk, over which hung a long loose robe, which
reached to the ground, having very wide sleeves,
which came down, however, very little below the
elbow. This robe was crimson, and manufactured
out of the finest wool. A veil of silk, interwoven
with gold, was attached to the upper part of it, which
could be, at the wearer's pleasure, either drawn over
the face or bosom, after the Spanish fashion, or disposed as a sort of drapery round the shoulders."

It is not uninteresting to note that the conversion of the Anglo-Saxons to Christianity would seem to have affected their sartorial habits and customs, since in a Council held in 785, certain hide-bound old Tories of the period were charged with wearing their habits "like pagans."

But in many respects the Anglo-Saxons were extremely up-to-date. Married women dressed their hair artificially with an iron ; wore necklaces, bracelets and rings, and "were fond of painting their faces with red cosmetics." Of colours and materials used in the female dresses there are notices of a dun tunic, linen and web garments, a white cyrtel with cuffs and riband, a golden fly adorned with jewels, golden head bands, and a gown of otter-skin. Women had already begun to regard the skins of animals as luxuries, and not as necessaries.

The chief materials of men's wear were silk, linen and woollen, and the silk was in all probability extremely costly and uncommon.

A cap, probably of skin, coming to a point in front, supplied the place of the modern Homburg ; a loose robe, reaching to the feet, and another, longer, fastened over the shoulders to the middle of the breast by a clasp or buckle, were the chief features of the Anglo-Saxon dandy's wardrobe.

These garments were, in the case of the smart set, lined with rich furs and decorated with gold embroidery.

The dandy of the period wore his hair long and flowing, and his upper lip was covered with as much moustache as he could evolve. It was the absence of moustaches in the invading Normans which led the unfortunate Harold's Secret Service Department to report that the invaders were not soldiers at all, but peaceful monks, which is a lamentable instance of a fatal lack of intelligence in an Intelligence Department.

The long hair, parted from the crown to the forehead, was combed and curled into ringlets, while the beard was a continuation from side to side, meeting at the chin, and terminating in a fork-like effect.

These facial adornments were not at all to the taste of the Norman conqueror, and bitter were the curses against William the First when he insisted, in his arbitrary way, on the clean shave for his new subjects.

The Danish costume in its prevailing character resembled the Anglo-Saxon. Danish rulers seemed to have worn a red habit embroidered with gold, and a purple robe. The mantle, or tunic, was fastened with fibula on the right shoulder, and chausses (or pantaloons) were worn with pointed buskins.

The Danish woman's dress also resembled the Anglo-Saxon, but was rather more so, in that it was richer. A short kirtle, hanging to the knee, braided hair, gold bracelets, rings and jewellery were the characteristic features.

The fashionable dress materials were cloths, silks, and velvets, which were brought principally from Spain, or the Mediterranean, as plunder from the Moors.

Furs of various kinds were used as linings, and the dresses were often richly embroidered and decorated with long fringes.

The lower orders amongst the Danes wore a loose tunic with brochs (or trousers) and pointed shoes, or buskins—a mariner-like costume adapted in consequence, probably, of their seafaring habits. Another article of clothing was a kind of short cloak, or mantle, which reached to the thighs and had a pointed hood attached to it. These garments were frequently of skins and were worn rough and hairy for keeping off the wet.

Clothing of the Anglo-Saxon lower orders was distinguished by its fitness for the occupation of the wearer, the chief feature being a close-fitting tunic.

" His garment was of the simplest form imaginable, being a close jacket with sleeves, composed by the tanned skin of some animal. . . . This primeval vestment reached from the throat to the knees, and served at once all the usual purposes of body clothing; there was no wider opening at the collar than was necessary to admit the passage of the head, from which it may be inferred that it was put on by slipping it over the head like a modern shirt. . . . Sandals, bound with thongs made of boar's hide, protected the feet, and a roll of their leather was twisted artificially around the legs and ascending down the calf, leaving the knees bare like a Scotch Highlander. But the bandaging and cross-gartering of the hose, which was the undoing of Shakespeare's Malvolio, was common in Anglo-Saxon times."

One wonders vaguely—it is a hideously commercial age, and its influence is over the best and noblest of us—what could have been the cost of an Anglo-Saxon gentleman's wardrobe; but Anglo-Saxon tailors' bills are all too rare, whatever they may have been in the days of Alfred. At this time of super-taxation and high cost of living, the prices of essentials, such as clothing, have a rare and painful interest, and if one is unable to give the price of Alfred's best suit, it is possible to quote the cost of an outfit supplied some few hundreds of years later to the poet Chaucer. In 1357 Chaucer was in the service in the household of Elizabeth de Burgh, Countess of Ulster, the wife of Lionel, the third son of Edward III. The Countess came to London, with Chaucer in her train, and probably feeling that the poet's outfit was unsuited for the whirl of a London season, she ordered him an entire suit of clothes, consisting of a paltock (or short cloak) and a pair of red and black breeches and shoes, the price of which, as it appears from the Countess's household accounts in the British Museum, was no less than seven shillings. Later—pleased, no doubt, with his improved appearance—she bought other clothing for the poet at much the same rate.

Again, one wonders if the world has really advanced so very much.

CHAPTER II

THE FRENCH KINGS

Artistic and far-seeing Norman pirates—Man's desire for plunder—Halcyon days of no battle coupons—Battle of Bosworth not as important as a Cup-Tie Final—When wars were little local festivities.

I

THE most perfunctory student of the early history of England cannot fail to observe that every war that convulsed it was predatory in its nature.

The Saxon expelled the Celt ; and with many and picturesque barbarities, settled down, developed a civilisation, accepted a religion and a scheme of life, only to be rudely interrupted by predatory pirates from Denmark and Scandinavia, who, in their lust for gold and women, shattered the rising civilisation.

For six generations massacre succeeded massacre ; fertile provinces were wasted, commerce practically ceased, and the right of the truculent few subdued the rights of the would-be peaceful many.

Then, for a space, the world became war-weary. Dane intermarried with Saxon, and old feuds began to be forgotten ; a people began to arise which loathed war and the exactions of war, when once again a pirate community set back the clock of civilisation.

The Normans were pirates on land and sea.

Unfortunately for their victims the Normans were educated men and artists, who planned their piracies with far-seeing wisdom.

The rude plenty of the Saxon household of the upper class, with its drunkenness and its coarseness, compared ill with the refinements of the Norman nobles, and long before the Conquest English princes were sent across the Channel to receive the benefit

of a Norman education. Says Macaulay : " The
court of Rouen seems to have been to the court of
Edward the Confessor what the court of Versailles,
long afterwards, was to the court of Charles the
Second."

With the Norman Conquest the progress of
England stood still for over a hundred and fifty
years.

Once again a rising civilisation was well-nigh
obliterated by a predatory band of aliens, for the
Conqueror and his descendants prided themselves
on being, above all things, Frenchmen, and the money
and treasures wrung from the inhabitants of these
islands were spent in France.

The England of that day was merely a source of
income to the rich Norman, amongst whom its lands
and revenues were parcelled.

So it came about that the very abilities of her
first six Norman Kings were nearly her ruin as
a nation, and the happy idiocy of John was her
salvation.

When John was driven from Normandy, his
Norman followers were compelled to make England
their home, and being no fools, realised that it was
pleasanter to live in unity with the Saxon inhabitants
of the island than in eternal warfare. The tyranny
and exactions of a bad king welded Norman and
Saxon into a common bond, and the Magna Charta,
the precious treaty wrung from a tyrant by Norman
and Saxon alike, is the real commencement of
English progress. By the fourteenth century the
amalgamation of races was complete.

II

Passion for conquest once more disturbed the
island.

Instead of England being a province of France,
the idea of the ruling classes was to make France a
province of England, and under Edward the Third
and Henry the Fifth British armies wasted France
in a vain war of conquest.

D

It was France's turn to be wasted, and England's turn to build abbeys, cultivate the arts, and gather harvests in security.

Happily for the world and mankind, the war of conquest failed. The French nation, after years of sufferings and depredation, compelled their would-be conquerors to realise the futility of the struggle, and the predatory armies returned to their island, their aims unfulfilled.

An apparently curious, but in reality perfectly natural, result immediately follows.

If you place a sword, a crossbow, an arquebus, or a Lewis gun in a man's hand and tell him that that is his only means of livelihood, and if for many years he has found it an exceedingly lucrative means of livelihood, you will find a difficulty in persuading him to exchange it for a dull plough or an uninspiring desk.

The predatory Englishman of those days had drawn his revenue from the wasted lands of France ; on the aged but infallible principle of " light come, light go," he had acquired expensive tastes. His habits were luxurious, and his source of income had disappeared. His arms, his war-like habits, and his desire for plunder still were left him, so he promptly proceeded to plunder his neighbour.

The long and devastating Wars of the Roses nominally arose from the rival claims of two branches of the royal family ; in truth they arose from a desire for plunder, and lasted long after all pretence of legitimate right to the throne had been abandoned on each side. " The adherents of Lancaster rallied round a line of bastards, and the adherents of York set up a succession of impostors."

Here you have war in its naked, stark reality, and stripped of every shred of illusion and of decency ; and it was only by the fatal process of economic exhaustion and attrition that the waning factions were reconciled, and a sobered and impoverished community merged all claims and united under the throne of Tudor.

III

It is an amazing proof of the inherent vitality of this country that through all these struggles and cataclysms there was a slow, steady, if often interrupted improvement in the social system ; an improvement not due to either peer or peasant, but to the rise of a hard-working, level-headed, agricultural and commercial middle class.

In spite of the constantly recurring shocks and calamities of civil war, this agricultural and commercial middle class—both essentially productive—thrived and prospered, and the cause is not far to seek.

It must be remembered that in those days, war was not an affair necessarily calculated to destroy the activities, to say nothing of the very life, of a nation.

The bloodiest battle was strictly a local affair ; most men could, at a pinch, pull a bow, or handle a sword, and professional soldiers were few and far between. While a popular chief could succeed in rallying a host of adventurers to his colours, a vast proportion of the nation went on sowing and reaping, weaving and spinning, taking far less interest over the issue of Bosworth Field than our modern mechanic takes over the result of a Cup Tie. Provided he were at a distance of a few leagues from the scene of the conflict, the issue would affect the workman less than a Cup Tie Final would affect his prototype of to-day. In that golden age there were no enterprising newspapers to issue Battle Coupons, and betting on battle results was no part of the social system.

It was possible for the country to exist in a normal state of civil war, and, with certain set-backs, to thrive and prosper under such a handicap. In the present state of civilisation, with its elaborate commercial system, its equally elaborate homicidal weapons, and its immense capital sunk in works, industry, and property of every description, the effect of one week of civil war would spell ruin, and far exceed in lasting evil the effect of one hundred years of the poetically named, sordid little struggles called the Wars of the Roses.

Even while the Wars of the Roses were raging, our country seems to have been in a happier condition than the neighbouring nations during years of profound peace. Commines was one of the most enlightened statesmen of his time.

" He had seen all the richest and most highly civilised parts of the Continent. He had lived in the opulent towns of Flanders, the Manchester and Liverpool of the fifteenth century, he had visited Florence, recently adorned by the magnificence of Lorenzo, and Venice, not yet humbled by the confederates of Cambray. This eminent man deliberately pronounced England to be the best governed country of which he had any knowledge. Her constitution he emphatically designated as a just and holy thing, which, while it protected the people, really strengthened the hands of the rulers who respected it. In no other country, he said, were men so effectually secured from wrong. The calamities produced by our intestine wars seemed to him to be confined to the nobles and the fighting men, and to leave no traces such as he has been accustomed to see elsewhere, no ruined dwellings, and no dilapidated cities."

Happy, happy days, gone, never to return, when wars were little local festivities, designed for the purpose of letting off the superfluous steam and giving vent to the exuberance of the " nobles and fighting men " !

One fact emerges ; wars were " profitable " only in so far as they served their purpose in letting off the steam from a truculent section of the community, and did not interfere with the industrial and commercial life of the country—a combination of circumstances totally impossible in these highly complicated days of higher civilisation.

CHAPTER III

WILLIAM I. (1066-1087)

*Birth of the Feudal System—Dividing the booty, and the
responsibility—No meanness about William the First—
Ingenious method of tolls and taxes—An Algernon introduces whiskers—Young knight's hairy dream.*

I

THE entry of the Normans into Britain brought about
a radical change in the constitution and in the habits
and customs of the people.

To some extent by force of arms, and to a still
greater extent, perhaps, by an elaborately designed
and strictly commercial system of forfeitures—every
badly managed revolt resulted in forfeitures, and
there were many badly managed revolts, and consequently many forfeitures—the first Norman sovereign
became the chief landed proprietor in the realm, a
position that at once enabled him to institute the
Feudal System, in which he had been nourished.

The Feudal System in all its exquisite simplicity
was probably derived from the exquisitely simple
political system of military conquest.

It was an easy and a natural thing for a military
conqueror to bestow portions of a partially conquered
country on his principal followers, and to leave the
rest of the fighting to them. Profiting by their
leader's admirable example, each stalwart also
divided his booty—and his responsibility—between
his inferiors, the booty receiving the names of Feuds,
Fiefs, and Fees (or rewards).

All such rewards were held under an Oath of
Fealty to the superior chief, and under the
liability of doing him military service at home and
abroad.

II

Prior to the Conquest, land under the Saxons was held in Socage (or Burgage) ; that is, by payment of rent, or by performance of certain services in husbandry or otherwise, but in every case for services strictly non-military.

Being a conqueror, William was generous to himself and to his followers—at the expense of the conquered. Such generosity invariably attracts much *réclame* and has the immense merit of costing the benefactor little or nothing.

In this case, the Conqueror appropriated some fourteen or fifteen hundred manors, with their lands and forests, for the support of the crown, and then, feeling that he could afford to be really generous, distributed the remainder of the country among his followers, being particularly mindful of his relations.

To his nephew, Hugh de Abrincio, he gave the whole of Cheshire ; to his half-brother, Odo, Bishop of Bayeux, he gave a paltry 430 manors ; to the Earl of Mortaighe he gave 970 manors ; to the Earl of Bretagne 440, Bigod 123, Clare 171, Percy 119—and there were many others.

There was no meanness about William I.

In return for his gifts of other people's property, he insisted upon certain services, military or financial, the chief of which was Knight Service, by which the tenant was obliged to attend his lord to the wars for forty days a year. A really equitable form of conscription of knights, which, were it applied in the wars of to-day, would have the salutary effect of considerably reducing the Honours List.

Before very long the happy recipient of a gift of land under the tenure of Knight Service found life very far from being a bed of roses. In addition to his military homage he was liable for such trifles as Aids, which were cheerfully initiated as " voluntary grants " for the purpose of redeeming his lord's person when prisoner of war, making his eldest son a Knight—a particularly costly ceremony, for Honours are ever expensive—and raising a marriage portion for his eldest daughter. Other expensive burdens attached to the present of lands were Reliefs, the sum the heir paid for the privilege of succeeding to his father's tenure ; Premier Seisin, or first possession, the payment of which exceeded the modern income-tax in that it amounted to a half of a year's rent ; Wardship, a delightful privilege under which the over-lord was entitled to retain the person and lands of the unfortunate heir, if a male, until he attained twenty-one, if a female, until she reached twenty-four, without giving any account of the profits ; Marriage, under which the happy guardians could own the best lands of their wards ; Escheat, under which on intestacy, felony or treason, the whole property reverted to the original lord.

Man's ingratitude is a proverb and a byword. The Normans found the gifts of their lords so onerous that they defrauded them of rents and services, and William I. was at last compelled to take stock of his own conquest.

To ascertain his losses and to estimate the rents and services due from his numerous and ungrateful tenants the King ordered the famous stocktaking of England which is yet extant, and is called the Domesday Book.

In imagination one lingers over the spectacle of the Conqueror balancing the cash in hand and searching his great ledger for defaulting debtors.

Other reforms—from the point of view of the reformer—instituted by the first William were the depopulation of whole districts to provide for the King's hunting and forests, the vesting of the sole property, and all the game in England in the King's Majesty ; the barbarous woodland laws, and an ingenious system of tolls and taxes.

III

Taxation under William I. was no joke ; the soldierly Norman understood the gentle art of squeezing the last shilling as thoroughly as any modern Chancellor of the Exchequer—which is high praise indeed—and William's feudal sources of wealth are estimated to have produced *daily* the sum of £1,061 10s. 1½d., no small figure if the rate of exchange is taken into account. It should be borne in mind that the total number of tax-payers cannot have exceeded two millions. But William's system of taxation was both extensive and peculiar. In addition to revenue from ordinary sources one finds sums paid into the royal coffers for all sorts of curious reasons ; William de Wile pays his King £80 and one hundred shillings that he may have his lands and be free of prosecution when accused of ravishing his ward, and Lucia, Countess of Chester, pays five marks in silver that she may not be compelled to marry for five years.

It is perhaps fortunate that no modern tax imposer has happened to think of those ancient and profitable sources of revenue.

But it is a quaint paradox that unbridled extravagance ironically benefits somebody, even if it is only a bankruptcy court official, and the very opulence of the Normans opened a way to privilege and freedom.

The merchants and the towns were still rich, and as their extravagance made the conquerors poor, the corporations were able to buy from their lords the services and rents they could demand, whereby the most important advances were made towards a free government.

The fashion of purchasing immunities grew, and while the great towns became more powerful, the poorer communities sank into the state of villeins and bondmen.

IV

Nine centuries ago simplicity and utility ruled the style of dress.

The Norman nobles and gentry wore a long and close gown reaching to the feet, the lower edge of which was embroidered with gold ; and over it a long cloak, buckled at the breast, and with a hood hanging behind.

The Norman knut put on his close gown over his head like a shirt, and fastened it round the waist with a girdle which was luxuriantly embroidered or set with precious stones His nether stock and stockings were of the finest and most costly cloth.

Loose trailing gowns, girdled round the waist, which would be the delight of a prim urban councillor, were worn by the Queen and Norman noblewomen. Married women had an additional robe over the gown, hanging down in front like part of a priest's dress, with a purse, or pouch, hanging to the girdle.

For at least a century the Anglo-Normans were a clean-shaven race, and it is said that the introduction of whiskers into the ranks of the men about town was also responsible for the introduction of the deplorable name of Algernon, not only into the Percy family, but also into the music-hall literature.

The story goes that William de Percy, who followed Robert Duke of Normandy to Palestine in 1096, was reckless or foolish enough to grow whiskers, whereupon he promptly received the nickname "Algernons," or William with the Whiskers. He would seem to have deserved his fate.

On the other hand, the hair was long. A few years later—Henry the First on the throne—its length aroused the wrath of the priest Serlo, who was moved by the spirit of his period to deliver a tirade against the habit. Such was Serlo's consuming eloquence that king and nobles, bursting into tears, repented on the spot, and the priest, producing a pair of scissors, with his own right hand trimmed the hair of his congregation before any had time to change his mind.

A long-haired young knight saw himself in a dream being strangled in his own hair by a grisly spectre ; the dream had such an effect on his nervous system that on awaking he summoned a barber and demanded a close crop, his example being followed, as soon as he had explained his horrible reasons, by all the courtiers.

CHAPTER IV

WILLIAM II. (1087–1100)

William's unanswered question : " Who is he that can per-
form all his promises ? "—A Norman tailor—Woman
realises possibilities of bodices and Welshmen wear loose
trousers to indicate morals—Innovation of long-toed
shoes.

I

WITH all his faults, and the faults of his age and
outlook, the Conqueror had certain virtues that
distinguished him from his unpleasant successor,
William Rufus.

The first William, within limits, seemed to have
rather studied the restoration of the ancient English
customs than their subversion, and according to
Ingulphus he made the laws of Edward the Confessor
the foundation of his own. He made a material
contribution to the abolition of slavery by pro-
tecting the slave's lands and forbidding undue
service. He permitted an easy form of emancipation
by enacting that if any slave lived a year and a day
in any city, burgh, walled town, or castle without
being claimed, he should be entitled to perpetual
freedom. This subtle philanthropic policy strengthened the crown against the Barons.

The Conqueror's best epitaph is to be found in
the Saxon Chronicle.

" . . . the good peace which he made in this
land is not to be forgotten ; so that a man who had
property of his own might go unhurt over the
kingdom with his bosom full of gold, and no man
durst slay him, though he had done ever so much
evil against him."

The second William early revealed his personal nastinesses.

He had bequeathed Normandy to his eldest son, Robert, but William the Red, the second son, rushed to England with his father's ring, and with the assistance of Lanfranc, the Archbishop, secured the throne.

II

William II. promised to restrain the iniquitous forest laws, provided he received the Crown in preference to his elder brother, yet when Archbishop Lanfranc recalled the promise to him, his answer was : " Who is he that can perform all he promises ? " And he unscrupulously left the prelate out of power for the rest of his life.

Even then, aspiring politicians hated to be reminded of old promises.

The profligacy and extravagance of William II. impelled him to find new sources of revenue. The old feudal exactions, increased up to breaking point, failed to fill the royal treasury, wherefore a new source of revenue was found in the Church.

At the close of this enterprising monarch's reign no fewer than one archbishopric, four bishoprics, and eleven abbeys, were found to be without pastors —to the vast benefit of the royal banking account.

A severe illness of the King, and his craven fear of death, resulted in the appointment of Anselm to the Archbishopric of Canterbury, but

> " When the devil was sick
>   The devil a saint would be ;
> When the devil was well,
>   The devil a saint was he."

With restored health the Red King saw red and drove the Archbishop from his presence.

Left without a check, he plunged the country into wars, and it was a happy and a lucky day for his subjects when some peasants found his body in a glade of the New Forest, with an arrow in his throat.

III

While the women made the men's dress the fashions remained undecorative. They brooked no risks when their husbands went abroad. It was only when a Norman tailor, named Baldwin, settled in England that an advance was made and rich fabrics and fine clothes were introduced.

Individuality crept into the reign of the second William. Women woke up to the possibilities of their bodies, and Welshmen wore loose trousers to indicate their morals. The fabric of women's garments became richer, and though by lacing she disclosed the shape of her breast, she was modest enough to hide her legs—at least to the multitude.

Perhaps the chief sartorial innovation were the idiotically superfluous long-toed shoes, which were introduced by a "fashionable" who quickly got the name of De Cornibus, and later became known as Robert with the horns. The fashion grew to such an indecent height as to call down the censure of the clergy.

CHAPTER V

HENRY I. (1100–1135)

Hectic men's tours in the Holy Land : fashionable expiatory pilgrimages—Arbitrary powers of Norman invaders— Little new in designs—Woman shows her hair—Queen Matilda and the poets and Henry and his harem.

I

THROUGHOUT the reigns of the Norman Kings, England was on the anvil, and a happy chance forged Norman and Saxon into one.

On the happy death of Rufus, Robert, Duke of Normandy, the rightful heir to the Conqueror's estates, was on his return from the then fashionable expiatory tour of the Holy Land—an experience which, besides broadening the mind with foreign travel, was popularly supposed to invest the traveller, whatever his hectic past, with the odour of sanctity.

Fortunately for England, Robert was abroad at the critical moment of the King's death, and in spite of the opposition of the Norman baronage, his younger brother Henry contrived to seize the crown.

This defection of the Norman barons forced Henry to rely on the support of the English, and the English exacted the price of their support in the abolition of certain kingly and feudal tyrannies, and the Charter which they wrung from Henry was not only the precedent for the Great Charter, but was the first definite check to the despotism and arbitrary power of the Norman invaders.

With exquisite diplomacy and happy tact Henry contracted yet another alliance with the English upon whose support his throne depended. He married the Saxon Matilda, who, in spite of her name, appears to have been a fascinating and spirited lady, and was moreover the grand-child of the Saxon, Edgar Aetheling. In her girlhood the delightful Matilda seems to have possessed a mind of her own ; she had violently resented her compulsory interment in the nunnery, and her elevation to the throne struck a blow in favour of England both at the tyranny of the Norman Barons and of the Norman Churchmen.

With the union of Henry and Matilda, the blood of Norman and Saxon was blended on the throne, and in two generations the fusion was complete in the cottage.

Moreover, the aim of Henry the First was Peace, and his proudest title was that of the Peace-loving King.

" He was a good man, and great was the awe of him," says a chronicler grudgingly.

Powerful, pitiless, just, cold, clear-sighted, an organiser to his finger-tips, unamiable, unwavering, constant, Henry was the ideal instrument for the forging together of two hostile races, the conquerors and the conquered.

In spite of famine, plague, and taxation, the people were at peace, and in this breathing space the new freedom was born.

II

The beginning of the twelfth century ushered in little that was new in the designs of clothes. The tunic with embroidered borders become longer and reached to the ground, and the mantles of the nobles were fur lined and full.

Woman kept on awakening. She went abroad with her hair in long plaits and clad in a loose silk coat hooked to define the waist. Hitherto the beauty of her locks she had modestly and dutifully reserved for the eyes of her spouse only.

In other ways feminine influence was making itself felt.

Queen Matilda, an accomplished woman with a leaning for the fine arts, liberally encouraged the poetry of the period, rude and imperfect though it was. Furthermore it was a source of complaint against her that she was so generous a patroness of music and its professors that she oppressed her tenants in order to obtain the funds to develop whatever talents her *protégés* possessed. Matilda was very attached to church music.

Henry, what time Matilda was with the poets and musicians, found artistic relaxation amongst the harem of mistresses and the poets and the jongleurs who infested the court. So the ideal balance was struck in the fusion of the domestic life of Norman and Saxon.

CHAPTER VI

STEPHEN (1135–1154)

*Exquisite modes of torture to wring taxes—Death of the
unlamented, disillusioned, disappointed Stephen—Simple
costumes donned in a minute—Woman displays her form
—When war is depleting menfolk instinct compels woman
to allure other men to preserve the species.*

I

WITH the death of Henry the thirty-five years of
productive peace came to an end, and the realm was
plunged into anarchy and tumult.

His nephew Stephen appeared at the gates of
London and persuaded the citizens to choose him as
king. Thanks to Henry's rule, the voices of the
barons and of the prelates were of less account than
the votes of the citizens, and the new king was elected
by the people.

But Stephen was the mere soldier, who found himself in control of the intricate and complicated
machinery set up by the statesman, and as was to be
expected, it was not long before a breakdown was
imminent.

The old vicious practices were resumed. Knights
and their retinues were hired from abroad to bolster
up the failing power of the throne ; desperate attempts
were made to fill the exhausted treasury by means of
base coinage and exactions. This rule speedily
brought about revolt, revolt grew into civil war, civil
war in its turn brought about a revival of feudalism
and faction, and England was speedily in the hands
of robber barons, who had no conqueror to restrain
them with an iron hand, and who plundered the land
and its inhabitants.

The castles of robber barons sprang up all over the
country ; the owners of the castles vied with one

another in devising exquisite modes of torture by which to wring contributions from unwilling contributors to their funds, and it was left to a religious revival of a remarkable character to rescue the land from anarchy.

A common peril bound the ecclesiastical power and the power of the people together, and just as once before crown and people had saved England from tyranny, so did prelacy and people save it now.

Stephen died, disappointed, disillusioned, unlamented, and Henry II. reigned in his stead.

II

Most of the men of the nation being occupied by war during the reign of Stephen, there was little finery in their dress. A simple shirt, a tunic to the knees, trousers of leather or wool, bound with straps of coloured cloth, a semi-circular cloak with embroidered border, and woollen socks and one button leather shoes—the entire costume could be donned in less than a minute.

Despite the sport of their menfolk in killing and torturing their fellow-countrymen ; despite the fact that in their castles were dungeons in which prisoners were fastened to beams and left to starve or dragged up to the tower and thrown into the moat below —despite these horrors woman's innate vanity developed, as it invariably does in war time. She displayed her form more, her gown fitting closely from the breast to the hips, with a loose flowing skirt of soft, thin material. Her hair was decked in ribbons, and artificial plaits added to its length.

When war is depleting menfolk, instinct impels women to allure other men to preserve the species.

CHAPTER VII

HENRY II. (1154–1189)

Trial by jury originates—Transatlantic free-and-easiness in Henry's ménage—Man's fur-lined cloak ; gay-coloured hose with crossed garters ; jewelled gloves — Woman protects her ears against uncouth oaths and her chin against unmannerly chucks—Excellent reasons for her demure, nun-like garb.

I

WHEN Henry II. ascended the throne of England in the twenty-first year of his age he found himself king of a single race.

The fusion of Normans and Saxons was complete and England was a nation.

Young as the King was, he had seen enough of anarchy to be sickened with it, and being of an essentially practical turn of mind he had a lively appreciation for the practical benefits of good government.

The Church had placed him on the throne, but he cared as little for the Church as he cared for the barons, and blissfully ignored the growing power of religious impulses or influences on his people and period.

The clash direct could not long be deferred, and it came with the royal insistence that clerics, equally with the barony and the laity, should be subjected to the ordinary laws of the land.

The whole jurisdiction of the Church courts was thus challenged ; the valuable rights of excommunication, of interdict, of sanctuary were assailed, and it was only human that the prelates, under Thomas à Becket, the Archbishop, should offer vigorous resistance.

The King was adamant ; the Archbishop fled to France, and the reforms were carried out.

Trial by jury originated in 1166 with the Assize of Clarendon.

For six years the quarrel between the King and the exiled Archbishop raged ; the Pope and the power of France were in turn invoked by the angry prelate, and at last, under the threat of an interdict, the Archbishop returned to Canterbury to meet his death at the hands of the passionate knights who were spurred on by their master's furious words.

It is highly significant of the slow growth of public opinion against clerical or baronial interference with the ordinary law of the land, that the murder of Becket, while the crime itself aroused horror, had little effect on the power of the King.

But domestic troubles were destined to cloud Henry's later days. His wife, Eleanor, for some time parted from him—even in those days the *ménage* of a king had a transatlantic free-and-easiness about it—urged his sons to take up arms against him. The sons were reduced to submission, but the domestic ill-feeling persisted, and culminated finally in a quarrel with Richard, his heir, who with the French king drove his father in flight from Le Mans.

At the head of the list of conspirators was the name of the King's youngest son, John.

" Now," said Henry, turning his face to the wall, " let things go as they will. I care no more for myself or for the world."

II

In the course of Henry's long reign the designs of men's costumes altered little, but the materials of clothes became richer. Silks woven with gold threads and cloaks lined with magnificent furs were worn ; gay coloured hose, with gold crossed garters, and jewelled gloves, completed the outfit.

Woman, in her eternal desire for change, adopted a demure and nun-like garb. She wore a chin band and covered her hair with a wimple—the linen folds of which protected her shell-like ears from the sound of uncouth oaths ; and she bound her neck up to the chin as a guard against unmannerly chucks.   Her gown was loose, shapeless, and apparently meaningless, but although the design appears unattractive to us now, she had excellent reasons for it then.

CHAPTER VIII

RICHARD I. (1189–1199)

Story about a Tottenham Court Road magnate—Two kings make a quarrelsome journey to the Holy Land—Lion-Hearted's merry career of blood and thunder—Men at war have little time for arts—Woman's sexless garments —The Ceinture de Chasteté attributed to the Crusaders' passion for foreign service.

I

RICHARD CŒUR DE LION was an adventurer neither pure nor particularly simple, and like many such adventurers, his name and fame have become famous in fable and myth. The story of his slaying an unoffending lion with his brawny, naked hands was told in every nursery of his period, and even in comparatively recent days the glamour of the Lion-hearted King added fresh glories to a Victorian title.

The story goes—malicious it may be, but it is of interest in showing the persistence of unreliable tradition—that when a Tottenham Court Road magnate figured in an Honours List he consulted appropriate experts for a pedigree and crest

The experts pursued their investigations, and at last submitted their report.

" We find," said they, " that you are a direct descendant of Richard Cœur de Lion's devoted minstrel, Blondel, and your family name is derived from an exciting little incident in the career of the King and a minstrel.

" When the King lay in his foreign dungeon, despairing of the past, the present, and the future, a distant lay stole upon his ears. He recognised the

voice of his faithful follower. Starting from his pallet,
' Ha,' he cried in the vernacular of the day, ' Blondel
M'appelle ! ' which, being interpreted, signifies
' Blondel is calling me.' And ' Blondel M'appelle '
became from that day the court patronymic of the
poet, whose descendants are now known by the
corruption ' Blundell Maple.' ''

For Richard the English throne was merely a con-
venient source of revenue, and he bled the nation to
its limits in order to provide funds for his continental
and Palestine excursions.

With Philip of France, this very unpleasant
sovereign quarrelled his way out to the Holy Land,
while his very unpleasant brother, John, made the
most of his chances at home, seized Windsor and the
royal castles, and prayed devoutly for his elder
brother's death abroad.

Hastening homeward Richard, to the delight of his
brother, was arrested in Vienna by Leopold of
Austria, one of the many for whom his cheery bon-
homie had no appeal, and was promptly held
up for ransom.

Owing to the exertion of the Archbishop of Canterbury, the huge sum demanded was raised, the devoted
nation subscribing a fourth part of its movable goods
in return for its expensive King.

Free once more, the Lion-hearted at once
resumed his merry career of blood-and-thunder, and
England groaned under the exactions which were
essential to supply the necessary funds for his continental wars.

At last a dim idea of '' value for money '' began to
infect the nation, and when Richard had matured his
plans against Philip of France the devoted country
'' struck.'' This ingratitude almost broke the Lion-
heart. Prowling greedily round a French castle,
which was reputed to contain a vast treasure, an
arrow from the walls put an end to the hero's desires
and life, and left England free to contemplate the
accession of another member of the same unpleasant
family.

II

During the reign of Richard I., civil and uncivil strife left little time for the arts, for the man who may in a moment lose both his goods and his life has little time to care for a beautiful picture, an inspiring poem, or a nice design. Even the cut of his clothes is a matter of merely passing interest to him.

So plainness still ruled in men's costumes, the only change being that the garments were more voluminous and flowing—quite possibly the hope of concealing minor valuables about the person influenced this mode—and the great majority of their lords being on foreign service the garments of the women remained sexless in design.

But it is worthy of note that it is to the passion of the Crusaders for foreign service that the introduction of the *Ceinture de Chasteté* is attributed.

CHAPTER IX

JOHN (1199–1216)

A particularly bad king—Tiresome spectacles : old men crushed
to death, ravished women, starved and tortured children—
Coincidences : John loses his baggage in the Wash, first
symptoms of fatal illness appear during stay at Swinehead
Abbey—Man's monk-like garb—Woman's dress shapeless
in spite of vogue in rich colours.

I

Not for the first time in our island story was a bad
King England's salvation, and John was a dread-
fully bad King.

Normandy being lost to his house, John was
forced to make England his home, and very speedily
England began to appreciate the compliment at its
proper value.

Much to his disgust the new King found that the
fusion of Normans and Saxons was now complete,
and that he was confronted with a common English
feeling and patriotism which declined to submit to
unreasoning tyranny and exaction.

There were even signs of an intellectual revival in
the land, and any intellectual revival was, in the
nature of things, bound to be detrimental to the
interests of such an individual as John. The
Universities began to be a power, and the growing
influence of the intellectuals threatened the reactionaries in Church and State. The towns and the
great Merchant Guilds were also powers that could
no longer be ignored, and powers which had nothing
in common with a blithe-hearted despot, who out
of sheer excess of high spirits plucked the beards
of Irish chieftains as they bowed in homage, and
" united in one mass of wickedness and insolence of

the Angevins, their selfishness, their unbridled lust,
their cruelty and tyranny, their shamelessness, their
superstition, and their indifference to truth and
honour."

It was a lucky chance for England that such a
King attempted to rule her in the critical hour of her
fusion into one people ; a people that was tired of the
hilarious spectacles of old men being crushed to death
under copes of lead, of ravished women, of starved
and tortured children.

" Foul as it is, hell itself is defiled by the fouler
presence of John," was the cheerful verdict of a contemporary critic, who had grounds for his criticism.

John defied the Church, and it excommunicated
him ; he defied the baronage, and it broke from him ;
he defied the people, and the people wrung from him
the Great Charter.

> " And still when Mob or Monarch lays
> Too rude a hand on English ways,
> The whisper wakes, the shudder plays
> Across the reeds at Runnymede.
> And Thames, that knows the mood of kings,
> And crowds, and priests, and suchlike things,
> Rolls deep and dreadful as he brings
> Their warning down from Runnymede."

There is an occasional appropriateness in history
which is uncanny. John lost his baggage in the
Wash ; the first symptoms of his fatal illness made
themselves apparent during his stay at the Abbey of
Swineshead, and a gluttonous debauch put an end to
the wholly unpleasant tyrant who, *malgré lui*, did
more for the liberties of England than many a hard-
working, conscientious, and early-to-bed King and
Queen—to say nothing of Prime Ministers and their
wives.

II

During the reign of John a monk-like garb for men
was still in fashion, but richer embroidery made an
appearance. Womenfolk took to showing a little

hair beneath their wimples. But, although rich colours and silks were in vogue, the designs of female dresses were shapeless.

This shapelessness is perhaps understandable, for John, though an amorous animal, took pleasure in torturing women ; therefore the wise sought not to attract his attention unduly.

CHAPTER X

HENRY III. (1216-1272)

Henry's Hohenzollern temperament—Bad Government is expensive Government ; good Government and economy go hand in hand—War and tyranny are bed-fellows, and their progeny is waste—Dress designs little more than drapery—Man takes centuries to shape his hangings—Woman's mask of demureness is wearing out.

I

ON the death of the unlamented John a child of nine ascended the throne, and as was to be expected the state of England during the long minority was a stormy one. Every self-seeker quite reasonably thought his chance had come, but due largely to the stern uprightness of Archbishop Langton, and of the justiciar, Hubert de Burgh, the anarchy of the bad days of Stephen was kept in check.

In 1227 Henry declared himself of age, and set about to rule in earnest.

Possessed of none of his father's cruelty and lusts, cheerful and pleasant in manner, and a lover of the pleasant things of life, Henry's character had threatenings of good, but he was also false, changeable, recklessly extravagant, unbridled in temper, and had a Hohenzollern craving for absolute power.

The shadow of the Charter hung over him like a cloud ; all his absolutist ambitions were thwarted by that precious instrument which he had by oath bound himself to maintain, and he looked to Rome to free him from the obligation of his oath.

Here were all the elements of civil and religious discord.

Rome demanded its price, and once again, as in the days of feudal strife, exaction followed hot upon exaction. But the English were now a united people and in no mood to endure exactions ; armed men seized the tithes and gave them to the poor, and the papal collectors were beaten and despoiled. The unrest was laid at the door of the justiciar, and there was a violent quarrel between the young King and his former mentor, ending in De Burgh's fall, and the delivery of the country into the power of the King.

Misgovernment and tryanny were soon rampant. The administration of the realm passed into the hands of the King's unscrupulous puppets and nominees, and robbery, corruption, and bribes became the order of the day.

Misrule inevitably brought about deficiency in the royal treasury, and deficiency as inevitably brought about renewed exaction.

Once again was the moral pointed—a moral as old as the hills, but imperfectly learnt even to this day : bad government is expensive government, while good government and economy go hand in hand.

Presently the Crown debts exceeded the Crown revenue by four times, and an appeal was made to the country for financial help.

Aid was granted on conditions which included a confirmation of the Charter, but the conditions were ignored, and further subsidies were refused.

To quicken the inevitable conflict, the King's forces had been defeated in France and the treasury was utterly drained.

There was another appeal for money, but by this time the barons had their plans of action ready, and were prepared to insist upon their terms.

The King was helpless, and the royal power passed into the hands of the Great Council of the Barons, which in its turn abused its power at the expense of the barons and the commonalty, who adopted Simon de Montfort as their champion, and in the battle of Lewes Simon and the barons routed the reactionaries.

And then it was that De Montfort immortalised his name in English history by creating a new force in English politics and instituting a constitutional change of vast importance.

He called together a Parliament, and not only did he summon two knights from each shire, but he summoned to sit beside those knights two citizens from every borough.

For the first time in England the merchant and the tradesman sat beside the baron and the knight and the bishop in the Parliament of the realm.

The De Montfort government fell, but Simon's reform was to stand for all time.

For more weary years civil wars and factions disturbed the weary realm. In the end the constitutional system was finally adopted by the crown, expenditure was brought within bounds, and taxation only imposed by consent of the Great Council.

After years of strife and suffering and of waste, the old lesson was learnt that war and tyranny are bed-fellows, and that their progeny is waste.

II

Dress designs were practically at a standstill during Henry's fifty-six years' reign.

Cut, which is the art of the originator, did not enter into the field of fashion. Clothes appeared in all sorts of beautiful colours ; silk, embroideries, and costly furs were worn in profusion by the nobility. But design was little more than drapery. People just wrapped themselves, as it were, in swaddling clothes, and the human form was little more than a peg for materials to be hung on. Man is a slow thinking animal, and it has taken him slow centuries to shape his hangings, and to arrive at any degree of elegance.

Towards the end of the third Henry's reign, however, women took to shaping the gowns to their figures again. Perhaps the mask of their demureness had worn itself out.

CHAPTER XI

EDWARD I. (1272-1307)

*Simple finance—No Norman Plantaganet tries to impose a
tax of ten shillings in the pound—Strike against the King's
taxation—Debt of Chambers of Commerce to Edward—
Heraldic ornament on gallant's surcoat—Woman finesses
with her hair.*

I

IN the reign of Edward I. war almost justified
its existence, for it was due to the financial crash
brought about by the eternal wars of conquest and
defence that the Parliamentary system had its rise.

In early times finance had been comparatively
simple. The outgoings of Government, as represented by the Crown, had been met by the Crown
Revenue ; local expenses were paid by local bodies,
and the national, let alone the international, financier
was an unknown figure in the land.

To ransom the land from the Danish invaders it
had been necessary to raise a tax, appropriately
enough called the " Danegeld," and the Normans had
been quick to see the advantage of universal taxation
for military purposes. To the Danegeld they swiftly
added the feudal burdens—the feudal " aids " and
the relief on inheritance and profits on wardship and
marriage.

Expenses of war soon exhausted these sources of
supply, and by degrees a system of emergency grants
sprang into being. and as commerce and manufacture
struggled into prosperity, grants of from a seventh
to a thirtieth of personal property were demanded.
But with a moderation that cannot be too highly
commended, no Norman Plantagenet attempted to
impose an income tax of ten shillings in the pound.

The immense charges of war with France and the

need of supplies induced Edward I. to call together for the first time the Parliament which has left its mark on the history of this land, and it was the financial difficulties of the Crown which led to the admission into the Great Council of those very important commercial personages, the representatives from the boroughs to sit with the militarist knights, nobles, and barons.

Wars with France and Scotland drained the treasury. The King demanded half their annual income from the clergy, which demand so terrified the Dean of St. Paul's that he fell down dead from sheer fright. Plain country gentlemen were compelled to buy knighthoods, or exemptions—times are indeed changed !—export duties were sextupled, and customs were levied exactly as the King pleased. And he did please.

Edward had gone too far ! The barons were the first to strike ; the clergy were infuriated, and the wool industry, the chief industry of the period, recalcitrant, and before Parliament met, Edward realised his powerlessness.

He adapted himself to the inevitable ; after a passionate appeal to loyalty he obtained an assent to the prosecution of the war on condition that he accepted additional articles to the Charter, wherein he renounced his right to tax the nation without its consent.

Here is a very notable instance of evil bringing forth good. The pledge that there were to be no more aids, tasks, and prizes, or heavy customs on wool, without the common assent of the realm, brought forth as great a victory as the Charter of Runnymede.

Edward I. disliked war, but he was a great soldier, and his very antipathy to bloodshed made his military genius more admired by his subjects.

He loved power ; he was a statesman and a politician, and as such had a proper contempt for just military glory.

If war was necessary to his statesmanship, then

war was to be accepted regretfully and as a necessity.

For the first time an English King ruled in a constitutional England, a King whose one aim was to consolidate and to build, to organise order and good government.

Wars with Wales and Scotland necessitated supplies—but the wars were forced and the King's demands were moderate—and the supplies were granted. In the midst of wars never did Edward the King forget the task to which he had set himself, the work of internal reconstruction.

Many and lasting were the reforms he initiated, and not least amongst them was the beginning of reform in the judicial system.

The commercial classes owe much to the memory of this first of truly English kings, and the Statute of Merchants alone should secure him a niche in every Chamber of Commerce.

The menace of war and economic pressure brought about an event which has made a lasting mark.

The threat of a French war found the King in need of supplies ; still more, in face of such a menace, did he need the united support of his people ; calling together a Parliament to advise with him on the dangers to which the realm was exposed, he gave that Parliament a shape and organisation which has left its assembly the most important event in English history. It was financial necessity induced by war which was primarily responsible for the presence of soberly clad citizens in the Council Chamber.

But in spite of all successful attempts at reform and organisation, war permeated the reign of Edward I. —war with Scotland, war with Wales, war with France—and the King died at the head of his army.

II

War—as it always does—impeded the development of art and design in dress. The gallant of Edward's thirty-five years of reign spent most of his

E

time in armour, and in his few moments of leisure shuffled into a comfortable loose gown. The knight perhaps would add an heraldic ornament on his sur-coat, whilst the knight of to-day must wear his cheque book up his sleeve.

Nor did women develop their modes ; their lords being so much occupied, where was the encourage-ment ? They finessed slightly with the dressing of their hair, and occasionally amused themselves by altering the shape of their wimples.

CHAPTER XII

EDWARD II. (1307-1327)

*Domestic jars in Royal household—The Queen has the pleasure
of seeing her husband bolt—Best popular education is
practical politics—Revolt against disguising the human
form—Cotehardie—Fantastic coloured tights—Fat men
reform—Basis of sex-attraction.*

I

WAR was responsible for the creation of Parliament,
and the hundred and fifty years of war which followed
its creation consolidated its position.

The eternal need for money for military purposes
was the salvation of the young power which was, in
time, to overshadow the Crown.

Arbitrary taxation was no longer possible ; so soon
as the Treasury was empty, Parliament, the only
power in the land which could fill it, of necessity had
to be summoned. And whenever Parliament was
summoned and asked for money, it betrayed an uncomfortable habit of asking something in return,
either in the way of redress of grievances or extra
Parliamentary power.

Paradoxically enough, war saved the liberties and
the Constitution of England. Her would-be despots
were no fools ; they saw the net about their feet.
None grew to realise better than they that the salvation of despotism was peace ; war and the cost of war
meant ceaseless appeal to Parliament for supplies,
and each appeal was answered only at the price of a
fresh concession—a fresh increase of Parliamentary
power.

In vain the despots struggled to escape the net they
themselves had woven ; but they were now hopelessly
in its toils, and war went on and the power of
Parliament grew.

About 1309 the Scotch war compelled Edward to meet his Parliament, and financial pressure brought about a notable concession to industry, for it was only by abandoning the right to impose import duties on merchants that the necessary subsidy was obtained. After a military failure in Scotland, Edward again met his Parliament. This time the terms were harsher. The custom duties imposed by his predecessor were declared illegal. Parliament was to meet once a year, and the consent of the barons in Parliament was to be needful ere any war could be declared. The commons were still regarded as mere tax-payers, but Parliament was a power and representative.

Another unsuccessful war against Scotland brought about a climax. A humiliating truce robbed the King and his councillors of their last shreds of popularity, for the pride of the country had been aroused, and although the immediate war pressure no longer compelled recourse to Parliament, that institution was now too strong to be checked.

Even monarchs are not immune from domestic jars, and the wife who hated him took advantage of Edward's unpopularity. Returning from France at the head of a vast conspiracy, she had the satisfaction of seeing her faithless husband bolt in ignominious fashion, and the still greater satisfaction of seeing him deposed by Parliament.

If there ever comes a moment in a woman's life when she feels life has been indeed worth living, such a moment must have come to Isabella of France.

Politically the reign of Edward II. was a period of amazing development ; the power of arbitrary taxation had been wrested from the Crown, a new system of government had been established, and the excellent principle that no supply would [be granted without redress of grievances had been settled beyond all power of dispute.

And as there is no popular education like practical politics, so were there developments in the social arts.

II

Here we arrive at the stage of the development of the artistry of colour in materials, the pied or first attempt at blending. Stamped velvets were produced, and designed brocades and shining satins, soft and illusive to the touch. A material culture manifested itself, as though timidly anxious to be caressed into the art of life.

An artist tailor was born to rescue humanity from the sexless shapelessness which hitherto had characterised its dress.

Until now the loose fitting robes afforded the tailor no scope in design or cut, therefore to the artist tailoring was merely a labour without opportunity to display art. Men and women were bodyless and legless creatures. Probably the fashions had long been cunningly controlled by obese men and pouchy women. But in the early fourteenth century an artist, maybe in the form of a shapely lordling, revolted against this long surviving disguise of the human form.

A revolution took place in men's dress. Man suddenly discarded his loose wrappings and the first appearance is recorded of the cotehardie, a body-tight garment reaching only to the hips, with sleeves tight to the elbow, and from there hanging loosely and showing the close-fitting sleeve of the under-vest. Gay coloured cloths and parti-coloured silks were made fantastic use of, the two legs of tights, for example, vying with each other in contrasting hues.

On the cloaks, which were worn in colder weather over these garments, was attached a hood, to the peak of which was fastened a long strip of material called a "liripipe." This was toyed with in all sorts of ways, by tying it round the neck, rolling it on top of the head, or dangling it like a pig-tail.

The conservatives and fat men, timid of exposing their nether limbs, clung to long robes. They were, however, influenced by the trend of style, and had garments fitted to their manly chests, flowing loosely over their parts of indiscretion.

It is peculiar that with this revolution in men's dress there was little or no response in woman's fashions. She adhered to the existing styles, and merely shaped the upper part of her gown to her breasts—the fountain of man's wisdom.

Maybe she was nervous of encouraging her lord in his new-found and more attractive freedom of attire And knowing man as he really is did not wish that knowledge advertised. Either that, or the subtle intuition of the allurement of the antithesis, which is the basis of sex-attraction in dress and all things, inspired woman to drape herself in an excess of wrappings in contrast to man's discarded wrappings.

It is illuminating in the study of fashion through the centuries to observe the subtleties of contrast between the sexes.

CHAPTER XIII

EDWARD III. (1327–1377)

*Pauperism and unemployment are always attendant on war—
Styles run riot—Saving grace : men shave their faces—
Wool tax—Woman dyes her hair—Alluring gown that
indicates the curves of the breast and the shapeliness of
the hips—Imaginative buckled shoes.*

I

THE costly political experiences of the last reign had
brought wisdom to the knights of the shire, who had
hitherto allied themselves into a political force with the
barons, and on their combination with the representatives of commerce the Commons sprung into being.
The four orders of clergy, barons, knights, and
citizens ceased to exist in Parliament, and the
knighthood, by adopting this new course, in reality
welded the baronage and the burgesses into one
order.

No inhabitant of this island during the fifty years'
reign of Edward III. could complain of political or
social dullness.

If ever " life was real, life was earnest "—to quote
the uninspired platitudinarian—it was so in the days
of this jubilee reign, and no peer, knight, or yeoman
who took the least interest in political or private
affairs, could complain of a dull moment.

But war was the background of the picture. The
Hundred Years' War with France, which filled the
lives of the third Edwardians, was a melting pot in
which English institutions were to be remoulded.
The long strain brought about a social, political,
and religious revolution, which advanced England
immeasurably on the path of progress.

The prolonged man-killing business taught the
yeoman that he was every bit as good as the noble in

the art of butchery—and if in the art of butchery, why not in other rôles ?—and the growth of pauperism and unemployment—invariable attendants on war—for the first time placed labour face to face with capitalism.

The Hundred Years' War was a European war on a huge scale. The so-called civilised world was not over-populated in those adventurous days—and Edward's army of 8,000 men-at-arms out of a total population of 4,000,000 reflected great credit on the combers-out of the day.

Here was a reign of constant excitement, of new ideas, of violent actions and reactions, of false prosperity, of real poverty, of revolution in thought and outlook, and, as is inevitable, the mental effervescence is reflected in the dress of the period.

II

Here we arrive at vicissitudes of fashion and a life of pageantry, of joy and pain, of gaiety and death. It is amazing that despite the Great Plague of 1346, which killed half the population of England, the pendulum of fashion swung with more passionate velocity.

Styles developed, approached their century's extreme, and occasionally ran riot. Colours were variegated. There was one great saving grace : the men shaved their faces.

The cotehardie—from which two modern garments are adapted—varied in shape. Some were as long as the knees ; some cut short, half-way up the thighs ; some buttoned down the entire front ; some buttoned only at the neck. Here is the origin of the lounge and the morning coat. The most fashionable of all was the cotehardie shaped close to the figure and made of fine figured silk. The sleeves were tight to the wrist, and buttoned to the elbow, and above the elbow was the tippet with its long streamer of silk attached. Tall crowned hats appeared, and into the long peak-shaped ones a feather was stuck.

Dress progressed, and the rulers annexed an advantage to themselves. They taxed wool and the tax yielded £30,000 a year. A fine sum, then, but sickly in comparison to the £60,000,000 our Government annexed by control during Armageddon.

In the face of plague and pestilence—or perhaps to combat it—woman evolved an artistic beauty, which had long been dormant, in her dress. She realised the asset of her hair, and the most elaborate modes of coiffure were invented. She adorned it with a metal fillet, to which were attached circular cases, ornamented with precious stones. Another fashion was to fling it loose in all its beauty. As the styles in design changed, so did those of colour. Yellow hair was the most popular ; the brunetted and chestnutted and auburned by nature sought the artifices of saffron and subdued Nature to a cult.

Woman's gown was perfectly beautiful, and alluring by sheer design. Picture her, with the sun shining in the gold of her hair and reflected a thousand times in the rubies of its ornament—her silken gown buttoned or laced from neck to waist, delicately indicating the invitation of her breasts, the shapeliness of her hips, and the invitation of the close-sheathed beauty of her arms. And beneath the hem of the graceful folds of a voluminous skirt peeps a dainty foot, encased in a buckled shoe, as a signal of the mysteries of imagination that it is her destiny to inspire.

CHAPTER XIV

RICHARD II. (1377–1399)

*Military successes won at price of nation's interests—Last
continental market for English goods closes—Loans and
grinding taxation—Extravagance in dress—Dandies wear
massive chains similar to those worn by the modern aspiring
and aspirateless mayor—Ridiculous houppelandes—Beards
and moustaches return—Woman demonstrates her aversion
against hairy lips by hiding her hair.*

I

THE military successes of the English army under
Edward III. were dearly purchased at the price of
the higher interests of the nation, and the trader and
the labourer cursed the name of Crécy and groaned
at the mention of Calais. To all intents and purposes France, the great enemy, seemed broken once
and for all, but military success and the plunder of
foreign cities were, in the end, poor compensation for
disease and poverty.

The Black Death swept the country, and accomplished what war had only partially accomplished ; it
completed the disorganisation of productive labour.

Owing to the scarcity of workers, the rate of wages
rose, and the labourer was almost worth his weight
in gold. So it appeared advisable to conscript him,
and the Statute of Labourers was passed by acclama-
tion of those interested in conscripting him. There
was, quite naturally, resistance, a resistance which
refused to be placated by such meretricious military
victories as those of the vastly over-rated Black
Prince, and as the screws of poverty and militarism
were ever tightened, resistance culminated in revolt.

Bitter poverty and defiant pride had been for long
face to face ; the clash was inevitable, and the terrible
measures of repression which followed the Peasants'

Revolt failed to destroy its effect or significance.
The frenzied panic against all reform which followed
tells its own tale.

Richard the Second ascended a throne rendered
more uncomfortable than most thrones by distress,
social disorganisation, panic and poverty, all induced
by war. The reduction of Ghent by the French
closed the last continental market for English commerce, and English forces were being squandered in
foreign wars.

Whatever his faults, the King had sense to see that
peace was essential, both for himself and his country,
and in the short period of peace which was won, men
had time to sing and listen to songs, and the voice
of the first great English poet, Chaucer, was heard.
English slang became a national language. A new
national life arose, and expressed itself in an
extension of commerce, in civil progress, and in the
growth of a free and vigorous yeoman class. It was
an age of talk, of speculation, of mental vigour and
inquiry.

And, curiously, the death of Chaucer synchronises
with the birth of a new era of bloodshed and
upheaval.

A mad extravagance on a plan of absolute
despotism—with the attendant forced " loans,"
grinding taxation, and war with Ireland—sent
Richard's crown toppling to the dust. In his attempt
at conquest he lost his throne.

II

Now we come to a stage of extravagance in fashion.
The dandies thirsted to make experiment. Bands of
gold and enamel encircled their heads, great rings
adorned their fingers and thumbs, shoes had spiked
points protruding many inches beyond the toe, sewn
with pearls and stamped with gold. Massive chains
hung from their necks, a fashion passed on to our
aspiring and aspirateless mayors.

A new and rather ridiculous garment, the houppe-lande, was designed to wear over the cotehardie and hose. It was a long, voluminous garment with a very high collar buttoning up to the chin and fitting only on the shoulders ; the sleeves, narrow at the top, became so wide at the wrist that they touched the ground. A long slit up the side of the leg was a concession to convenience.

Daggers were, of course, a necessary part of the equipment of the gallants ; just as with the development of our modern system of civilisation it is possible in the near future that we shall all walk about with a tin of poison gas in our waistcoat pockets.

Daggers were carried in many sorts of fantastic ways, some hanging from the necks and some between the legs, some carelessly cast over shoulders to flap in the middle of backs.

Woman displayed no originality or individuality in her costume ; she was content to adapt her dress from the existing fashions of the man. Her short skirted cotehardie was adapted into a kind of houppe-lande. For riding, and she rode astride, she was habited exactly the same as a man.

But she played the very devil with her hair. Here she proved the theory of the attraction or the distraction of sex antithesis.

Men had beards and moustaches in every conceivable form, and their hair came to the nape of the neck. Therefore, in her contrariness, woman not only hid her hair in a tight coil and shaved it well and high at the back of her neck, but plucked out her eyebrows. Perhaps this was her means of showing her aversion against bearded lips. She adorned her brow with chaplets and her head with crowns and bags of gold net studded with precious stones. Thus she made man pay the penalty for his hairy exuberance.

CHAPTER XV

HENRY IV. (1399–1413)

*Youthful Henry as theologian : attends a burning-alive
ceremony—Epaulettes, leg-of-mutton sleeves, waistcoats
—Enter the pleated skirt—The mystery of woman's legs
puzzles the author.*

I

THE House of Lancaster was a Parliamentary
creation. Parliament deposed Richard and set Henry
in his place, and for sordid financial reasons alone
Henry was more in the power of Parliament than any
former king.

War and insurrection had exhausted the Treasury,
and both his title and his credit depended on
Parliamentary sanction.

Both Henry the Fourth and Henry the Fifth in
their dealings with Parliament and people betrayed
a very proper appreciation for and deference to the
power behind the purse.

But the fashion of war is difficult to modify, and
the Scotch, the Welsh, and the Percys forbade peace.
But Parliament, having learnt its lesson, was
grudging in supplies, and the military party in the
State had to study finance and to attempt to fight
revolution and war on a more economic basis—if
revolution and war can ever be waged on an
economic basis.

In addition, there was constant disaffection within
the realm, the legacy of past wars and present
privations.

Times were unsettling for a wearer of the crown,
and Henry's position was not made easier by the
fanfaronades of his son, who as a bright boy of
thirteen started his military career by leading an

incursion into Scotland. At fifteen this ingenious lad fought at Shrewsbury, and at seventeen he was a general in Wales, but not a too successful general.

Hot from the battlefield, the Prince returned to England to secure the domination of the Lords over the Commons, and personally assisted at the burning alive of Mr. Thomas Bradby for a denial of transubstantiation—a doctrine on which the youthful warrior held himself an expert.

Heavy taxation had destroyed the King's popularity, and for some obscure reason the future Henry the Fifth was the popular idol and actual ruler before an attack of epilepsy translated his beloved parent to other realms.

II

The vogue of the houppelande continued into the fifteenth century, but in a variety of shapes, some reaching to the ground and some cut short to the knees. The epaulette appeared, and from the shoulder the sleeve was enormously full and very tight at the wrist. The first hefty leg-of-mutton sleeve in which a dozen rabbits can be kept was seen, and baldricks were worn over the shoulder to the knee, with bells attached to acclaim each movement. Waistcoats were introduced, and trimmed with fur or embroidered were worn over the tunic.

The fashionable lady condescended to expose her neck and shoulders. Her gown defined her figure to the hips, and was laced down the front to below the waist. Houppelandes, surcoats, and cotehardies were still worn, and all the skirts were voluminous. The only innovation was the pleated skirt, which made its debut.

It is an unquestionable fact that woman possessed legs, but they were never seen.

CHAPTER XVI

HENRY V. (1413–1422)

*War's three handmaidens : " fire, blood and famine "—Garbled
records of valour : kings, rulers, and leaders keep in
rear of battle fronts—Conquerors and megalomaniacs are
merely devastators and destroyers—Costumes adapted from
the past—Hair ornaments invented for women.*

I

" WAR," once said Henry V., " has three handmaidens ever waiting on her : fire, blood, and
famine," and nothing in the career of Henry V. or
in the subsequent history of the world induces one to
give him the lie.

It is wise not to accept all the accepted and
decorated detail of history. Henry the Fifth
undoubtedly possessed the ambitions and egotistical
mind of the conqueror and the warrior. But the
psychologist is entitled to refuse to accept the garbled
records of valour. It sounds magnificent in reading
history books to hear of kings personally leading
their armies into battle, and the more remote the
history the more prominent in the frontal attack
appear the kings and generals.

But the philosopher knows that though manners,
poses, conventions, and fashions change, human
nature and instinct remain the same. Therefore
since we know that kings, rulers, generals, and
leaders in modern history take good care to keep well
in the rear of every battle front, seldom receive a
scratch, and suffer only the pain of an occasional
twinge of mental indigestion, it is logical to conceive
that Henry the Fifth was wise enough to direct and

observe the battle of Agincourt from the shelter of the woods to which the English army after its frontal attack strategically retired. At least we know that Agincourt had no definite result, for the English army made its way to Calais and returned to England. Henry the Fifth spent most of his time fighting in France, and though unwounded, he contracted a disease at Courbeuil from which he died.

Conquerors and megalomaniacs are merely devastators and destroyers. They are the enemies of happiness and prosperity. which are ruthlessly sacrificed to their individual aggrandisement.

II

There was little progress in the art of dress during the nine years of the fifth Henry's reign. The gallant had neither time, money, nor inclination to study fashion. His civilian garb was a careless conglomeration of the styles of the previous century.

War does not encourage men to think of dress. The glorious victory of Agincourt was all-sufficing. Here, according to reports, which may have been slightly censored and judiciously edited, the British army, facing great odds, lost merely one hundred men against ten thousand Frenchmen slain. Yet had a battle of the size of Agincourt been fought in 1914 our War Office would doubtless have blazoned forth the news by the statement " On the rest of the front there was nothing to report."

Woman continued to adapt her costume from the fashions of the past, but she played with her head-dress. She crowned her head with horns—no doubt an interesting piece of symbolism. The caul had grown to grotesque proportions and assumed comic protuberances, towering so above her head that men must have felt like pigmies. Then some fair lady invented the use of horns, the fronts of which were anything from four to fourteen inches; thus was designed the shape of her caul. The top of this peculiar head-dress was covered with a wimple.

Women are strange creatures, and their whimsicalities decorate the world.

CHAPTER XVII

HENRY VI. (1422-1461)

Subtle purpose of Statutes of Apparel—Lavish colours in civilian dress—Man's grotesque head-dress—Forerunner of hat worn by modern clowns—Cap and bells—Gaby Deslys's wildest extravagance is modest simplicity compared with woman's fashions—Sleeves as comprehensive as the wings of love.

As a nine-months-old baby, Henry the Sixth was King of England, and heir to the throne in the realm of France, a legacy from his ambitious and aggressive father. But wars continued, until the north of France was reduced to a desert, and misery and disease killed one hundred thousand people in Paris alone. The militarism of Henry the Fifth availed England nothing, for by 1450 every yard of Norman ground was lost.

Justice in England was ill administered and taxation was unequalled and extortionate. Political strife was rampant. The Statutes of Apparel show a peculiar subtlety in their anxiety to curtail the dress of the labourer and the farmer, lest the wearer should gain power by the influence of better clothing.

The War of the Roses, with its long succession of treachery and corruption, bringing misery and persecution to the people, ended the thirty-nine years' reign of a weak and imbecile king.

During the intervals of campaigns in France and

civil wars at home, the sporting of lavish colours in the civilian dress of the nobles developed.

In design, comfort was considered the first essential. A loose tunic was worn, with balloon sleeves, open at the neck, and reaching to the knee, edged perhaps with fur or with a different material in a contrasting shade. The belt was low, giving the wearer a long-waisted and short-legged appearance. Tights were worn beneath. The cold weather coat had no more shape than a sack, which, in fact, it was. The head was pushed through a hole at the top, and the arms through long slits cut into the sides.

Tunics and gowns were made of fine, double-piled velvets, which were of beautiful designs raised over a ground of gold. The one original feature of man's apparel was his hat. That was the roundlit, with a long liripipe twisted round and hanging on one side, and a coxcomb of silk decorating the other. There were also the tall, conical hats, with brims of fur; broad, flat-brimmed varieties; the sugar loaf affair, the headgear of the clown of to-day; and—probably making its first appearance as a burlesque in the diversity of styles—there was invented a three-peaked cap and bells and hood.

Woman went perfectly mad in the matter of hats. Nothing was too extreme. Conceive the wildest extravagance of Gaby Deslys in her zenith, and it would be a modest simplicity in comparison to the fashions of the fifteenth century ladies. Never had the world seen such wonderful erections, nor in such fantastic shapes. Some were twenty-four inches or more high; some enormously fat; some thin and long like a minaret, or a lighthouse to the rock of woman's chastity; some great circular shapes, like the arena of woman's understanding; some great canopies supported by horns, thirty inches from end to end, and covered with gold tissue and rich falling draperies of blazing colours.

In sympathy with the lofty head-dress, the waists of the gowns were abnormally high, reaching almost to the breast, and as a natural sequence of the intermittent wars, the bodice was abnormally low, tapering to a point at the bottom, and flirting with the tapered waist. And the sleeves were as wide and comprehensive as the wings of love.

CHAPTER XVIII

EDWARD IV. (1461-1483)

*Comparison with modern conditions : arbitrary taxation, spy
system, arbitrary imprisonment—War means loss of
freedom to victor and vanquished—Edward and the
merchants' wives—Codpiece appears ; woman hides her
feet and keeps her skirts voluminous—Shoulders are bare
to the waistband.*

I

PRIOR to the reign of Edward the Fourth England
had, by Parliament, established securities of national
liberty—the right of freedom from arbitrary taxation,
from arbitrary legislation, and from arbitrary
imprisonment.

With the Wars of the Roses and the succession of
the House of York, this liberty disappeared, and the
progress of English freedom was arrested for more
than one hundred years.

Mark the significance of this era in comparison
with that of to-day. Arbitrary taxation reappeared
in benevolences and forced loans. A formidable spy-
system was instituted and personal liberty was almost
extinguished by the constant practice of arbitrary
imprisonment.

Under the reigns of the House of York and the
Tudors, the people of England were ruled with a
despotism as complete as the despotism of the
Turk.

Will the peoples of the world ever learn to understand that war in its design means the loss of all
freedom for both victor and vanquished ? And that
the call to arms to fight for " A War for Freedom "
is the transparent lie of a call to accept new bonds of
slavery ?

Edward the Fourth annexed everything for himself; he secured the grant of the customs to his own purse, filled his treasury by forfeitures and confiscations, and degraded justice by the prodigal use of bills of attainder, and stripped hundreds of knights and squires of their estates to his own profit.

Yet despite his greed, he had an attractive personality, and a gay but determined carelessness, which he used to further his popularity. He was not conservative in his loves, and though attentive to his recognised mistresses, he was democratic enough temporarily to annex the wives of the London merchants when the mood seized him.

II

Gentlemen of fashion, who were fortunate enough to escape the block, began to wear their tunics shorter and shorter. The most popular mode was made in pleated velvet and trimmed with fur, the jewelled belt placed low to give a long waisted effect. Sleeves were wide and slit open from the shoulder and narrowed at the wrist, leaving the arms covered in a rich silk, free and independent of the sleeves.

The extremist's tunic came only to the waist and displayed a pair of legs clothed in tights and a codpiece daintily fastened with ribbon. This is the first mention of the codpiece, in England, and since Rabelais has written three classic volumes on the subject, in his masculine style, there is no need for it to be enlarged upon here.

There is little wonder, in view of this exhibition, that the ladies hid their feet and kept their skirts voluminous. The waists of their gowns remained very high, but their shoulders and the V of their bodice were bared to the band of the waist. The more modest had an under-garment of silk drawn beneath the V. Tired of horns, woman drifted into steeples, eighteen inches high, and worn at an angle.

On the end of the steeple, and the tall hennin, a long veil floated, suggesting illusiveness.

It is interesting to observe with regard to the fashionable long pointed shoes, that only an esquire or one above that rank was permitted to wear them more than two inches beyond the toe. It is recorded that a tailor was fined twenty shillings for making wide sleeves, presumably under the Statute of Apparel.

CHAPTER XIX

EDWARD V. (1483)

Purple lives render most monarchs unprofitable subjects for insurance companies—So fashionable is the block that black velvet is all the rage.

ON the death of Edward IV., a victim in the early forties to the purple life which has rendered so many monarchs unprofitable subjects to the insurance companies, the crown passed to his son, Edward V.

The succession of a boy of thirteen was a godsend to the axe grinders ; a child and king who could be used as a puppet appealed to the ambitions of every faction, and the nation suffered in consequence.

Sick and tired of wars and civil jangles, the country as a whole longed for peace, and was quick to realise that peace was impossible under an infant monarch who was a pawn in the hands of its various oppressors.

That those oppressors should cut one another's throats was a matter of little moment to the Englishman of that day. What was of moment to him was that the country should be at peace ; that he should be at liberty to live his life, and to enjoy the fruits of his labour ; and that an active ruler, who could and would put a stop to costly and wasting internal jars, should occupy the throne.

Therefore, the sudden appearance on the scene of the somewhat maligned Richard of Gloucester was at first not unpopular.

At the least he put an end to the intrigues of the Woodvilles, and the Parliament which called him to the throne probably reflected the desires and hopes of the majority of the people.

The boy King and his brother disappeared mysteriously into the Tower, and the news of their suspicious deaths in that sinister fortress was for long withheld from the public.

Richard was quick to realise the necessity of enlisting the nation on his side, and once again a despot's needs proved to the national advantage. Parliament was summoned, and sweeping measures of reform designed to rally the all important mercantile interests to the new King's standard, were enacted.

The reign of the unfortunate boy King of thirteen lasted only two months, when his hunchbacked uncle, Richard, caused his murder, together with that of his younger brother.

So many nobles were sent to the block that it is not strange that black velvet was all the vogue during this short reign.

CHAPTER XX

RICHARD III. (1483-1485)

*Comparison with modern conditions : levy of benevolences
in defiance of Statute—Men wear open-breasted tunics,
rich-coloured waistcoat-like undergarments, and black
velvet stiff-brimmed hats—Woman lowers her gown and
tightens her sleeves—She regards her eyebrows with
disfavour.*

I

To conciliate a nation sick of internal strife and
monarchial conspiracies, Richard convoked Parliament and made sweeping reforms. The extortion of
money by benevolences was declared illegal. The
policy of rule by terror was reversed, pardons were
granted, and remission of forfeitures were made.
But like our modern statesmen, directly he felt
himself secure Richard threw off the pretence of
constitutional rule in 1485, and to replenish his
exchequer caused the levy of benevolences in defiance
of the statute. The resultant disaffection, together
with the latent nausea at his brutal murder of his
brother's children, caused widespread conspiracies
against him. He met a well-deserved fate at
Bosworth Field, when his armies deserted him, and
Henry Tudor gained his crown.

II

The Renaissance was at hand. Tunics, in compliment perhaps to the gowns of the ladies, were open-
breasted and cut low in the neck. Skirts were longer
and pleated ; beneath the tunic was a rich coloured
under-garment like a waistcoat, and showing above
was the top of a fine pleated white skirt. Over this
came an overcoat with lapels to the collar, and loose

flowing skirts with comfortably wide sleeves. Add a small, black velvet stiff-brimmed hat, with square-toed natural shoes, and you have got the man about town.

The waist of my lady's gown was lowered, the sleeves got tighter and were folded back with deep cuffs of linen or fur. The corsage was higher and the skirts were very full and swept the ground in a train.

The fantastically tall head-dress disappeared, the huge steeple being replaced by an embroidered bonnet, or jewelled cap, fixed on the back of the head at a right angle. Behind this, stretched on wires, was a linen wimple extending perhaps eighteen inches back and falling on each side of the face to the top of the shoulders.

The hair was drawn firmly away from the forehead under the bonnet, smaller and recalcitrant hairs being plucked away lest they should show. Eyebrows were regarded with disfavour.

It is amazing that women had not yet discovered the beauty of their hair as an adornment. But perhaps in their generosity they deemed it more delicate to inspire my lord to conjure the beauty of the tresses concealed beneath the virgin whiteness of the linen of their wimples.

CHAPTER XXI

HENRY VII. (1485-1509)

Henry's prudence loses him a share in Columbus's adventure —Sovereigns at forty-two shillings each—Gowns of men and women are rich in gorgeous colours, beautiful in texture, artistic in design—Codpieces are now garlanded with gay ribbons; woman's bodice is shaped to the figure.

I

THE long financial and political strain of the Wars of the Roses had one pronounced beneficial effect ; the last remains of the old aristocracy of war was enfeebled to the verge of impotence, and the new nobility was closely allied to, if not at one with, the commonalty, its ranks being largely recruited from the mercantile class.

On the benches of the House of Commons sat the draper and the lord of the manor, the merchant and the younger son of the great noble, and, in the words of Macaulay, from the effects of this fusion " our democracy was, from an early period, the most aristocratic, and our aristocracy the most democratic in the world." This peculiarity has lasted unto this day and has produced many important moral and social effects.

So it came about that although the sovereigns of the House of Tudor were " arbitrary gents," the exercise of their arbitrary power was very strictly limited, and as no Tudor was politically a fool, limitations were recognised, and accepted after one or two subtle trials of strength.

Henry the Seventh possessed the commercial instinct in a marked degree, and with a lively appreciation of the value of money, was a friend to trade.

Dispatching his Almoner to Naples to establish a treaty of national traffic, the King observed in his instructions : " . . . the earth, being the common parent of us all, what can be more desirable and praiseworthy than by means of commerce to communicate her various productions to her children ! "

Deeply imbued as he was with such laudable ambitions, one is not surprised to see the first Tudor becoming the owner of a small line of merchant ships and making a handsome private profit out of trade.

Incidentally, he made a valiant if unsuccessful attempt to standardise weights and measures. In one unhappy instance, however, his commercial prudence cost him dear.

His extreme caution caused him to delay acceding to the proposition of Bartholomew, the brother of Christopher Columbus, who had urged the King to " go shares " in the discovery of America. By the time Henry had made up his mind to accept, the expedition had been financed by Ferdinand of Spain and had set sail.

But it is to his credit that he was the first English King to coin a golden sovereign of forty-two shillings, and a half sovereign in proportion, both of which he religiously maintained at their standard value.

Henry the Seventh was a wise man, a lover of art, and a determined lover of peace. He was merciful and generous. When he quelled the revolts which chequered his rule, he spared the heads of the rebels and imposed heavy fines instead. Benevolences were again revived ; subsidies granted for the support of wars which Henry politically evaded, the revival of dormant claims of the crown, the exaction of fines for the breach of forgotten tenures, and the extortion of " gifts " to the exchequer from men of wealth so swelled the royal Treasury that at the end of his reign the King was enabled to bequeath a hoard of two millions to his fleshy successor.

II

This was the era of beautiful materials. The gowns of the men and the women were rich in gorgeous colours, beautiful in texture, and artistic in design. Double-piled velvets, damasked silks, and diapered stuffs were worn in gay profusion. From Bruges came world-famous silks and satins ; from Ypres the finest of linen ; from Germany elaborate and wonderful embroideries ; from Florence fine velvets in strangely enchanting designs.

Gentlemen of fashion wore a long and graceful gown reaching nearly to the ground, with a deep wide collar rolling to the waist, displaying a gorgeous patterned waistcoat laced across the breast and a shirt ornamented with fancy stitching and finely gathered at the neck with ribbon.

The sleeves were wide, with a slash from the shoulder to the elbow, through which the arms could be pushed at will. Tights of every conceivable colour were the rage ; the somewhat indelicate cod-piece, tied with charmingly coloured ribbons, was seen everywhere.

The extremist went about in a short jacket or petticoat in order that he might show to full advantage his wonderful waistcoat and other attributes, while his large felt hat was decorated with a splendid array of feathers.

Women's gowns were simple in cut, the waist being defined in unison with nature. Many were lined with fine fur, and to prevent them trailing in the mud the trains were fastened by a brooch to the waistband. In the absence of a train, the gown was cut to show an underskirt of silk. The bodice was shaped to the figure, cut square below the neck and trimmed with an edging of fur, and above the V shape was the white crimped chemise.

Sleeves were either tight from the shoulder to the wrist, or tight at the shoulders and graduated.

The end of the age of women's fantastic head-gear was approaching. Its last form was its most artistic.

It was diamond shaped, converging to an apex in the front, like a gabled roof. The stiffened border of the outline was sewn with gold and pearls—denoting the purity of the wearer's soul—and the hood, surmounted by a jewelled stole, hung over the back and shoulders, sheathing shell-like ears, and delicately caressing neck and bosom.

CHAPTER XXII

HENRY VIII. (1509-1547)

The axe as a solution for domestic difficulties—Lloyd Georgian finance—Fat Monarch's influence on clothes—Breeches stuffed with hair—Wolsey's apparelled pomp—Restrictions : purple for royalty, cloth of gold for dukes, velvet for commoners of distinction—Jewelled codpieces—Comment : When the modern woman loses her head she loses her character, in this reign she loses her neck—Woman experiments with her hair.

I

THOUGH well aware of its solid benefits, Henry the Eighth understood less of the practical side of commerce than his father, and as his money sense developed it brought him into severe conflict with his so-called " devoted people."

Encouraged by his success in granting monopolies of various kinds—prohibiting, for instance, his subjects not residing in certain named towns from making or selling cloth—he went a step too far, when, without undergoing the tedious formality of obtaining the consent of Parliament, he purposed that his subjects should contribute one-sixth of their goods to the Royal Exchequer. That might be a moderate enough demand in these enlightened days, but it set Tudor England in a blaze.

One county alone promptly raised an army of four thousand men as an active protest, and with enormous tact Bluff King Hal withdrew his demands and apologised publicly and solemnly for his momentary lack of good taste.

Possessed of a fair share of Tudor tact it was rarely indeed, even in his most arbitrary moods, that Henry the Eighth overstepped the border line which had been set up between arbitrary power and popular right.

His household affairs were another matter. Sad and callous as it may sound, the nation at large cared little for his matrimonial adventures, and he was at perfect liberty to use the axe and the block for the settlement of his domestic difficulties as long as he did not interfere with the cost of living or the private affairs of his subjects. Henry's house was his castle, and if he chose to run a permanent scaffold in connection with it, that was his own affair.

Fully appreciating his father's mercantile adventures, he turned his business attention to the problems of navigation, encouraged naval adventures, and generally made improvements in harbours and rivers. Over £60,000—then a vast sum—was expended on the harbour of Dover ; Southampton was widened and deepened, weirs and shoals were removed, and the corporation of the Holy Trinity received its first charter from Henry's hands, the charter which gave it power over all the shipping of England.

To his commercial debit must be placed the fact that Henry towards the end of his reign began the bad practice of debasing his coinage ; in 1545 his silver had one half alloy, and when he was gathered to his wives and concubines, the nominal pound was worth a bare 9s. 3¾d., thus anticipating the Lloyd Georgian Treasury Note.

II

The inflated personality of the King had its effect on the habits and customs of the age ; and as his figure increased in size, the clothes of his courtiers were stuffed to make his advisers resemble him—a custom which appears to have descended even to domestics, and is still partly commemorated in the habits of the Yeoman of the Guard.

The hood of the preceding century was exchanged for a coarse, round felt hat, cap or bonnet, with a single jewel in front, for the men ; and a plain coif, composed of a roll of false hair on a velvet bonnet,

F

for the women. Maidens left their heads uncovered, their hair hanging down or simply braided. At the Court of Henry the Eighth it was considered advisable that maidens should be distinguished.

Growing tired of long hair in men, Henry ordered his attendants and courtiers to cut their hair short, a move which was promptly countered by the first introduction of the peruke. Is it not recorded that twenty shillings was paid for a peruke for Saxton, the King's fool ?

In another of his purple moods, Henry directed that purple was to be worn only by the Royal family ; cloth of gold and tissues only by dukes or marquesses ; embroidery by earls ; silks and velvets by " commoners " of " distinction." The ordinary leg coverings were cloth boots, and a pair of black silk stockings brought all the way from Spain was a present literally " fit for a king."

The enormous trunk breeches, as a tribute to the ever-increasing King, were a smart set vogue, which vogue was carried to such an absurd degree of magnitude that in Parliament House there was a low sort of a scaffold around the building for those members who wore great breeches stuffed with hair to rest their weary thighs upon. Another instance of imitation being an uncomfortable form of flattery.

To illustrate the pomp of priestly dress, could any-thing in history equal that of Cardinal Wolsey—this son of a butcher and servitor of another ; this corpulent Cardinal, this fully blown flower of priestly prosperity, expanding through life in his magnificent silken vestments as a covering for his obesity, and as an advertisement of his opulence ?

Could anything be more significant of the power of apparel than the incident of the Cardinal's hat, which was sent to him to York Place by the Pope through the hands of an ordinary messenger ? The messenger was clothed by Wolsey and sent back with the hat to Dover, from whence the cavalcade went and fetched him. The hat was set on a sideboard full of plate, with tapers all about it, where dukes and lords made curtsies thereto.

Did ever a minister of Christ make more material show of apparelled pomp and magnificence and authority than this prince of profusion ? His household consisted of a dean (his steward) ; a knight (his treasurer) ; an esquire (his controller) ; a cofferer ; three marshals ; two yeomen ushers ; two grooms ; an almoner ; a master cook (who was clothed in damask, satin or velvet, with a chain of gold about his neck) ; a high chamberlain ; a vice-chamberlain ; twelve gentlemen ushers ; daily waiters ; six gentlemen waiters ; nine or ten lords (each allowed two servants) ; forty carvers, servers, etc. ; six ushers ; eight grooms ; forty-six yeomen of his chamber to attend upon his person ; sixteen doctors and chaplains ; two secretaries ; two clerks of his signet ; four councillors.

As Chancellor of England Wolsey had four footmen, apparelled in rich running coats, whenever he rode a journey.

Then he had a Herald of Arms and a Sergeant of Arms ; a physician ; an apothecary ; four minstrels ; a keeper of his Tents ; an armourer ; an instructor of his words ; two yeomen in his wardrobe ; and a keeper of his chamber in the Court.

In the wonderful and splendid arrayed retinue of the past is perhaps shown the origin of the black coated bureaucracy of to-day.

When Wolsey appeared in public he would issue forth apparelled in the red habit of a cardinal—which was of satin, taffeta, damask, or caffa, the best that could be bought for gold—and upon his head a round pillion, with a noble of black velvet set to the inner side and a tippet of fine sables about his neck. Borne before him, first came the great seal of England, and then his cardinal's hat carried by a bare-headed nobleman. At his hall door there was an attendant for him and his mule, the latter in crimson velvet and gilt stirrups. When he was mounted, with his cross bearers and pillar bearers, upon horses also trapped with scarlet, he marched forward with his four foot-men, with gilt pole-axes in their hands.

He served his sovereign before his God. He studied Harry's wishes well and secured their accomplishment, whether for the signature to a treaty or the procuration of a new mistress.

His august master, Henry the Eighth, was a great moralist—inasmuch as he was a believer in the insular morality of marriage. That is why he murdered his wives in order to marry his mistresses. He was always in a quandary as to which commandment to break, the sixth or the seventh, and usually chose the former. We in the twentieth century are more humane in our choice.

Henry inherited the crown of a prosperous country ; he left behind him a bankrupt people, a weakling son, and a record of marriage only equalled later in America.

III

Since in this age there lived such men as Michael Angelo, Raphael, Leonardo da Vinci, Botticelli, Holbein, Luther, Erasmus, and Rabelais, it is natural that styles, fashions, and designs in clothes developed and were many and various. The most characteristic perhaps was the overcoat cut to reach the knee, with tremendous folds and an enormous collar of satin or fur, coming well over the thickly padded shoulders, and rolling back down the centre of the front. The sleeves, barred with fur or rich applique, were very wide, and puffed at the top and tapered to the wrist. The cut of the coat with |its swelled effects was probably originated as a compliment to Henry's robust figure. A richly ornamented waistcoat, in satin or brocade, showed a white shirt, the front of which was sewn with fine designs in black silk. The collar, which reached high in the neck, was also embroidered in black and had a tiny frill hem at the top. A shirt wonderfully artistic in effect !

Then there was the skirted frock-coat, open to the

waist, and held by a sash of silk tied in a bow ; from the waist it was either cut full to the knees or cut away in the front to show the coloured fronts and the still popular and protuberant codpiece, which had now arrived at the stage of being highly decorated and even jewelled. Club-toed shoes, and the little flat hat of the period adorned perhaps by a feather, completed the picture.

Breeches of various odd designs and shapes were introduced ; these were slashed and " blistered "— to show the shirt underneath—in an extravagant fashion. Some were cut straight to the knee, and then puffed and sagged ; others cut close but slashed around the thigh ; and some slashed and puffed at the knee and swelled out to balloons around the thigh. On all the breeches the universal codpiece was made in a variety of fantastic shapes.

The Irish were forbidden by law to wear shirts or smocks of linen dyed with saffron ; nor were they allowed to wear in shirts or smocks more than seven yards of cloth.

Restrictions in dress were autocratic. Only royalty were allowed to wear black genet, only viscounts sable, and martin and black trimming were allowed to those with an income of two hundred marks a year.

In design the fashions of the women during the reign of the fat and sensual Henry were not nearly so attractive as those of the men. This is natural, since England was ruled by an obese murderer.

Perhaps women were nervous of the consequences of allurement in those vicious days. When a modern woman loses her head she suffers only the loss of her character, but at Henry's court she lost her neck as well.

In her cloaks woman followed man's lead, and they were voluminous, full and broad at the shoulder to accommodate the widest of sleeves, with a huge fur collar to elaborate the effect.

The bodice of her gown was cut square at the neck and fitted tightly from the bosom to the waist. On some the front would be laced and the waist pinched to an extreme. Beneath the lacing was seen her shift, daintily embroidered with black silk. The skirt graduated stiffly to a considerable width at the feet, and sometimes panelled in a V shape from the waist to show an underskirt of brocade. The sleeves were narrow at the shoulders, and very full and square below the elbow, showing an under-sleeve of silk or brocade.

The diamond-shaped head-dress continued to be worn and elaborated, but woman was getting tired of exhibiting her head as a box of tricks, and towards the end of the reign she commenced the experiments from which woman has never ceased—the dressing of the crowning beauty of her hair.

CHAPTER XXIII

EDWARD VI. (1547-1553)

Book of Common Prayer due to unscrupulous Somerset's bid for power—Agrarian troubles, rise in prices, debasement of coinage—Pendulum of fashion swings back—Reaction from pomp and pageantry—The jerkin (and its insanely puffed sleeves) ; the partlet (the origin of the modern collar) —Woman's clothes suggest a weariness of the desire to attract.

I

ON the death of Henry VIII. the religious storm, which had only been kept in check by that wily Tudor's personality, broke on the devoted head of his successor, Jane Seymour's child, Edward the boy-king.

Ever since his father's health had been seen to be failing, the child had been a centre of intrigue, political and religious, and again the nation suffered under and by reason of the rule of an innocent minor.

Before Henry's death artful suggestions of a rival to his son in the person of the Plantagenet Surrey had brought that noble to the block, and only the ruthless, relentless, remorseless monarch's death saved Norfolk from a similar fate.

The boy's uncle, Hereford, lost no time in profiting by his position as Protector and Governor of the child King to elevate himself to the Dukedom of Somerset, and he did not forget his friends and supporters.

Nor did he and his followers forget the financial possibilities of the situation, and though the treasury was beggared, public money was found to gild the coronets of the new peers. And more, a new patent, in the boy-king's name, made the devoted uncle supreme.

But hastily acquired supremacy has its disadvantages, and Somerset found it advisable—even necessary—to bring the nation to his side. So popularity was attempted to be purchased by the repeal of arbitrary enactments, and the Protestants being the more likely party in the State from which support could be hoped, wholesale Protestant reforms were speedily introduced.

It is somewhat ironic that the Book of Common Prayer owes its inception to the utterly unscrupulous Somerset's bid for supreme power.

A disastrous campaign against Scotland, religious changes which became unpopular owing to the rigour with which they were enforced, agrarian troubles due to the rise in rent under new masters, a general rise in prices, and the continued debasement of the coinage were all contributory factors to Somerset's fate.

Under his successor, the Earl of Warwick, things went from bad to worse.

German and Italian mercenary troops were introduced, and the rule of the Council of Regency became a rule of terror, the sole aim of its members being to elevate their fortunes at the cost of the State.

An intensification of religious persecution added fresh delights to the life of the ordinary citizen, and that there was no revolution was due to that ordinary citizen's patient belief that when the young King came of age in two or three years' time and was his own master, life would be worth living.

But the lad's health was failing ; his death would bring Mary to the throne, and her accession meant the overthrow of the gang which had for so long ruled England.

Something had to be done ; the boy-king was induced to sign a will naming Lady Jane Grey as his successor, and he passed away leaving the country a legacy of religious and political chaos.

II

Back had swung the pendulum of fashion ; style was retrogressive, its progress arrested by simplicity.

The reaction from pomp and pageantry was shown. Monarchies have an actual and a subtle influence on dress.

The boy-king reigning nominally from the age of ten to sixteen years, possessing no power politically, influenced the trend of the dress of the men and women of that day in some subconscious way.

The exaggerated effect of the enormous broad shoulders of the obese Henry remained, but the design was tampered with until it became silly. In came the jerkin, which Puritanism under Cromwell developed a century later into a garment of disgustingly severe simplicity.

In the boy Edward's time the jerkin was thrown over the head ; was tight at the waist, had insanely puffed sleeves at the shoulder, and was worn over trunks which were puffed at the knee. Altogether the wearer looked what he probably was—a fool. The embroidered shirt remained, and was added to a partlet, which was a detachable frill fixed to the neck of the shirt—the origin of many fashions and of the modern collar.

The effect of the previous reign was shown in the dress of woman which was peculiarly timid and undesigning. Evidently she was nauseated by the power of the block. More often she would wear a simple loose gown—sexless in shape—cut high in the neck, consisting of a few trimmings of ribbons, a slightly puffed shoulder, and generally conveying an impression of weariness of the desire to attract, which is understandable.

CHAPTER XXIV

MARY (1553-1558)

*Barren specimen of decayed virginity—Spanish influence on
men's dress—The ruffle appears—Woman's gown is loose
in deference to the maternal aspirations of the sterile
Queen.*

I

By the right of her poisoned blood this fanatical,
degenerate, and withered spinster of thirty-eight
ascended the throne of England. Fortunately, her
reign was short, and stricken in body and in mind
her perfidious career was ended after five horrible
years.

In the history of the world so many foul deeds have
been perpetuated in the name of religion that the
very word stinks in the nostrils of decent men and
thinkers. One is forced to make one's own solitary
religion, and choose one's own individual God.

II

Man's dress evinced a Spanish style and tendency,
the result no doubt of the political marriage of young
Philip of Spain with this barren specimen of decayed
virginity. England was spared an issue of this
unsavoury union, for though often imagining herself
with child the bloody queen achieved nothing but
burnings and slaughters, and produced nothing but
the impotent hallucinations of her own sterility.

The high-peaked Spanish hat came in—a velvet
erection with a narrow brim. The short Spanish
cloak or cape reached just below the waist. The first
appearance in England of the ruffle is recorded ; in
its origin small and neat. Then the cape became
longer and was made with sleeves, and the collar

was turned up and stood high above the back of the neck, fastened with a clasp or a brooch at the front.

The doublet was shaped to the body with a long skirt, and the opening at the top showed a portion of the shirt, or the partlet strip, or collar.

Ladies' gowns were long and loose, with a high standing collar and sleeves very wide at the end, with a deep turned back cuff.

Around the waist was a loose girdle with an ornamental pendant attached ; the figure was not defined and the waist was full, in deference, perhaps, to the aspirations of the Queen, which were as misplaced as her principles.

CHAPTER XXV

ELIZABETH (1558–1603)

A straight-laced, tight-laced Queen, whose commercial epitaph might be : " She overdid it "—Monopolies for value received—Exorbitant prices—Elizabeth's acrobatics unrivalled in history—Human form is a peg for bombast —Fashion mixes its breed in wild confusion—A new misery is introduced : starched cambric—Inventor of yellow starch is hanged, but for another crime—Spanish hats, Italian ruffs, German hose, Flemish shoes—Women wear masks in the streets.

I

ON the latest medical authority we have it that the Virgin Queen was a strait-laced, not to say tight-laced lady, so one is relieved from the disagreeable necessity of re-writing any scandal about Queen Elizabeth. Apparently her morals were all that could be wished, if her digestion left much to be desired.

With Tudor business aptitude Elizabeth determined to do all that lay in her power to encourage commerce and navigation, and like a true Tudor determined to make business profit out of the Royal encouragement.

For long the nation was too occupied in the struggle to exist as a nation to pay much attention to purely commercial matters. Reformed Europe and the old Catholic regime were at death-grips ; France had ceased temporarily to be of account, and England stood alone against the Catholic Prince " who ruled Spain, Portugal, Italy, the Netherlands, the East and the West Indies, whose armies repeatedly marched to Paris, and whose fleets kept the coasts of Devonshire and Sussex in alarm."

At this time it was plain that whatever her faults, the fates of the realm and of all reformed Churches were sealed in the security of Elizabeth's person and the success of her administration. The very subject who suffered from her bigotry realised this, and it was in this spirit that the fanatic whose hand had been lopped off for punishment, waved his hat with the hand which was left him and shouted " God save the Queen."

But the series of events comprising the defeat of the Armada at last brought breathing space, and both Queen and people began to turn their attention to business.

Characteristically, Elizabeth sought to turn what no doubt in her opinion was an honest and desirable penny by the grant of monopolies, but her zeal outran her discretion, and her commercial epitaph reads " She overdid it."

" For value received " the Queen granted monopolies by scores, and in consequence the cost of living soared almost to modern pinnacles.

The most ordinary necessaries—iron, oil, starch, coal, lead, vinegar, glass, leather, and so forth—could only be bought at exorbitant prices, and through the House of Commons the nation voiced its protest.

Passions were high, disaster and revolution seemed at hand, when the Tudor tact saved the situation.

With a political agility many a modern politician seeks in vain to rival, the Queen placed herself at the head of the reformers, redressed the grievances with ostentatious grace, and thanked the Commons in dignified and touching language for bringing the matter to her notice.

An amazing feat in political acrobatics which stands unrivalled in history.

" She gained more honour and love by the manner in which she repaired her errors than she would have gained by never committing errors " is a magnificent epitaph on an extraordinary woman.

If monarchs be judged by the company they keep what a fame is that of Elizabeth, and what a group is that which lends lustre to her throne !

Sydney, Spenser, Essex, Raleigh, Bacon, Walsingham, Burleigh, Sackville, Ben Jonson— great names these indeed ; but one name there is greater than all, a name which it has been left to a modern young woman dramatist to degrade into a " fancy "—the name of William Shakespeare.

A queen who achieved fame in such an age of famous men must be accepted as exceptionally queenly.

II

If, in the arts, this was the period of the renaissance, in the matter of dress, it was the era of revolution.

In reviewing the fashions of Elizabeth's time, one must curb one's exuberance lest one's dissertation becomes as windy as the inevitable draught beneath the skirts of the Elizabethan woman.

It was the age of fantasy. In clothes it was the period of gestation of design. Styles ran riot. Comicality had free play. Experiment was hailed. Grace had a following, but the grotesque had a vogue. Things were not what they seemed, and the human form became a peg for bombast. National character in dress lost its insularity, and merged into that of the continent. Fashion mixed its breed in wild confusion. Convention was cast aside and the old formality became a feeble force.

The Spanish hat gaily sported itself on top of the Italian ruff, and the ruff held itself starchily aloof from the French doublet, while the German hose looked arrogantly down on the Flemish shoes.

The great ruff cockily and uncomfortably encasing the neck was the distinguishing feature of the reign. Then a she-devil in Flanders discovered the art of starching cambric, and added to life a new misery from which we fools of men suffer unto this day. Another fiend in England, by name Mrs. Turner, gained notoriety by inventing a receipt for yellow starch. She was afterwards hanged at Tyburn for another crime.

The fantastic revelled in extravagance. Up sprang the clown and pantaloon, and the harlequin ruled the herd.

Man became a monstrous creature. He was swelled with pride, which exhibited itself in strange places, for his belly was stuffed in his doublet, and his breeches stuck out a foot all round him. To solidify the illusion his trunks were stuffed with rags or bran. In the Houses of Parliament special accommodation had to be made for the swollen seats of the mighty.

To accentuate his inflation the gallant was tight-laced to the waist, and his breeches were made of wide striped silks or velvets with bands of contrasting colours or slashed and panelled with bars of gold lace.

But from the chaos of the various extravagances a design of grace was evolved for the figure of the Elizabethan in his jaunty hat, high-collared Italian cloak, slimly defined waist, moderately full trunk, gay coloured hose, and top boots cross-strapped from the knee to the thigh. Such is a pleasant picture of the good old days, which were probably infinitely worse than we imagine.

Under the influence of a rule of virginity, one would imagine woman would incline to a fashion of adolescent simplicity. But apparently the irritation of this exampled condition drove her to excesses. At any rate, in dress, she went stark, staring (this reiterated adjective is so applicable that it is unavoidable) mad.

Woman can show only one sense at a time, and in that she is artistic, as some of us know. In this case she only showed the artistic sense of displaying her hair in all sorts of becoming and alluring styles ; and if her own hair did not please her, she showed some-one else's. Some of the periwigs were beautiful and dressed with pearls and rings of gold, and a false love-lock would rest upon her shoulder to be caressed by a faithful lover.

Beyond this and her pretty face she was not a

woman at all. The bodice was so tight-laced that she could not breathe her love song ; her skirt was a huge parachute, already inflated and waiting to be dropped.

Around her neck was hung a starched ruff, as a warning—or a symbol—to the suitor. Her sleeves were puffed and the epaulettes wide to ward off the intruder, or perhaps there were false sleeves in addition hanging loosely down in sympathy with the love-lock.

Her gown was open in front to show the stiffly embroidered undergown and the edge of her fine linen chemise, and from the waist it hurriedly parted contact with the body and spread itself around the frame of the great farthingale on which had been placed half a dozen petticoats to give the necessary fullness. But lest one's pity is aroused by the thought of what the wearer must have suffered by the intolerably many garments enumerated in their entirety, it is comforting to point out that the entire construction was so much a thing apart and separated from the silk stockinged nether limbs, that she in fact suffered even less from the lack of hygiene than the average lady of to-day, who dances in a confection of georgette, to which at least is added a daintily unobtrusive undergarment of *crêpe de Chine*, or some such stuff as dreams are made of.

It was the custom in the sixteenth century for the ladies to wear masks in the street. On occasions masks were a useful shield to their modesty.

CHAPTER XXVI

JAMES I. (1603-1625)

A Court of drunken women—The King's stiletto-proof doublets—Man's clothes a medley of adaptations—Woman displays her bare breasts—Court ladies regret the passing of the farthingale : an odd reason.

I

DESPITE his big head, ugly face, slobbering tongue, rickety legs, buffoonery, coarseness of speech, and personal cowardice, James possessed an acute shrewdness and a ready wit, and was a lover of beauty.

War and its cost in inevitable taxation had dimmed the popularity of Elizabeth towards the end of her reign, so the policy of James was to evade war but annex all the taxation for himself.

English commerce was growing and James availed himself of the right of the Crown to levy custom duties for the replenishment of his individual purse. His impositions were greater than those of any previous monarch.

Guido Fawkes, an insignificant person and conspirators' tool, had fame thrust upon him by being connected with a plot to blow up James and Parliament with extreme thoroughness. Fawkes was merely the keeper of the cellar, and although he lost his head, he made a great name for himself. He made but little noise in his time, but since his death he has been responsible for more noise than any man in history. At the sound of his name even children's faces light up. A great achievement !

The profligate Court of James was so prodigal in expenditure that the exchequer was seven hundred thousand pounds in debt. Parliament refused to grant supplies, so he flouted Parliament as he flouted the law. But money and credit were as essential in those days as in these, and James, though a Scotchman, was a spender; and being quick-witted, he conceived an original idea. The number of peers at the time of his accession was sixty; for two centuries only ten new peerages had been created. To relieve his embarrassment James sold baronies at ten thousand pounds a piece, created ten in one batch, and managed to bestow forty-five during his reign.

James's little idea is still exceedingly popular with modern governments, but the price, with the times, has advanced.

Lucky James the First was lucky perhaps only in so far as that he wore the crown of England. Then the Court showed a falling off in decency. Drunkenness became a fashion even with the women at Court. The ladies abandoned their sobriety and were seen to roll about in intoxication.

James and his brother-in-law, Charles IV. of Denmark, finding Bacchus an affinity, were wont to get drunk together. The feasts organised by James degenerated into carousals. At one of these some of the Court ladies appeared in various guises, one as the Queen of Sheba, three richly clothed as Faith, Hope and Charity, and two others as Victory and Peace. The Queen of Sheba, whose part was to carry precious gifts to James, having overmuch enjoyed her cups, fell down with her casket at her monarch's feet. Hope did make one effort to speak, but being incoherent was excused on account of her hopeless condition. Faith, good though her intent, found her feet unstable, and left the Court in a staggering state. Charity, covering the multitude of her sister's sins, attempted an obeisance and then returned to Hope and Faith, who were both sick in the lower hall. Victory, after some lamentable utterances, was led away like a silly captive and laid to sleep on the outer steps of the antechamber. Peace was the only one of the party virile and aggressive, and turning in wrath upon those attending her, made war upon their heads with her olive branch.

James, gallantly inspired with a desire to dance with these fair ladies, arose, but unfortunately fell down at the feet of the Queen of Sheba, and was carried to an inner chamber and laid on a bed of state.

He was no lover of clothes, but was faithful to those he wore, for he would never change them until they were in tatters. He studied fashion only so far as having his clothes made large and easy to make his body appear more corpulent. In this there was reason ; being of a timorous disposition, he had his doublets quilted so that they might be stiletto-proof.

With all this debauchery, it was in James's reign that the poetical atmosphere of the masque was introduced. Here was the age of poetry and literature. From the Court mummeries of Henry VIII. and the pageants of Elizabeth developed the fable, fantasy, poetry, gorgeous dress, and dances of the masque. Ben Jonson was the great poetical master at the Court and Inigo Jones the artist.

II

Men's dress of this reign had no distinguishing character. It was more or less a medley of adaptation, with perhaps a Spanish tendency—like the king's politics.

The tall stiff hat with a feather was worn. The ruff was smaller and cut square in front, or took the form of a plain wide linen collar standing high in the neck. The doublet was looser, and the buttons set closely from the waist to the neck ; at the waist was a very short pleated skirt. The sleeves were narrow to the wrist with a turn back cuff of linen or stuff. The breeches and fronts were loose but not bombasted ; at the knee of the breeches was a ribboned bow.

Women continued to look grotesque. The great farthingale was still popular. Bodies of gowns were cut so low as to display bare breasts. The waist was low and tight-laced and reached to a point in the front, marked with a narrow sash of ribbon tied into a bow. Woman's huge skirt was divided and showed a large square panel and embroidered petticoat barred with gold lace. In place of the ruff she wore a tall, upstanding collar or rebate of fine lace, and round the wrists of her narrow sleeves a cuff of pointed lace.

The day of the farthingale was nearing its end, to the regret only of those ladies at the Court who welcomed it as a concealment of a condition in which they had no right to be.

CHAPTER XXVII

CHARLES I. (1625-1649)

*Peace and economy policy—Rulers should be judged by the
effect of their reign upon the people—Long wigs for men
with two elegant love locks—Sleeveless bodices—Beauty
spots and feather fans add to woman's attractiveness—
Women equal to men in some designs.*

I

WITH Charles I. drunkenness disappeared and
decorum and comparative virtue were restored. The
King maintained a royal dignity and stately reserve
and enjoined a strict Court etiquette on the personnel
of his household. But despite the magnificence of
his Court the atmosphere was dull, for the monarch
was stiff and repulsive in his manners. He was
without a sense of humour and consequently more
easily lost his head.

It was unfortunate that in ascending the throne he
had to pay, in more ways than one, the penalty of
James's extravagances.

Parliament was adamant on the matter of supplies.
So Charles, who was by no means weak in financial
matters appertaining to himself, proceeded by the
divine right of kings to trample on the law. Finding
a poor reception given to his endeavour to raise
money by " voluntary " loan in the form of
Benevolence, he met the needs of his purse in 1627
by the levy of a forced loan. Poor men who refused
to lend were pressed into the army and navy, and
recalcitrant tradesmen flung into prison. Buckingham, his friend and sharer and spender of spoils,
undertook the task of squeezing the nobles and the
gentry with considerable success.

Buckingham was a rich liver and generous lover,
a poor soldier and a bad diplomat. Having made

a ghastly failure of his campaign to relieve the Huguenots at Rochelle, the treasury of the Crown was again bankrupt, and Charles had to summon a new Parliament. But the Court candidates were defeated everywhere at the elections, and the king was forced to waive all claims to levy taxes not granted by Parliament.

Money ruled the world then as it does now, and since supplies were not forthcoming, Charles very wisely—though of course of necessity—determined on a policy of peace and economy.

Unhappily, however, his ordinary income was insufficient to pay the laundry of his lace cuffs, so he resorted to every conceivable shift to fill his exchequer. He created fifty-six new peerages at a price not divulged, doubtless obtaining more than the inventor James. He forced knighthoods on the peaceful landed gentry, and if they refused he squeezed them into submission. He developed his commercial mind by reviving monopolies, and the companies who undertook them agreed to pay a fixed duty on their profits and a large sum down for the original concession. Consequently almost every article of domestic consumption fell into the hands of the monopolist and prices rose out of all reasonable proportion. Charles was no fool, and had he lived to-day he would probably have kept his head and exploited America.

Individually his policy was sound ; he reduced the National Debt, which was then the King's Debt and had risen to £1,600,000, to half that amount, and he raised the personal revenue of the Crown to £800,000 a year.

In reviewing the rulers of the past it is wise and logical and just to judge them not by the lying accounts of their great military victories, but by the effect their reign had on the people they ruled. Were their subjects on balance, peaceful and prosperous, or decimated, miserable and poverty-stricken.

Thanks to Charles's policy of Peace, England was prosperous for many years. He was unlucky to reign during a century of mad fanaticism. The curse of religious strife, fostered and inflamed not by Charles, but by political place-seekers, broke out afresh in Civil War.

The King was condemned to the block by fanatics, but he met his fate with brave dignity and died like a nobleman. Less than ten years later the Puritan Cromwell died snivelling in bed, muttering his sanctimonious imprecations and protesting hysterically his fear of the Lord—a fear which was probably justified.

II

Charles had a manner, and the dress of the men during his reign attained an elegance. His bosom favourite, the Duke of Buckingham, was a dandy of magnificence, and infuriated Parliament by his excesses and by the arrogant splendour of his attire.

The man of fashion wore his hair or wig long, the tresses reposing gracefully—or otherwise—on his shoulders. Sometimes two elegant love-locks, tied with a dainty ribbon discreetly annexed from some fair lady, adorned each side of his languid face. His broad brimmed hat sported a wonderful feather, and his vandyke beard nestled on the top of a vandyke collar. The doublet became graceful. It was buttoned only from the neck to the waist, and from there the long straight fronts, embroidered on the edges, reached to the thighs. Sleeves were wide and loose with one big slash down the centre through which the shirt was seen, the cuffs narrow with point lace edges being turned back. The breeches of satin were comparatively close-fitting, and below the knee appeared a ribboned garter with a bow. A large silk cloak used was lightly thrown across the shoulders, or fixed by a strap so that it could hang over the arm.

With the rise of Puritanism, the Royalist carried his clothes with a studied air of carelessness.

The ridiculous farthingale, and the somewhat uncomfortable revatoe had disappeared and the woman favoured a rich simplicity, or a comparative assumption of simplicity. The bodice of her gown was cut low, leaving her neck and bosom the freedom they had so long sacrificed to fashion. Over this sleeveless bodice was a short satin jacket, opened and laced in the front to show the contrasting coloured bodice underneath. Sleeves were moderate in width and came just below the elbow, the cuff edged with lace being turned back. Skirts were very full and hung loosely to the ground ; sometimes they were tied back or hooked up in a variety of ways to show the rich satin petticoat of the same colour as the bodice.

A beauty spot on the cheeks, and a big feather fan added to women's attractiveness.

In point of graceful design in dress the lady of Charles's reign hardly vied with the men, but in all other designs she was doubtless more than his equal

CHAPTER XXVIII

CROMWELL (1649-1660)

An ex-kaiser Wilhelm of his period—Rules by force and fraud—Ugliness is godliness and beauty satanic—Battle of Drogheda is won by Belfast linen factories—Woman denudes herself of every frill—Her symbolic strip—Two things wise men doubt—Men and women are instinctive lovers.

I

THE people of any nation, in all times, are a strange, conglomerate mass ; ignorant, always ill-educated, stupidly infantile in political love, led eternally by silly parrot cries in the guise of religion, ideals, patriotism, and freedom. Impotent individually and impotent in their various sections, they must be governed as a whole ; and the manners and the thought of the mass are dependent on its rulers.

In the seventeenth century, with the chaos of religious upheaval, the masses were abnormally susceptible to the ruling influence. The pendulum swung rapidly, vibrating with the force of fanaticism.

Culture was at a discount for the term of ten years under Oliver Cromwell. Give power to a crude, unrefined mind, and brutality will reign.

Cromwell's first act on attaining power was to behead those nobles who disagreed from his religious principles. Almost his first words to a Council of State, when referring to the many of his own fellow-countrymen who opposed him were, " We must cut these people to pieces."

Having succeeded in achieving this he went to Ireland to teach the people the true religion. His storm of Drogheda in 1649 was the first of a series of the most ghastly massacres recorded in British history. Here are his own words from his terrible dispatch :

" Our men were ordered by me to put them all to the sword. And indeed, being in the heat of action, I forbade them to spare any that were in arms in the town, and I think that night they put to death about two thousand men. A few fled to St. Peter's Church, whereupon I ordered the steeple to be fired, when one of them was heard to say in the midst of the flames, ' God damn me, I burn, I burn.' In the church itself nearly one thousand were put to the sword. I believe all their friars were knocked on the head promiscuously but two."

Of the remnants who surrendered, says Cromwell :

" When they submitted their officers were knocked on the head, every tenth man was killed, and the rest shipped for Barbadoes. I am persuaded that this is a righteous judgment of God upon these barbarous wretches, and that it will tend to prevent the effusion of blood for the future."

These blasphemous words of this bloody fanatic remind one of the invocations of a modern bloody tyrant, ex-Kaiser Wilhelm !

Under Cromwell merciless oppression continued for years and was completed as it began. Thousands perished by famine and the sword. Those who surrendered were sent like cattle in shipload after shipload over sea, for sale into forced labour in Jamaica and the West Indies. All those who proved to have borne arms were sentenced to banishment or death. Catholic proprietors, even though they had taken no part in the war, were punished by the forfeiture of a third of their estate ; and those who had borne arms were made to forfeit the whole.

It was veritably " the curse of Cromwell " and the doom of any real peace between England and Ireland for centuries onwards.

Were it not so tragic it would appear comic that throughout his rule he carried as his banner "Political and Religious Liberty"! It was by the sword that he ruled, yea, though he called it the "Instrument of the Lord."

He was more autocratic than any king. He defied constitutional law and placed the Press under a strict censorship. Catholics and "Malignants," as the Royalists were named, were excluded from the franchise. His elections were even more farcical than those of to-day. In 1655 the sixty members returned by Scotland and Ireland were all Government nominees. Two hundred members, or one half of the entire House, were bound to the Government by ties of profit or place, a diplomacy still fashionable in our twentieth century. One hundred members of the remaining half were excluded from admission to the House on grounds of disaffection and want of religion. Thus Cromwell made certain of his majority.

Taxes were levied by his sole authority, and payment was enforced by distraint. When a collector was sued in the courts for redress, the counsel for the prosecution were sent to the Tower.

Theatres were closed, Sunday sports were prohibited, racing was abolished; cock-fighting and Maypole dances, Christmas junketings, and even mince-pies were forbidden.

Joy was a crime, merriment an offence, happiness a sin: such was the religion of the Great Cromwell, the despot and the fearer of the Lord. He ruled by fraud and force, and prostituted liberty, but his endeavour to entail a doctrine of slavery failed.

Towards the end of his short rule the traditional instincts of England revolted against this miserable conception of human life, and as a natural consequence the pendulum swung to the other extreme. The younger generation, who had grown up amidst the horrors of Civil War and in the ghastly atmosphere of Puritan suppression, were irreligious and sceptical in temper. Even the children of the leading

Puritans contemptuously stood aloof from the Protector's idea of God, and when Milton was conceiving his chilly " Paradise Lost " his nephews, reared in his house, saddened his simple heart by the satires they wrote against Puritan hypocrisy, and by their numerous contributions to the obscene songs of the day.

This blighting influence petered out to the tune of Cromwell's death-bed groans, and life came into its own again.

II

So far as the dressing of the gloomy stage on which Cromwell performed is concerned, the supers looked and played their mirthless parts.

Ugliness was godliness. Beauty was satanic. Restraint was a virtue. Expression was a vice. Clumsiness was holiness. Elegance was ineptitude. Delicate fripperies were devilish futilities. Pointed lace was so pointed that it was lascivious.

All dress became plain and miserable in sympathy with Cromwell's policy.

Man clothed himself like the tyrannical fool he was. Picture him in his broad-brimmed hat with the tall narrowing crown of the clown, and in his deplorable loose doublet. Black, brown, and grey were his giddily popular colours. His breeches were beastly and shapeless, hanging straight and loose to below the knee. His large wide-topped boots created a vacuum, in company with his mind. His plain linen Eton collar proved that the battle of Drogheda was won by the linen factories of Belfast. His sloppy cloak was capacious, but not capacious enough to cover the multitude of his hypocrisies.

Woman ? How she must have laughed in her contempt for these men and pandered to their transient whims. Purity is the vogue ! Then, says woman, let us pose in the picture.

She dressed her hair plainly and severely under a linen cap, and only rarely a curl was seen astray.

She denuded herself of every frill. All the little strips she removed from her bodice, but in the middle of her back she left one little strip, like a tail, symbolising her opinion of the age. She wore a very deep linen collar and modest linen cuffs. Her skirt was loose and plain, and occasionally she coyly lifted it to show the neat little roses on her shoe. What matter her clothes, since her eyes were a dream and dressed in ten thousand moods ?

The part that women played in Cromwell's time is unrecorded—like all truly great deeds—but it may be assumed that, irritated and unamused by the gloom, the horror, and the bloodiness, they subtly determined through the aid of their men to end this brief phase of annihilating fanaticism.

Morality is the same on balance in every era ; it is only manners that change. There was probably no more morality or immorality in Cromwell's time than in Charles the Second's time. In one Court the manners were cultured and open, in the other narrow and confined. One Court presented its gaiety, the other propounded its purity.

Two things, however, the wise man doubts : the man who overmuch propounds his fear of the Lord, and the woman who overmuch protests her virtue.

All men and women arc born instinctive lovers, but it is an achievement to practise the art gracefully. Such a culture did not exhibit itself under the Protector, and so England and the women joyously welcomed the advent of a merry monarchy.

CHAPTER XXIX

CHARLES II. (1660–1685)

Merrie England clothed in delicate untruths—The King's open love affairs—Blind historians—The stocks of Royal bastards—Love triumphant over convention—The author addresses the reader on the subject of death—Sweeping change of fashion in dress—Ancestor of the frock coat—Locks and curls, and painted faces—Without art man is merely a peg upon which clothes are hung—Pepys's picture.

I

WITH splendid laughter and a magnificent pose of studied carelessness, the thirty-year-old Charles makes his way through the cheering throngs to Whitehall.

England awakes from her nightmare of gloom, freed from the miserable manacles of the doctrine of fear, which had enchained her soul, released from the fetters of fanatical oppression. No longer gagged or subject to the bitter tyranny of hate, England, merrie England, finds her soul her own again.

It was England's armistice from Hades. To laugh was no longer a crime, and the people got back their maypoles and their mince-pies.

At the Court frivolity and excess ran riot for a time. But it was a Court gracefully clothed in delicate untruths, and not clumsily masked in barbarous and hypocritical lies.

With England's return to life and freedom, culture, science, and industry rapidly developed and progressed. It was the great age of the dawn of science, which even became a fashion. It is significant that the nausea of the wars, stimulated by the false cry of " religion," turned the thinkers of the day to salvation in science. Of the scientists, Halley and Isaac Newton lived, and of the poets, Dryden and Cowley.

If Wycherley, the dramatist and cynical commentator of the period, was lewd in his frankness, the vicious freedom of his expression is easily understood. Sterilised for so long by suppression, he vented his fury in reactionary disgust at hypocrisy and penned his pictures with extremity.

And Charles—the greatest and most attractive figure of all—made his entrance on the world's stage at the right dramatic moment ; and his bow was in great contrast to the frightened exit of the fearsome Cromwell. Charles was an actor who knew how to mask his intelligence in the pose of idling indifference. He was the Sir Charles Hawtrey of his age. He was a clever diplomat and used his diplomacy first for himself but considerably for his people. He was tolerant, even when irritated by bigots. He possessed a marvellous sagacity, the instinct of perfect manners, and the charm of a pleasant wit and humour. Beyond all things, he was human ; and he was loved by the people.

He was a great lover. Mistress followed mistress, but his was not the love of dark and secret passages.

Historians condemn him for revelling in the pleasures of life. But the philosopher is tempted to ask the critics to search the recesses of their mind to see whether such condemnation is not merely a blind to their envy of openness and a cloak of their timidity and secrecy. For men are much alike, but manners are strangely different.

To assume, as some presume, that Charles was incapable of real love, displays the limit of a " finished " comprehension. Charles was a polished and unfinishing lover.

To the world in general his attitude was one of refined but amused contempt, which attitude was kingly ; he was beyond the pettiness of despotism and above the meanness of tyranny.

In the election of 1661 Charles gave back to the

Catholics the right to vote, and half England was able to go to the poll. Only fifty Presbyterians were returned. The new House of Commons was mostly filled by virile young men, who determined to have no military rule, and justly hated the very name of a standing army. Obsessed, however, by the spirit of revenge for their sufferings under Cromwell, the new Parliament brought about the renewal of the Act of Uniformity. Charles signed the Act against his will and Parliament alone was responsible for the law by which on St. Bartholomew's Day two thousand Nonconformist rectors and vicars were driven from their parishes. Another scandalous instance of the devilry of religious intolerance.

Religious beliefs and differences were the responsible lever for outraging England and the Continent for centuries. Statesmen looked on religious questions purely as politics to be exploited to their own ends.

Charles did not want to go to war with Holland in 1665, but he was won over to assent. During the war London suffered from two great calamities. The Plague broke out in May, and six hundred thousand died. Parliament was drawn from London and assembled in Oxford, whilst a year later the great fire of London reduced the city to ashes from the Tower to the Temple, burning thirteen hundred houses and ninety churches.

Parliament voted £2,000,000 for the continuance of the war, but the money was not forthcoming, and in 1667 the Dutch fleet sailed up the Thames to Gravesend and England was forced to make peace.

Later Charles was forced to turn his attention to family matters. His marriage with Catherine of Braganza had proved barren. His brother James, the Duke of York, had become converted to the Catholic Faith, and was heir presumptive to the throne. It evidently was no fault of Charles that there was no offspring from Catherine, as he begat several by various other ladies. These Royal bastards, for whom he had a genuine affection, were many nobles and are the ancestors of many famous lines, including the Duke of St. Albans (Nell Gwynn's stock), the Duke of Grafton (dam, Barbara Palmer), the Dukes of Richmond (ancestress, Louise de Quervouaille), the Dukes of Buccleugh (co-founder, Lucy Walters).

Charles foresaw that England would be unlikely to wait patiently for the advent of a Catholic king of James's bigoted temperament, unless forced to by diplomacy. In view of this he entered into a secret treaty with France, agreeing to support her claims in Flanders, and then to announce his own conversion to Catholicism, in consideration for which he was supported by the French army, and received from France a subsidy equal to £100,000 a year. Religion was a profitable principle to monarchs at times.

In consequence, England was intrigued into war with Holland in 1672. After two years of indecisive warfare Parliament refused supplies and Charles was compelled to make peace. To the credit of the Parliaments of Charles's reign is due the passing of the Habeas Corpus Act in 1679, incorporating amongst many liberties the freedom of the Press. This great act of individual justice was annihilated by Dora during the Great War of 1914–18.

Then the King realised how adverse England would be against the acceptance of a Catholic on the throne—which foresight was fully justified during James's subsequent short reign—and brought about the marriage of the Duke of York's fifteen-year-old daughter, Mary, to William of Orange. At all costs the throne must be kept in the family, and in this aim Charles succeeded.

Despite his faults, which were very human, Charles was a great man and a great king. Whilst he lived he stilled the internal unrest that had tormented and crushed the English people, and he was generally loved by them as he was loved by his intimates, and his memory will be eternally revered by artists.

All his children—except Monmouth—begotten by

G

his mistresses, were gathered at his death-bed. Each he took to his heart and embraced and blessed, commending him to his brother's protection; a kingly act of love triumphant over convention. Tortured with pain, but brave and witty to the last, he begged the bystanders to forgive him for being so unconscionable a time in dying.

Ask yourselves, you moralists and hypocrites, is not this greatness? Compare this splendid adieu of Charles to the beaten end of Cromwell, terrified of facing the hereafter.

To the few who drink generously from the joyous cup of life death holds no terrors, for love abides eternally in the heavens it has conceived. The fearing ones, the hypocrites and liars, repudiate their mean and paltry passions from very shame. These whited-sepulchres, frightened lest their surreptitiously begotten brats may learn to know their fathers' hallowed names, crawl, with their tails between their legs, to answer the inevitable call, and, trembling at the prospect of the sordid hell of their imagination, make a miserable and cowardly exit from the earth they have befouled.

II

Back from the clouds to the material stage on which the spirits of Charles's reign paraded in new and gay disguises.

Never in history was there such a sudden and sweeping change of fashion in dress. The clothes of yesterday were impossible to-day. To appear in them damned one as of a bygone age. With a cry of joy at relief from her bondage of sobriety my lady tore the Puritan garb from her back and one is amazed to find that silken undergarments with pointed lace and dainty embroidery had remained hidden beneath so severe a mask. Imperiously she demanded the harassed costumier to drape her in a gown of gay colours post haste.

My lord threw his shapeless doublet to his

servant, and donned a little coat cut short to the
waist and wide open in the front to display his fine,
loose pleated shirt. Over his breeches he wore a
short petticoat, from the waist to above the knees, or
petticoat breeches sewn with bunches of ribbon.
His cravat was knotted tightly at the neck, with wide
lace ends, and his broad-brimmed hat groaned under
its great cluster of feathers, and his magnificent
periwig fell gracefully over his shoulders. He was
ribboned all over, even to his high-heeled shoes.

Later came a new and distinctive fashion
of this graceful reign. This was the long
coat from which the frock-coat is more or less
derived. Though this garment has degenerated into
ugliness, it was conceived in beauty. It was a body
fitting coat reaching to the knees, and shaped from
the shoulders to the hips, and carefully fitted to the
waist ; from the hips it was gently sprung to the
bottom. The collar was covered by the ends of the
lace cravat, and the long straight front was made with
a single row of buttons all the way down and set very
closely together, and fastened to below the waist from
where the coat was left open. The sleeves were
close-fitting to the wrist, where they were belled and
embroidered, showing the fine frilled linen cuff of
the shirt. This was the origin of the coat worn by
Charles, made in black velvet, in which he stands
as a picture of the times.

My lady threw away the Puritan collar which had
stiffened her character and neck, and exposed her
bosom in its natural delicacy ; and that her arms
might caress more freely she bared her sleeves to the
elbow. The *perruquier*, coming with a revived joy
into his own again, aided the dressing of her hair
with his art, and playing with her curly locks gave
them such a character that they were christened with
names. The little loose curls on the forehead were
called " favourites," and the locks over the ears
were " heart-breakers," and the coy little curls flirting with the blushes on her cheek were unquestion-
ably " confidants."

Woman's bodice, or what was left of it, defined her shapely breast, her sleeves were ribboned and slashed to show her fine linen under-sleeve and cuff. Her skirt of satin—full and forming a point in the front—was cut or held up on the left side to the hips to show a rich satin under-skirt of a contrasting shade, and it had a long train, but Nell Gwynn and others with shapely ankles wore their skirts shorter and gave suggestion to their dainty legs.

My lady's face, which had been pale so long, was highly painted. She assumed the robust colour of a robust dawn. As many patches adorned her as she willed.

It was a great age for style. It was the evolution of design. The pen can only give a vague impression. But beyond all was the fine manner with which the clothes were worn. There was a gloriousness, carelessness, a studied unconsciousness, without which spirit wonderful garments cannot be gracefully carried. When that art is not possessed, men and women become mere rough pegs upon which clothes are hung.

Lavishly as they dressed, the women of Charles's time were not nearly so extravagant as the men, nor, as a matter of fact, were they throughout history until the twentieth century. Here is a passage from Pepys's inimitable diary :

" This morning came home my fine camlet cloak, with gold buttons, and a silk suit, which cost me much money, and I pray God to make me able to pay for it.

" To my great sorrow find myself £43 worse than I was the last month, which was then £760, and now is but £717. But it hath chiefly arisen from my layings out in clothes for myself and my wife ; namely —for her about £12 and for myself about £55 or thereabouts ; having made myself a velvet cloak, two new cloth skirts, black, plain, both ; a new shag gown, trimmed with gold buttons and twist, with a new hat, and silk tops for my legs, and many other things, being resolved henceforward to go like myself. And also two periwigs, one whereof cost me £3, the other 40s. I have worn neither yet, but will begin next week, God willing."

Master Pepys displays a very proper and pious sense of obligation as a debtor, but since his father was a tailor he was probably assisted by good credit. . . .

Men's clothes were certainly expensive, as Pepys shows :

" After dinner I put on my new camlet cloth, the best that ever I wore in my life, the suit costing me about £24.

" To Hampton Court, where I saw the King and Queen set out towards Salisbury, and after them the Duke and Duchess, whose hands I did kiss. And it was the first time I did ever, or did see anybody else, kiss her hand, and it was a fine, white and fat hand. But it was pretty to see the young, pretty ladies dressed like men in velvet coats, caps with ribands, and with laced bands, just like men. Only the Duchess it did not become."

But Pepys had an eye for economy, for, in case he might be rushed into mourning, with a charming disregard for sentimentality he cancelled a coloured order. Says the diarist :

" This morning, hearing that the Queen grows worse again, I sent to stop the making of my velvet cloak, to see whether she lives or dies."

Then again, during the Great Plague, he displays a wise concern for his health.

" Up, and put on my coloured silk suit very fine, and a new periwig, bought a good while since, but darest not wear, because the Plague was in West-minster when I bought it, and it is a wonder what will be the fashion after the Plague is done as to

periwigs, for nobody will dare to buy any hair, for
fearing the infection ; that it had been cut off the
heads of people dead of the plague."

As a man posing in the fashion, he conceived his
own extravagances necessary to his bearing, and he
was cunning enough to pass a pretty but inexpensive
compliment to his wife on her two-year-old gown.

" Up betimes. My wife extraordinarily fine with
her flowered tabby gown, that she made two years
ago, now laced exceedingly pretty and indeed was
fine all over. And mighty earnest to go, though the
day was very lowering, and she would have me have
on my new suit, which I did. And so anon we went
through the town with our new liveries of serge, and
the horses' manes and tails tied with red ribbons, and
the standards thus gilt with varnish, and all clean,
and green reins, that people did look mightily upon
us, and the truth is, I did not see any coach more
pretty, though more gay than ours, all the day ; the
day being unpleasing, though the Park full of
coaches, but dusty, and windy and cold, and now and
then a little dribbling of rain ; and, which made it
worse, there were so many hackney-coaches as
spoiled the sight of the gentlemen's and so we had
little pleasure."

This was Pepys's first ride in his own coach ;
previously he had always ridden in hackney-coaches.
There is a delicious humour in his newly acquired
superiority.

It is with a pang of regret that one bids adieu
to the graceful Charles and the sage Pepys.

CHAPTER XXX

JAMES II. (1685-1689)

*A fanatic and a fool on the throne—Grim reason why men
discard ribbons—Sudden deaths make black fashionable
—Woman covers her bosom and adopts the pinner.*

I

JAMES was a fanatic and a fool. Under him England
was plunged into misery by religious bigotry.
Ecclesiastical supremacy he regarded as a weapon to
achieve his ends. Under Henry and Elizabeth it had
been used to turn the Church of England from
Catholic to Protestant, and James imagined he was
powerful enough to turn the Church back from
Protestant to Catholic.

From the outset of his reign England was thrown
into a state of suffering and revolt.

Monmouth rose against him in the West but was
defeated at Sedgemoor and sent to the block. Then
James, with the brutality which is characteristic of
the fanatic, instituted the most terrible methods of
repression. As Chief Justice he appointed Jeffreys
and sent him on his " Bloody Assize " of judicial
murders. Three hundred and fifty rebels were
hanged, and eight hundred were sold into slavery.
Women also suffered. For harbouring they were
sent to the block, and Elizabeth Saint, for an act of
charity, was burned at Tyburn.

The reign of terror was short-lived. The birth of
an heir—who later caused considerable trouble—was
unwelcome to the people, who feared that the child
had inherited his father's vices, and the event
hastened the revolution. James lost his crown
and fled to France, where—by the grace of God or the
devil—he died.

II

In so short a time there was naturally little change in the fashion of dress. Men discarded the use of ribbons, probably because they were too symbolic of hangings. They wore buckles on their shoes. The long Persian coat, made popular by Charles, became more closely fitted to the figure. The two pockets were placed so low that the finger-tips could only just reach them. The sleeves were narrow and from below the elbow showed the full white shirt tied at the wrist, or had a wide turned back cuff of the same material as the coat. The distinguishing feature of the period was the cross braiding of the fronts of the coat ; from top to bottom, reaching two inches on either side, these narrow rows of braid giving the garment a very attractive appearance. Black materials were quite fashionable, and were extremely useful for the many sudden deaths.

In general design there was little change in woman's gowns. The tendency was slightly inclined towards more simplicity. She covered her bosom and adopted a pinner. In addition to her neck she also disguised her opinions, lest the disclosure of the latter might cause the loss of the former.

CHAPTER XXXI

WILLIAM III. AND MARY (1689-1702)

*Finding no emotion in the creation of life, decadent William
seeks his thrills by the infliction of death—Ruinous wars
and high taxes—The dandy's powdered wigs, small
muffs, and claret-coloured suits — My lady's idiotic
vagaries—Commode head-dress—Style stiff and Dutch
like.*

I

JAMES having made his hurried exit, Mary, his eldest
daughter, ascended the throne by hereditary right.
She was not a strong character and is hardly a figure
in history. William of Orange, refusing as Regent
to become his wife's gentleman-usher, was crowned
with her.

The Dutchman brought little profit to England.
He was a man of cold and sickly presence ; completely
ignorant of letters or art ; unattractive, sullen,
asthmatic, and consumptive. Happily there was no
issue from the royal pair.

Finding no appealing emotion in the creation of
life, William, like all decadents, sought his thrills by
the infliction of death. To redeem the grievances
and defeats of Holland, which he politically ascribed
to a desire to knit England and Holland together, he
immediately plunged England into war with France ;
a terrible war which, with one short break, lasted
for two reigns, or twenty-five years. In the naval
fights the allied fleet was defeated at Beachy Head in
1690 and the French landed and burnt Teignmouth.
In 1692 the French fleet was defeated at La Hague,
but despite the victory at sea, England could not win
a victory on land, and the French privateers were
able to ruin English trade.

The cost of the war was ruinous and the people

were aghast in their bitter resentment of the taxation. Taxes had risen to double their pre-war standard, and when peace was signed in 1697 it had bequeathed twenty millions of debt and a fresh six millions of deficit. That was the result of William's foreign policy.

Meanwhile James had gone to Ireland. Under his rule, being a Catholic, every Englishman had been turned out of office, and with the memory of Cromwell's devilries in their hearts it was perfectly simple to raise an army of fifty thousand in his support. The Irish policy of " Ireland for the Irish " was good and wholesome, but James's policy was to use this cry to enable him to regain the English crown. So again poor Ireland was intrigued into war. William, with his hands full on the Continent, determined to end this rising with expediency, and in the battle of the Boyne, in 1690, with a superior force averaging three to two he forced the Irish army to retreat on Dublin. James following the motto of " Safety first ! " abandoned his troops and took the first fast boat to France, where he stayed until he died in 1701.

Ireland held out against hopeless odds until the following year, when her forces were compelled to surrender. By the military treaty the whole of Sarsfield's force of ten thousand men chose exile in France rather than life in a land where all hope of national freedom was lost.

For one hundred years there was peace in Ireland, but it was the peace of despair. She was doomed to suffer under the most terrible tyranny under which a nation has ever groaned. No Englishman with a sense of equity and justice can look back without sorrow and shame upon that century of guilty oppression, the bitter fruits of which have poisoned for so long the unity of two peoples, whose interests are alike and whose kinship is close.

The reign of this man of Orange with his hacking cough brought little but misery to Britain. Had he

been blessed with a better stomach, the history of
England might have recorded nobler incidents

II

It may be a small consolation that trappings of the
few gay spirits of this reign stood in pleasing contrast to the mood of the monarch.

It was natural that the graceful coat of Charles's
time should develop in graceful variations. It was a
design which lent itself to experiment. The square
cut fronts were worn open to display the splendid
waistcoat worn beneath. The coat was tightly fitted
to the waist, and the skirts sprang sharply out in
generous fullness to the knees; the straight embroidered fronts of the long waistcoats reached to
within two inches of the bottom of the coat. The
sleeves were narrow to the elbow, belled to an extreme
width at the wrist, and the deep turn-back cuff, held
back by two or three buttons, was faced with brocade.
The pockets, placed at arm's length, were buttoned
and cut either vertically or horizontally.

The breeches were cut close to the knee, with just
sufficient fullness above for comfort. The cravat was
loosely tied, and the long lace ends hung down over
the top of the coat and waistcoat. The broad-
brimmed hat, trimmed with gold lace, was perched
at any cocky angle the wearer willed—one brim turning to heaven and the other smiling on earth.

It was the age of powdered wigs, with curls
innumerable and colossal, some brown and some
smothered in meal.

The dandy carried a small muff, and the high heels
of his ribboned shoes were red. His cane hung by a
ribbon to his wrist, enabling him the more elegantly
to take a pinch of snuff from its dainty box. When
he walked abroad his stick languidly dangled after
him, aping the manner of its master as if resenting
the necessity of taking the air.

Claret coloured suits were the rage. It was the
age of blood.

My lady's dress was by no means so graceful as
my lord's. She was affected perhaps by the peculiar
scents of his wig. She was inclined to be idiotic in
some of the vagaries of her fashion. On her head
she carried a commode, which one hastens to explain
is a wire frame over which great masses of curls are
piled on the forehead. On top of this a large bow, or
top knot. Standing defiantly and erect on her hair
she wore a " fontage," a weird, stiff, fluted head-dress
about eighteen inches high, and covered in layers of
ribbon and lace.

The bodice of her gown was cut low in the neck,
and very long in the waist. The front was widely
opened and laced across the breast with ribbon like
the broad rungs of a ladder, up which one's eyes
climbed to the lure of her lips. The skirt of her
gown was lopped into wired side panniers, which met
the short black apron of silk which adorned her
exaggerated stomach. Her sleeves were short with
a turned back embroidered cuff above the elbow,
covering which was the frilled lace of the undersleeve.

On the whole her style was stiff and Dutch-like, in
which perhaps she displayed her instinctive subtlety.
William gave so many plums to his Dutch favourites
who followed him to England that probably the
Court ladies, by complimenting their taste, managed
to share the fruits of the Dutch invasion.

CHAPTER XXXII

QUEEN ANNE (1702-1714)

*The joke—Generals' strategical plans to save their eyebrows
—Picturesque, unhygienic Ramillies wigs—First morning
coat—Woman fills her cheeks with plumpers and hides
a dozen lovers under her capacious skirts—Queen Anne
is dead, but Venus lives for ever.*

I

THE second daughter of James was the last of the
Stuarts' breed to reign. She was weak and feeble
and historically a nonentity, her only claim to
distinction being that her death provided England
with a standing joke.

Anne and England were both dominated and ruled
by the Duke of Marlborough, who was king in all
but name.

In 1702 England and her allies were again at war
with France, and the war continued until 1712. In
the fluctuation of the struggle France offered peace
in 1708, but it was refused, and again in 1710 a
further peace offer of France was rejected.

Anne wanted peace ; and so did England, which
was being ruined in trade by taxation. But war
suited Marlborough's personal policy. He was
greedy and mercenary and regardful only of his own
interests. He would betray Englishmen, or lead his
army to butchery for his own profit. He amassed
a great fortune by his peculation.

When peace was rejected in 1710 the smouldering
passion of discontent burst into flame. At St. Paul's
Dr. Sacheverell preached a sermon maintaining the
doctrine of non-resistance, and was impeached. He
was found guilty, but the light sentence passed was
regarded as an acquittal, and bonfires and illumina-
tions were lighted all over the country in his honour.

A significant commentary which might be contrasted modernly.

Swift, writing in bitter irony against the war, says : " Six millions of supplies and almost fifty millions of debt. The high allies have been the ruin of us."

Marlborough was ridiculed and reviled, and accused of insolence, cruelty, ambition, corruption, and greed. Even his personal courage was assailed, and since we moderns know what war is and since there is no record of Marlborough's battle wounds the possibility is certainly an open question.

One is justified in refusing to regard as sacrosanct either the accepted great generals of the bygone centuries or of yesterday. A great general is so often a strategist who is brave enough to sacrifice tens of thousands of men's lives, but takes infinite strategical pains not to get his own eyebrows singed.

The hatred of the people for war in Marlborough's time was so great that they determined peace should be made. Marlborough was dismissed his command, charged with peculation, and condemned as guilty by the House of Commons.

It is recorded that he " withdrew " from England. Interpreted in modern colloquialism one presumes that he " ran like a rabbit." He died an imbecile about 1716.

The war petered out, none having won and all having lost. But the Treaty of Utrecht was naturally framed in such a diplomatic manner that plenty of valid excuses were left for future wars of " freedom " and magnificence.

II

The effects of Anne's impotent reign did not retard the momentum of fashion and style. In truth, the eighteenth century was an age of extraordinary extravagance in dress. Powdered wigs and red-heeled shoes were the vogue. It was the millennium of the bald-headed gentleman of uncertain age, but the gallant confused him with his close-cut satin breeches and silken stocking round his shapely calf.

The picturesque and unhygienic Ramillies wig came in with its white hair puffed over the ears, and the long plaited tail reaching almost to the waist. The coat of the man of taste was of flowered satin and pinched in at the waist, and fastened with a button or a link. In cut it was like the morning coat of to-day. The skirt was sprung from the hips with expanding pleats on each side. The waistcoat was slightly shorter, and long points hung open from just below the waist. The lace cravat was now worn inside, so that the cut of the front of the coat could be seen. The dandy's frilled shirt and his wide laced cuffs were a dream to his lady love, and a nightmare to his laundress.

My lady, unable to keep pace with the elegance of the gentlemen of the period, extended her circumference. Man, she must have thought, must be kept in his place. Her hair was simply dressed and her fontage became fragile, and the comparatively new wired side-pannier was discarded for an enormous hooped skirt. Her cheeks protruded with plumpers, an artificial contrivance for filling them. An obvious invitation! Her waist was still pinched and crossed-laced to a point. Her neck was beautifully bare and her bosom was invitingly natural, but from the waist her anatomy ceased. Somewhere in the vast space there were legs, else how would it be possible for this great balloon to slither? But her feet were furlongs from her furbelows. And beneath her capacious skirt it was possible to hide at least a dozen lovers.

Queen Anne is dead, but Venus lives for ever.

CHAPTER XXXIII

GEORGE I. (1714–1727)

Beaux, bucks and dandies—German on the Throne—" The most pernicious circumstances in which the country can be are those of war, as we must be losers while it lasts, and cannot be great gainers when it ends "—Fruits of misrule fall upon all—A statesman is judged by the evils he avoids—Difficulty of finding an honest statesman—Coloured silks, satins, velvets, brocades ; fine clothes, gold lace, flowered embroideries—My lord's painted shoes and my lady's bodice tribute.

I

WE are in the age of the beaux, bucks, and dandies, even though a German sits upon the throne of England.

Fortunately for England, the first of the Georges was an insignificant character, and was conceded little power. He made a vain attempt in the interests of Hanover to drag England into a war with Russia. He then concentrated his attention on getting as much money as he could for himself and his favourites, and kept his peace as England kept hers.

With the exception of a slight skirmish with Spain, England entered upon a long era of peace, wherefore commerce and industry flourished and exports were increased : Manchester and Birmingham doubling their manufactures in thirty years and the little country town of Liverpool leaping into the third port in the kingdom.

The real ruler and leader of the country was Robert Walpole, a great Prime Minister ; the wisdom of his policy should be the pattern for to-day. He pursued a determined policy of peace. Here are his own simple words : " The most pernicious circumstances in which the country can be are those of war, as we must be losers while it lasts, and cannot be great gainers when it ends."

He was the ideal type of statesman, realising that the only help a statesman can give to industry and commerce is to remove all obstacles in the way of development. The wisdom of this is clearly seen to-day, when the clumsy, grasping hands of our Lloyd George Government annihilate our trade until the nation is brought to the brink of bankruptcy.

Under Walpole there was established in England the right to free government—to freedom of commerce and freedom of speech. Yet, with all the general prosperity of his time, Walpole maintained a policy of rigid economy and accomplished a steady reduction of debt and a diminution of fiscal duties.

The years of his power are without parallel for political stagnation. With his entry into office legislation and political action practically seemed to cease. There was no tampering with personal freedom or with the Press.

A good statesman is judged not by his deeds, but by the evils he avoids.

If a country has the misfortune to be ruled by an autocrat or a demagogue as Prime Minister, who is corrupt, unscrupulous, and dishonest, the fruits of his misrule affect every individual of the State. Political difficulties are deliberately invented for ulterior motives, and can easily be overcome by an honest statesman. But the greatest difficulty of all is to find the honest statesman.

II

One must switch the mind, however, from the black-coated, black-hearted politicians of Mr. Lloyd George's Coalition to the gay-coloured gallant of the Georgian reign of peace.

In this lucky thirteen years there was a galaxy of colour—silks, satins, velvets, brocades, fine cloths, gold lace, flowered embroideries indicated the giddy spirit of the age.

My lord with his painted shoes, my lady with her painted face.

The golden beau in his three-cornered hat, cocked at a saucy angle, twirled his cane and stared impudently through his quizzing glass at the first attractive hoop which came his way. His wig was short and white, with a loop on each side and one at the back. His face was clean-shaven. His coat was cut just short enough to show the tops of his stockings, rolled loosely above his knees. His waist was as tight as his high living permitted, his skirts were as generous as his heart affairs, and the folds were as loose as his faithfulness. A profusion of gold lace showed the wisdom of his riches, and the embroidered front of his coat was scooped to the waist in a curve, like that of his waistcoat, to flaunt the frills of the shirt which covered his manly chest. The gauntlet cuff was wide and adorned by gold buttons, and he buckled his shoes instead of his sword.

My lady's bodice was tight—a tribute to the occasional condition of my lord. Her skirt was large and hooped, and when she sat it demurely lifted itself and formed a vast and silken canopy above her dainty feet and flounces. Beautiful butterflies were sewn on her gown, which flew into life with each movement of the limbs, and when my lady was in repose they remained still and sphinx-like. In movement and in repose they remained as if in sympathy with flight and fancy of my lady's mood.

CHAPTER XXXIV

GEORGE II. (1727–1760)

*An unpleasant King with the manner of a drill sergeant—
Politicians rinse their unclean minds in the blood-bath
of others—France's insular and mediæval politics—An
honest Parliamentarian is always lonely—A story about
George's challenge to the King of Prussia—Fashion is
fancy free—Beau's elegant outfit—Woman is no longer
legless—The author is disturbed by the cunning minds
which control our destiny.*

I

THE second German George was an unpleasant
person with the manners of a drill-sergeant. He
was aggressively stupid, and while imagining himself master of the realm, was in reality under the
dominion of his wife and repeated the lessons of
her impolicy.

Walpole, however, soon exerted his influence and
succeeded in keeping the royal pair in hand. The
peace of Europe was broken in 1733 by the con-
testants to the throne of Poland, and Austria and
France were drawn into the strife. The war party
in England were jealous of the French designs,
and George and Caroline, with their German
sympathies, were eager to join in the fray. Walpole
stood firm for neutrality, was adamant on maintaining England's peace, and defeated the aims of those
who were anxious to rinse their unclean minds in
the blood-bath of others.

Walpole's patriotism was the preservation of his
fellow-countrymen. As the war went on he made
the boast that " there are fifty thousand men slain
this year in Europe and not one Englishman." He
exerted his diplomacy to bring the war to an end,

and in 1736 the intervention of England and Holland restored peace.

France's greed for conquest and her ambition to dominate persisted throughout the eighteenth century. She was jealous of the martial supremacy of Britain and entered into a compact with Spain to ruin it. Walpole battled stubbornly against the renewed cry for war in 1738, a war which he knew to be not only unjust but impolitic. His efforts were in vain and negotiations were spoilt by the frenzy stimulated on either side. In England he was derided and lampooned and called " the cur dog of Britain and spaniel of Spain."

The trading classes were incited by the cry for a commercial war, but it was not until he stood utterly alone in 1739 that he consented to a war against Spain.

When war was declared peals and bonfires welcomed his surrender. " They may ring their bells now," the great minister said bitterly, " but they will soon be wringing their hands." England found his prophecy right.

France was playing her cards for French supremacy. She saw the opportunity of breaking Europe up into weak sections and leaving herself without a rival on the Continent by placing her puppets on the thrones of the weaker powers. This has been the fixed aim of French policy for centuries —an obsession which appears to be bred in the blood. It was her dominating policy in this twentieth century of ours in the Treaty of Versailles. The disasters of that Treaty were soon apparent. French political thought is not only insular, it is mediæval and impracticable in our modern commercialised civilisation.

In 1741 by subtlety and promises she succeeded in embroiling Europe. A treacherous act of George the Second in Hanover by binding himself as Elector to neutrality in the war was shamefully laid to Walpole's charge. Walpole, in 1742, resigned.

At the conclusion of peace at Aix-la-Chapelle in

1748, a peace brought about by financial exhaustion, England surrendered her gains at sea and France her conquests on land. Fools had achieved nine years of misery and nothing else.

War took a holiday for eight years, but peace was intended as a period of convalescence for human fodder. A fiercer conflict than ever broke out in 1756 with the Seven Years' War, in which France, Russia, and Austria were involved against England and Prussia.

It was fortunate for England that at this time arose another great statesman, William Pitt, afterwards Earl of Chatham. He refused to support the intrigues of George and was in consequence hated by the King, which hatred was praise indeed.

Dramatic in the Cabinet, in the House, in Office, Pitt possessed all the tricks of the actor's technique. For a politician he was unique in his honesty, loathing political corruption. When in his early days Pelham appointed him Paymaster of the Forces —which post was considered the most lucrative in the administration, but its profits were illicit, and the emoluments depended on the unscrupulousness of the administrating thief—poor as he was, Pitt refused to touch one farthing beyond his salary.

An honest man in Parliament, however strong, is always lonely. Pitt's ministry fell in 1761, chiefly through the influence of George the Third, who ascended the throne on his grandfather's death. England, sickened with war and debt, refused further subsidies to Prussia and the Peace of Paris was made in 1763. The same old bartering of territories were made in the Treaty, but Britain, as usual, made her gains far from the real battlefields, and gained supremacy in India, Canada, and America.

George the Second died before the end of the war, entirely unregretted except by a few sycophants. He had only played a walking-on part in history, and that he did ungracefully.

But " little cocking George " deserves his due. He

had a certain personal courage, which, had it ever become the fashion amongst rulers and statesmen, would have saved the world millions of lives and millions of treasure.

When George quarrelled with the King of Prussia, he challenged him to single combat, and being possessed of the animal virtue of pluck, would probably have given a good account of himself. Unfortunately the duel did not come off, and not only had Europe to put up with the two sovereigns for some years longer, but a valuable precedent just failed to be established.

II

It is like the morning sun after a feverish night to turn one's thoughts from politics and death to the fantasy and life of dress. It is amazing that, in the midst of horror and gloom, brave men should carefully deck themselves in respect for the dignity of life and express their gay contempt for the power of Death.

Notwithstanding the megalomaniacs of that day, the period was a great one for the development of fashions in dress.

It was the age of design. Fashion became fancy free. The variety of experiment was alluring. Style became a cult. Individualism was esteemed. Self-expression in dress was the mask of superiority. Clothes expressed the man and manners expressed the clothes. The carriage of a coat was an art ; the handling of a cane a gift ; a pose was a study of perfection ; a walk a journey of romance.

All wonderful adornments hung on the peg of the human form, framing the mask of a delicate lie.

There was no timidity in style ; self-consciousness was out of date ; colour was life ; conservatism was provincial ; invention was fashion's capital.

To attempt to describe all the fashions of the men would damn one with impudence.

From the middle of the eighteenth century, fashion

was a riot of revelry, an exhibition of exuberance, a battle of flowers and favours.

Let us select just one type of beau at random as one would select the first attractive woman in an over-crowded assembly.

His wig was curled and powdered and tied at the back with black satin, the ends coming round his neck and tied in front in a bow. His three-cornered hat, which he carried in his hand, he never wore lest it should disturb the set of his curls. His coat was waisted, and sprang out in a bell-like fullness, being either sympathetic or antagonistic to my lady's hoop. The fronts of his coat were cut straight and stood well open on the chest, and the back had a long slit up the centre, and on either side the material was buttoned back. Beneath the coat, reaching almost to the knee, and fringed, was a wonderful flowered waistcoat, to the top of which daintily fell his lace cravat. Dreamy lace ruffles almost covered his tapering fingers. His satin breeches were as dreamy, their closely fitting shape disclosing the elegance of his thighs. In the winter he would carry a muff, more as a plaything than a protection. The muff was of a variety of sizes, sometimes big enough to be used as a cushion, and sometimes so small that it would barely warm a forefinger.

But there were a hundred wigs and hats and coats, each of them vying with the other in delicate points of fineness.

There was about my lady, though she assumed eccentricities, a daintiness and a peculiar demureness.

She was delightfully perfumed, in which she showed her wisdom in those graceful but unhygienic days. She was powdered and patched, and she was also a painted lady, though entirely unlike the modern creation of the popular but provincial novelist of our day.

She wore a dainty little cap, the ribbons of which were coyly tied around her neck. Above her wasp-like waist, which, conducive to the vapours, came down in a V, a flower adorned her bare bosom. Her skirt was hooped with large panniers on each side and her sleeves were short, displaying an under frill of lace.

She was no longer legless ; her bell-like skirt disclosed the beauty of her ankles. In her vivacious movement new and more intimate discoveries were being made by the observer.

Even the Teutonic George was so affected by fashion that the Duchess of Bedford's blue riding habit with white silk facings inspired him to perform his only action of account in history. He ordered the officers of the navy to change their uniforms from scarlet to blue and white. In that he also set the tradition for our Air Force, whose leaders' minds have not recovered from their playful habit of toying with shades of colour.

The knowledge that at least ninety-nine decimal nine hundred and ninety-nine per cent. of the people of the universe are fools or madmen does not disturb the philosophical observer so long as his individual life is not temporarily affected by the outbursts of collective action. He is, however, slightly disturbed by the few cunning minds which control the destiny of our civilisation.

The bluff of a policy of disarmament of navies and armies is a meatless bone thrown as a sop to a suffering humanity. The world is controlled and governed by fear—and by fear alone. The idealistic disarmament would be that of a new spirit, a spirit of confidence in our neighbours. It is only the fear of bankruptcy that compelled a discussion on disarmament, but any such discussion of reducing armies and navies is futile unless the Air is acknowledged as the one colossal method of attack and defence.

If the people cannot learn the obvious lessons of the disaster of war to both victor and defeated, and will persist in their policy of a world armed to the teeth—in defence, of course, as each power will say —then the only future policy is to so strengthen and develop a Force in the Air that the victors in the next war will have the joy of flying over an obliterated civilisation and like carrion crows hover over the dead body of a dead world.

All of which has nothing whatever to do with George the Second and his blue navy.

CHAPTER XXXV

GEORGE III. (1760–1820)

George : small-minded, mean, petty, grasping, jealous, vindictive, callous, treacherous, cowardly—The historian looks at America (fighting for freedom), at Ireland (turned into a hell), and at the most unscrupulous Coalition Government until that of Mr. D. Lloyd George—Napoleon's one emotion : war—Mimics of Napoleon are suspect—Power an exertion of craftiness.

I

IN a scene of tumult the curtain rises on the sixty years' reign of the third of the Georges ; in effect, the most momentous reign of English monarchs. The reign is interrupted by the intermittent fits of madness of the King, and distinguished by the perpetual fever of the madness of the world.

It is an era of conflicting passions, curiously divergent in trend. It is an age in which is exhibited the fickleness of fashion and the futility of force ; in which the colour of life carelessly contrasts with the blackness of death.

Europe pursued its mad policy of destruction, and Death, mindful of the fruitful harvest of the reapers, spared the chief administrators to a ripe old age.

Wretchedly educated, small minded, mean, petty, grasping, jealous, vindictive, callous, treacherous, and cowardly, George the Third determined, since he could not act the walking-on gentleman, to play a leading part in English politics. He succeeded in so far that in a few years he reduced government to a shadow, and turned loyalty into disaffection. Within twenty years he forced the American colonies into revolt and independence, and brought England to the edge of ruin.

The election of the members of the House of Commons was reduced to a farce. Great towns like Manchester and Birmingham remained without a member, while small boroughs were represented. Purse and influence were the keys to Westminster. Out of eight millions of English people only 160,000 were electors at all. Seats were bought and sold in the open market at a price which rose to four thousand pounds ; George seized on bribery and borough-jobbing as the base of the power he proposed to give to the throne. He used the Royal Revenue to make his corner in the buying of seats and the buying of votes and employed bribery on a scale which mentally staggered competitors and physically staggered electors.

Nowadays votes are not purchased with gold ; in their economy politicians have found it cheaper to offer the bribe of sugar-coated lies and Utopian promises.

Such was the condition at the time that William Pitt, Lord Chatham's youngest son, in the height of his popularity with the people but with George's influence against him, had great difficulty in finding a seat.

It was natural that such a character as George should detest the instinctive honesty of Pitt, whom he lyingly called " a trumpet of sedition." But for *lése-majesté* Pitt might have retorted that the King's instrument was the " trombone of seduction."

In examining the policies of the mean King and the great man, one observes that all intelligent minds in England had now realised that her Empire lay in her Colonies. Incidentally—and how ludicrous the word sounds in so vast a project—England, with the aid of only a few thousand men with blunderbusses, had become mistress of India. This, in fairness, must be instanced as a case in which the aggression of war yielded a recurrent material profit.

And Captain Cook discovered, on a voyage of

adventure, both New Zealand and Australia, and planting a flag upon a fragment of soil, claimed a continent as British property.

II

America

Far earlier still, and of more immense importance, the continent of America had been gained as the colony of England by the arms of an odd battalion or two. This marvellous country was in its virile infancy and since then has increased from a white population of about one million to one hundred millions within two centuries.

England's wealth was provided on the right she assumed to monopolise American trade. She adopted the attitude of the plebeian parent making its off-spring support it. She meddled with America's self-government, and having saddled herself with debts which had risen to heights hitherto unknown, pro-ceeded to extract as much as possible in every form of taxation. But all proposals for such taxation in America were bitterly opposed.

Unrest was growing in America at British monopolies. Smuggling was resorted to, and there were constant bickerings with the Board of Trade and constant refusal of supplies. Britain did not like America's democratic principles and endeavoured to force her to bear the burden of the war debts by plans for raising both external and internal revenues.

George the Third regarded Americans as rebels and resolved to assert British Sovereignty by levying import duties at American ports. Pitt had said " This kingdom has no right to levy a tax on the colonies. I rejoice that America has resisted." But the King was supreme, and the shame of England lies on his tombstone.

Pitt's efforts for conciliation were of no avail, and war with America was declared in 1775.

The British Army, largely reinforced by German

mercenaries, was concentrated at New York. During the war American resistance was nerved by the outrages committed by the Indians who, employed by the British, used their scalping-knives.

In 1778 Spain joined the league of France and America against Britain and in 1782 England was forced to make peace and also forced to acknowledge without reserve the independence of the United States.

America, with her freedom, advanced with rapid strides to a greatness which changed the face of the world during the nineteenth century, and which before the end of the twentieth century will probably again change it beyond the conception of our modern European civilisation.

III

Ireland

The American war naturally found a responsive echo in Ireland. The threat came of a French invasion, and England called upon Ireland to provide for its own defence, and forty thousand Protestants were called to arms in 1779.

Every Catholic Irishman, although there were five Catholics to every one Protestant, at that time was treated as a foreigner and stranger in his own country. Catholics were excluded from the House of Lords, the House of Commons, the magistracy, all corporate offices in towns, all ranks in the army, the bench, the bar, the whole administration of government or justice. The very right of voting for the representatives in Parliament was denied them. All their property had been confiscated. They were the slaves of Protestant masters. A damnable indictment of England's principles of liberty !

For more than a century Ireland was the worst governed country in Europe. Since the time of William of Orange, England had vindictively and stupidly done her best to annihilate Irish commerce and ruin Irish agriculture, not realising that Ireland's prosperity would be England's gain. Poverty, therefore, was added to the curse of misgovernment, until famine turned the country into a hell.

With the peace with America the Irish Protestants demanded independence for Ireland, and England was unable to refuse. The two countries were then simply held together by a common monarch.

The independence of Ireland, however, meant merely the rule of a few noble Protestant families No Catholics could claim admission to the franchise. The ruling class found government very profitable. "A corrupt aristocracy, a ferocious commonalty, a distracted Government, a divided people" was Lord Hutchinson's description of the times.

With such a government and after the endurance of a century of oppression and wrong, it was inevitable that during the Napoleonic wars the opportunity would be taken to revolt.

Ireland was again turned into a hell. Soldiers and yeomanry marched throughout the country, torturing and scourging, robbing, ravishing, and murdering at will.

There is a miserably weak saying that "history repeats itself"; it would be wiser to say that "history belches its own bestiality."

The outrages in Ireland were so hideous that even the blindest Tories thrilled with horror. In the poor, fear-stricken country-side, their sufferings galvanised the peasants to action. Fiendish cruelties and massacres and butchery without mercy occurred on both sides. There is no solution to any problem by the brutality of force. Force breeds a like power of the same sex, and the result is impotence.

Pitt, disgusted and nauseated by the bigoted fury of the Irish Protestants, determined to end the farce of an independence, which was the slavery of the majority. He proposed at the opening of 1799 to unite the English and Irish Parliaments. If he adopted the methods of the times—which, though now more closely concealed, are still as fashionable —and brought the Irish borough-mongers over with a million of money, he may be excused by those who appreciate his purpose. With a liberal distribution of pensions and peerages, his object was accomplished, though it was merely a temporary solution of the Irish problem which remained poignant for more than a century afterwards.

In June, 1800, a hundred Irish members became part of the House of Commons. Trading privileges were thrown open and commerce was freed from restrictions, and taxation was proportionately distributed.

Pitt's great liberality of mind, wise statesmanship, and sympathy for freedom of opinion were exemplified by his fight for Catholic Emancipation, a fight which was defeated by the bigotry of George the Madman, who, trading on the bigotry of the bulk of his subjects, succeeded in resisting and defeating Pitt's purpose and achieving his resignation.

Pitt was left with the knowledge that it is easier to guide an assembly of able men than to lead one power-possessing fool.

During the ten years that had followed the disgraceful aggressive strife with America, the industrial prosperity of England was remarkable. Here were laid the original foundations of the great industrial era which made such enormous progress during the nineteenth century. Wool, cotton, linen, silks, coal, iron, lead, copper, tin—all were developed rapidly with the invention of the steam-engine, and Britain's practical monopoly of the woollen and cotton trades raised her into the greatest manufacturing country the world had seen.

Men of business, however, were no more content with the manner in which they were governed than they are now. They were indignant at the selfishness, the corruption, the facetiousness, and the administrative inefficiency of the ruling order. They revolted against the waste and mismanagement which seemed to have become normal in all departments of government. Though the face of the world may change, the methods of governments appear to remain the same for ever.

In 1783 was formed the most unscrupulous coalition known in history until that of Mr. D. Lloyd George, but, of course, the twentieth century is a record-breaking age in all things. The coalition then were as heedless of the power of public opinion as they are to-day. So long as governments can evade open rebellion, they entirely disregard and covertly sneer at public opinion.

Pitt was one of the rare exceptions, and though surrounded by political thieves, he was strong enough for a period to reduce public expenses, and appointed commission after commission to introduce economy into every department of public service. It is conceivable that within the last few years Pitt's body has not only turned in its grave but has been perpetually gyrating in agonised contortions.

IV

Napoleon

The French Revolution in 1789 with its attendant horrors and inevitable chaos afforded young Napoleon Bonaparte an opportunity to annex power, which he proceeded to use by drenching Europe in blood for twenty years.

War was his one emotion, and in war he realised his only chance of raising himself from his natural position of insignificance. His ambition, like that of many fools before and since, was to terrorise the people into an acceptance of him as world conqueror. His only chance to greatness was based on the efficiency of his ruthlessness.

When chaos reigns, force is the only weapon of account, and Napoleon was quick to seize his opportunity and paint a career for himself in scarlet letters. The unintelligence of the frightened herd is more easily goaded by the inflammation of war than governed by the wisdom of peace. That has been the accepted political philosophy of the various governments of the world throughout all history, and is the ruling creed of the twentieth century. The effects of our Great War—the greatest war in human knowledge—and the economic disaster of the subsequent peace have proved that the peoples of the world are entirely dependent upon our modern commercial system. The development of commerce has automatically become international and the finances of all countries have become interdependent. Our civilisation exists on the fruits of commercialism and its sustenance will depend in future on this recognition and the welding together of all nations as one unit. The commercial system is now a complicated machine in which every nation is a cog, and the smashing of any one nation or group of nations by war can only result in the economic breakdown of the rest.

Napoleon, inspired by his passion for destruction, revelled in the misery of Europe. The policy of aggression soon found France at war on every frontier. Austria, Prussia, Holland, Spain, and Sardinia were allied against her, and though Pitt struggled hard against intervention and clung stubbornly to his policy of peace, France forced the war on England in 1793.

The allies, however, found it more easy to agree on a common enemy than to agree amongst themselves. The many intrigues destroyed cohesion, and within two years Spain sued for peace, Prussia withdrew her army from the Rhine, Holland was lost, and the wretched remnant of the Duke of York's ten thousand men re-embarked for England, and only English subsidies kept Austria and Sardinia in the field.

On the sea England won a naval victory off Brest, and with her usual acumen added the West India Islands, the Cape of Good Hope, and the Island of Ceylon to her colonial acquisitions.

Privation told its tale in England however. There was a serious outbreak of a London mob against the dear price of bread. This was deemed so unpatriotic that it was answered by the suspension of the Habeas Corpus Act and the introduction of a Bill for the prosecution of seditious meetings.

Pitt was sick of the strife and the wretchedly inefficient conduct of the war by our generals, whom Lord Grenville described with refreshing candour as "old women in red ribands."

The costs of the war were terrible and taxation mounted to heights undreamed of. Debt rose by leaps and bounds. Sardinia concluded a humiliating peace, and in 1796 England negotiated for peace but her terms were refused, so the war continued until in 1797, when Austria sued for peace, and France was left at war with England alone.

Napoleon had meanwhile not only plastered his banner with honour and glory on the continent, but believing that peace was priceless had annexed from the conquered every penny he could lay his hands on. His merciless exaction poured gold into his exhausted treasury and gave him the wherewithal to proceed, as he probably explained, to free Egypt from a foreign yoke.

England achieved a naval victory under Nelson at Aboukir Bay in 1798, and Russia, fearing the supremacy of France would reduce the balance of power to a featherweight against the Napoleonic welter, entered into an alliance with Austria and declared war. Pitt raised the income tax to the then terrible amount of two shillings in the pound, and with the proceeds lavished subsidies on the two much needed allies ; but all the efforts of the allies were abortive, and at the peace of Luneville in 1801 the Continental War was brought to an end and France was again dominator.

The sudden withdrawal from office of Pitt in the very month of this Treaty was significant. His whole political life was one of tragic irony. A great states-man and a firm advocate for a policy of peace, he was dragged without option into the costliest war. The position of England then is allegorical of her position since 1914, but had the honest, economical Pitt been Prime Minister, the costs of our war would probably have become reduced by at least one or two thousand millions.

Free from armed oppositions on the continent, Napoleon determined to be master of the world and concentrated on Britain. The sudden uprush of her industries was making her the workshop of the world ; and the world and its treasures Napoleon regarded as his birthright. He was the gambler in power and blood. He staked for the world. Had he conquered the world and lived to-day, he would have been miserable until he had sent aeroplanes on voyages of discovery to deliver ultimatums to the planets, and would have safely, but restlessly, awaited their return hardly even consoled by the arms of his mistresses !

Despite their victories on sea England had, until now, proved no match for the French soldiers on land, but a force of 15,000 men under General Abercrombie, in 1801, recaptured Egypt from the French, and in the negotiated Peace of Amiens in 1802, Napoleon made terms by which England restored all French colonies save Ceylon and Trinidad, and arranged to return Malta within three months to its old masters, the Knights of St. John.

Napoleon only made peace because it served his purpose to gain a respite in which to mature fresh plans of aggression. Peace was anathema to him, blood only titillated his nostrils. He was a vulgar conqueror ; a despot seeking only his own profit. By his victories tyranny was made possible, and his suppression of the Press destroyed all freedom of opinion.

His determination to subdue England was merely postponed for further preparations. The pledges given at Amiens were ruthlessly set aside and his plans were so obvious that the British government anticipated his attack by a declaration of war in 1803. Pitt was recalled to power, but he was a broken man and died within two years. Assisted by Pitt's offers of subsidies, Russia, Austria, and Sweden joined in an alliance to wrest Italy and the Low Countries from Napoleon's grasp. Their efforts failed, and in the Battle of Austerlitz the combined Russian and Austrian armies were defeated.

England achieved a famous victory off the Cape of Trafalgar in October, 1805, and Nelson annihilated the French and Spanish navies. The bravery of Nelson, who died at his post, stands in brilliant contrast to the diplomacy of Napoleon who died in his bed.

Fox, who succeeded Pitt after his death on January 23rd, 1806, endeavoured to obtain peace, but was foiled by the evasiveness of Napoleon, who had now assumed the title of Emperor. The blood-thirsty megalomaniac pursued his career of slaughter, revelling in the human sacrifices to his ambition, and undertook a new war against Prussia, which he defeated at Jena. From Berlin Napoleon marched behind his men through Poland, and though checked in the winter by the stubborn defence of the Russian forces, his victory at Friedland in 1807 compelled the Czar to consent to the Peace of Tilsit.

He placed his brothers on their puppet thrones and created fresh wars, and possessing the one efficient army in Europe he continued a triumphant career of annexation.

England, despite the defeats of her armies, still controlled the seas, and declared the whole coast occupied by France and her allies from Danzig to Trieste to be in a state of blockade. It was impossible for her to enforce the order, and in retaliation for this paper blockade Napoleon issued an equally absurd decree from Berlin, which, without a ship to carry it out, placed the British Isles in a state of blockade.

Naturally, a wide contraband trade was carried on, and despite these nonsensical and bombastic decrees on each side, it is ironical to observe that the French army which marched to Eylau was actually clad in great-coats made in Leeds and shod with shoes made in Northampton.

Under such conditions, prices in England rose to unprecedented heights, and the fortunate but conscienceless profiteers waxed probably as fat then as they did after 1914. Wheat rose to famine prices, and the value of land rose in proportion to the price of wheat.   Agriculture assumed a feverish and artificial prosperity, but the scarcity of the necessaries of life caused a terrible pauperisation of the labouring classes.

Unfortunately England, in a violent stretch of her rights, had adopted on the seas the same aggressive attitude as that of Napoleon on land.   The effects were serious in America.   She was justifiably aggravated by her Orders in Council.   The English Government exercised a right of search and asserted a right of seizing English seamen found on American vessels.   American commerce ceased to exist, and the deplorable result was that in May, 1812, America declared war on Britain.   General Rose, with an invading force of four thousand, captured Washington, and before evacuating the city burnt its public buildings to the ground.   This act was done under the strict orders of the English Government, and must be recorded as one of the most shameful pages in our history.   The two expeditions designed to penetrate the States from the North and from the South proved failures.   Sanity prevailed in 1814, and both sides being anxious for peace, the warring claims of each were set aside in silence in the Treaty of 1814.

Still bent on satisfying his war lust Napoleon, by his peremptory and impossible demands, forced Russia into conflict in 1812.   Wellington with his army of forty thousand achieved a few successes, but were eventually driven to a hasty retreat on the Portuguese frontier, during which time Napoleon had marched on Moscow.

Victorious in the battle of Borodino and arrogant with continual successes, Napoleon impatiently awaited the proposals of peace from the Czar.   But they never came.   The psychology of the conqueror, like the body of the leech, had become bloated with blood.   Nauseated as his enemies were by the perpetual wars, they were more sickened by his transitory concessions of peace, his broken treaties, his impositions, and his fresh declarations of strife when his thirsty spirit moved him.   Alexander remained silent.   Words had become meaningless.

The inhabitants of Moscow kindled a fire with their own hands, and reduced the city to ashes. Napoleon could do no more than watch. The dying embers of the flames marked the flickering of his power. The gathering horrors of a Russian winter bent his stubborn will to retreat. Nature, cold and invincible, used her weapons in defence of humanity and proved herself the Nemesis of the destroyer. Of the four hundred thousand of Napoleon's Grand Army only a few thousand crossed the Niemen in December.

The reign of terror was nearing its end. A freshly gathered army of two hundred thousand men gained some temporary successes in 1813 ; but Wellington, with a force of ninety thousand men, overtaking the French forces in retreat at Vittoria, drove them in utter rout across the Pyrenees. The forces of Austria, Prussia, and the Czar overthrew Napoleon at Leipzig in October and forced the French army back in rout across the Rhine. The struggle with Napoleon ended in March with the surrender of Paris, and was at once followed by the abdication of the Emperor and the return of the Bourbons.

It is easier, however, to make war than to adjust peace, and, following the usual precedence, the allies, as conquerors, quarrelled over the spoils. Napoleon, who had been allowed by the Treaty to retain a fragment of his former Empire, the Island of Elba, still conceiving war as his only salvation, seized his last opportunity with avidity. Landing near Cannes, with a thousand of his guards, by the spell of his name he succeeded in 1815 in raising an army of two hundred and fifty thousand. In face of the common danger and knowing Napoleon of old, the allies ceased their strife and consolidated their forces against him.

Napoleon's final effort, desperate as it was, proved his last spasm. His army was defeated by the allies at Waterloo, and it is interesting to note that the Imperial Guard—his own reserve—took no part in the battle until the last moment, when in despair it was thrown into the fray.

Napoleon fled to Paris. It is astonishing to

observe how immune from wounds great fighting generals contrive to keep! Think how magnificent it must be to direct the onslaught from the rear, to enjoy the emotions of viewing the contest in safety and awaiting its decision in comfort! Then, if the fates have been unkind, and the human fodder one has gambled is lost, how advantageous it is to be in the van of the retreat, and in the indisputable position of being the first with the right to run. Napoleon exerted this right, and his modern prototype, William Hohenzollern, followed his example. What would have been the punishment of their misguided soldiers had they dared to exhibit this glaring fear?

Ask the average fool to enumerate the great men in history, and with characteristic stupidity due to imbecile education the first names to occur to him will be Napoleon and Cromwell. A veritable *entente cordiale* of greatness! Ask him to enumerate the great men of modern times, and he will become insularly patriotic and mention Mr. D. Lloyd George, Mr. H. Bottomley, Mr. Steve Donoghue, and Mr. Charles Chaplin. Being timid, it is amusing to note that these names may even occur to him in an inverted order of merit. Thus he exhibits his political apathy, his proneness to inflammation, his instinct to gamble, and his comprehensiveness for broad comicality.

Napoleon was not a great man. He was merely a notable example of personal force. Greatness is the ultimate achievement of a determined purpose. In his purpose of military domination, after ephemeral successes, Napoleon failed utterly. He and his kingdom fell like a house of cards. He traded on lies. " False as a bulletin " was a proverb in his day and war despatches have been edited on his principle ever since. He trampled on the world and treated humanity as a worm, which, turning, devoured him. His record is one of failure. He was a middle-class vulgarian, small in stature, and, beyond war, limited in imagination ; his stomach was fat, his mind was as inflated with his own importance as the breeches of Henry the Eighth.

His personal glorification depended only on upheaval, and realising this, tribute is paid to his method by modern mimics. One sees in our Parliament, our War Office, and on our Press, types seeking to emulate him. And, as Napoleon, they all start as democrats and will end as outcasts. From Parliament and safe security, the boast is thrown by one of " having won the war " ; from the War Office, irritated by peace, pinchbeck conquerors seek disaster by fresh campaigns ; from the Press, posing before a looking-glass and bludgeoning the ignorant by senseless reiteration, a pseudo-dictator vainly strives to sway the world to his unripe crude opinion.

Each of the three imagines himself to be the twentieth century Napoleon. Each is of the same breed, each regarding his typical predecessor with the slightly superior contempt one possesses for an earlier-born relative. Each futilely imagines that, with his fostered opportunities, he can rule the world. Each looks on the world as he views a golf course ; he optimistically anticipates the force of his drive, and eventually lands in the inevitable bunker of false ambitions.

Napoleon is assumed to have possessed a magnetic personality, but his magnetism was merely his influence on ignorant minds, weakened by the fear of his blatant force. Of this calibre is the magnetism of our modern minister, who succeeds in impressing the mob by frenzied phrases and muddled metaphors. Such magnetism may impose upon the herd, but against the cold reason of a critical intellect, it becomes impotent and is subjected to its place.

Power is an exertion of craftiness. It adopts the garb of force ; and though force is a charlatan, she must be stripped before her ugliness is uncovered. The philosopher, despising the usage and the impositions of power, casts it aside as a base implement, and feeds his emotions on the subtleties of suggestion.

CHAPTER XXXVI

GEORGIAN BEAUX AND BEAUTIES

*Century of personality in fashion, free of convention or vogue
—Man's limitless wardrobe—Origin of the top hat—
Eccentricities : zebra cloths, macaroni wigs, nevernoise
hats—Foolishness is contagious ; and woman outdoes man
in stupidity—Artificial bosoms— Hoops are discarded—
Woman discovers the artistic value of form—The Empire
gown—Form revealed to the world much as God made it
—Simplicity is an expensive virtue.*

FOR dress this Georgian era, extending over a century,
was a wonderful era. It was a century of personality
in fashion ; design, free from the shackles of
convention or vogue, became exhilarated in its liberty
and expressed itself promiscuously.

It was the era of the bacchanalia of style. Fashions
were conceived in a spirit of revelry, germinated in a
joyful acceptance, and were cherished with an air of
languor during the period of gestation. As the
sturdy stomach rebels at the banquet, and proud
capacity in a few fleeting moments is beggared by
beauty, so is description rendered impotent in any
attempt to pen the pictures of this age. Fecundity
defeats facundity.

There was no limit to the wardrobe of the man of
fashion. Coats of crimson velvet, of white satin, of
various coloured cloths, all embroidered and trimmed
with gold or silver lace and buttons of gold. Waistcoats of gold brocade, of every conceivable shade of
satins and silks, embroidered or fringed with lace.
Crimson and black velvet breeches. Silk stockings
in black or white. Ruffled shirts and neck-cloths.
Hats laced with gold point *d'Espagne,* or gold binding
or lace scalloped ; silver buckles for his knees and
shoes ; diamond stock-buckles and dainty tortoiseshell
snuff-boxes.

During the earlier part of the reign of George the Third coats were cut on lines from which our morning coat has been derived; some were frogged and others buttoned. Double-breasted coats with the fronts cut sharply away from the waist were worn. Collars appeared on all coats and were cut in a variety of ways. Also appeared long-tailed coats and short-tailed coats, coats elegantly tight and coats carelessly loose; all possessing character and style and carried by the beau as if he owned all London Town.

It is from this period that the few simple civilian garments of the Englishman of to-day have been adapted, but all sense of beauty of colour has degenerated into drabness and all inclination to the faintest elaboration has surrendered to timidity.

Towards the latter part of this reign men wore Napoleonic hats among a conglomeration of hats of every description, including the origin of the top-hat of to-day. Coats of the cut familiarised by the pictures of Napoleon were worn by civilians.

In the wild orgy of changing fashions, eccentricities appeared from time to time. Midway a few wore zebra cloths, often comically made to button high in the chest and cut sharply away over the hips to hang in long tails behind, the short zebra vest coming down in a V to the top of the stomach. The wide crossed stripes of these garments were peculiarly grotesque in effect.

Another ludicrous style of the beau was the macaroni; a colossal wig built a foot high on his head, and on the top perched lonely and desolate was a silly little nevernoise hat—a tiny rimmed affair like a nob on a loaf. His wig was made with three fat sausage-like rolls hanging from each side of his forehead to his neck. His cravat was tied in a great wide bow under his chin; his breeches were loose with many coloured strings or beribboned bows at the knees. Indeed he looked the fool he probably was.

Foolishness is contagious, and, for a short period, woman became afflicted, and being in all things an extremist, she proceeded to outdo him in stupidity. Responding to a call of madness, she erected her wig to a crown of absurdity, towering a foot and a half above her innocent brow. To keep its shape it was stuffed with sufficient meal to feed a regiment of fools. But she was pleasant-humoured in her comicality, and if she approved of the navy she wore a straw ship on the top ; if she was inclined towards a sporting squire she adorned it with a coach ; if she was a lover of horticulture she was solaced by a garden of flowers poised high above her eyes.

At this fantastic period some of the gowns were worn with a coy little cape on the bodice, the waist cut so long at the back that it strenuously endeavoured to reach the top of her legs. Later, when the erection of her wig had reached its point of futility, it suddenly collapsed to a normal proportion. But in discarding one eccentricity, she adopted another. Contemptuous of her own natural endowments, by artificial aids she swelled her bosom to a degree beyond the wildest dreams of nature's bounty. What she conceded in one way she contracted in another, and her waist was as tight as she could endure. The front of her gown was straight, but at the back it projected proudly and largely. The picture is that of a pouter pigeon, pouting so petulantly as to make a bull's eye for Cupid's arrow.

The shapes of woman's hats were multitudinous, some appealing to one's sense of beauty, some to one's sense of humour. The very broad-brimmed hat adorned with feathers was an artistic balance to the wide-hooped skirt ; the poke bonnet protruded so generously that it could almost canopy a family.

Then suddenly, after centuries of experiments and wild extremity, the hoop was discarded. With the French Revolution, woman, responsive to any move-ment of force, accomplished her revolution in dress.

For centuries, despite the period in which she had made herself gorgeous, impressive, monumental, elaborate, fantastic, grotesque, brazen, seductive, she had from an artistic point of view failed to vie with man.

To the artist and philosopher the development of the subtlety of the sexes is an interesting study. Almost to the beginning of the nineteenth century woman's inventive powers were dormant. She simply adapted or elaborated man's designs. Man puffed out his shoulders and bagged his breeches ; woman swelled her sleeves and hooped her skirt. Thus throughout the ages she copied her lord and master, but never attaining his grace nor his symmetry and form.

But towards the end of the eighteenth century she discovered the artistic value of form, and discarding every extravagance of design which contorted her figure, arrived at grace by evolving the simple Empire gown. This was made in such transparent materials that for the first time for ages she was enabled to reveal her form to the world more or less as God made it. With her simple little shoes, simple little turban, showing the simple little fringe of her hair, she leaped from a towering absurdity to a height of simplicity.

Simplicity, however, is an expensive virtue ; it has a variety of expressions, is dressed in a thousand disguises. The Empire gown marks the dawn of woman's emancipation in dress. Little by little she ceased to copy man, and to create styles of her own. Her inventiveness, which had been curbed for centuries, leapt ahead, and soon she outstripped man. To-day she has ten thousand styles, and man is employed as a black foil to the beauty and glory of her colours.

The gorgeous garb of the men of the Georgian era has now become a dream picture of the past, but that our eyes may be relieved from the gloom of our modern reflections, woman adorns herself in gay magnificence and concedes only the inspiration to man to work like hell to pay for it.

CHAPTER XXXVII

GEORGE IV. (1820–1830)

The author is unable to solve the mystery of George's popularity—Curtain falls on Georgian era of dress— Origins of some modern garments : pantaloons, full frock-coat, waistcoat, glossy silk hat—Woman's simple styles—The Georgian era is left in the spirit one leaves a garden of flowers for a pathway of weeds.

I

ONE of the most interesting of the unsolved problems of the nineteenth century is the popularity of George IV., for popular he was—in the baser sense of the word—both as Regent and King.

The best proof of that popularity is that thirty years after his death Thackeray, as a super-journalist and super-society-lecturer, gained enormous *réclame* and enormous profit by his famous attack on Prince Florizel.

In the face of cold record it is difficult to understand the grounds for this popularity. A bad friend, a worse husband, a treacherous lover, a poor sportsman, a feeble wit, a contemptible politician, a great drunkard, and a would-be dandy, George IV. nevertheless managed to captivate the imagination of men whose intellects are beyond dispute.

Even the cynical and Bonapartist Byron was, for a time, impressed by the manners of the Regent, and the great and good Sir Walter Scott lost his gigantic sense of humour in the presence of Florizel " in full Highland garb."

Lockhart says that the King at his first levee in Scotland diverted many and delighted Scott by appearing in a Celtic toilette which had been carefully supervised by the Laird of Garth, who had with his own expert hands arranged the Royal plaid of the Stuart tartans.

"And he did look a most stately and imposing person in that beautiful dress when mounting the 'cat-dath,'—but his satisfaction therein was cruelly disturbed, when he discovered, towering and blazing among and above the genuine Glengarries and Mac-Leods and MacGregors, a figure even more portly than his own, equipped from a sudden impulse of loyal ardour in an equally complete set of the self-same conspicuous Stuart tartan." The "figure" was that of Sir William Curtis, the Guildhall baronet, henceforward "Vich Ian Alderman," who apparently was rigged out as a—Guildhall baronet. Such was the glamour of Florizel.

It was that same glamour which induced the Wizard of the North to wrap up and carefully place in his tail-pocket the sacred glass which His Majesty had drained, to forget the precious relic, and to sit upon it. It is comforting to know that the damage was not serious : " The scar was of no great consequence, as even when mounting the 'cat-dath,' or battle garment, of the Celtic Club, he adhered, like his hero Waverley, to the trews."

As Regent and as King, Florizel's intimates and boon companions were brilliant men, and not all of them were toadies. The Carlton House set and the Brighton Pavilion set included men who added lustre to their great names.

How is it to be explained ? The answer is not found in Thackeray's society lectures. Nor is it to be found in the memoirs of the period.

In modern eyes the Fourth George appears merely as an untrustworthy, unscrupulous, tippling roué, of a distinctly uninviting appearance, in spite of his attempts to live up to the mode of the dandies. He may have had the manner, but he speedily lost the figure.

Says Creevey, malignantly : " Prinny has let loose his belly, which now reaches to his knees ; otherwise he is said to be well." A delicate way of saying that the Regent had, on medical advice, left off stays !

With the economists of the day George IV. was not popular, but the majority of the people not only tolerated, but would seem to have furtively admired him, and the only possible explanation that occurs is that his reign was one of comparative peace after the long strain of the Napoleonic wars, and that the throne shone in the reflected glories of Trafalgar and Waterloo.

In addition, whenever a fresh scandal broke out the nation probably consoled itself with the reflection that George IV., like his equally disreputable brothers, York, Clarence, Cumberland, Sussex, and Cambridge, was in the beneficent nature of things unlikely to leave legitimate issue, and the phase could therefore be regarded with amusement.

One would give volumes of dreary and would-be "spicy" memoirs of the Fourth George for a film record of the momentous interview, inimitably described by Mr. Lytton Strachey, between the King and the future Queen Victoria.

"The old rip, bewigged and gouty, ornate and enormous, with his jewelled mistress by his side, and his flaunting court about him, received the tiny creature who was one day to hold in those same halls a very different state. 'Give me your little paw,' he said, and two ages touched. Next morning, driving in his phaeton with the Duchess of Gloucester, he met the Duchess of Kent and her child in the Park. 'Pop her in!' were his orders, which, to the terror of the mother and the delight of the child, were immediately obeyed. Off they dashed to Virginia Water, where there was a great barge, full of lords and ladies, fishing, and another barge, with a band ; and the King ogled Feodora, and praised her manners, and then turned to his small niece. 'What is your favourite tune ? The band shall play it.' 'God save the King, sir,' was the instant answer. The Princess's reply has been praised as an early example of a tact which was afterwards famous.

But she was a truthful child, and perhaps it was her genuine opinion."

But Florizel had a glamour—how and why, God alone knows, for history is silent as to the causes whilst chronicling the effects.

An era of peace after long war was undoubtedly George the Fourth's biggest asset.

II

With this chapter the curtain falls on the wonderful Georgian era of dress. The gorgeous masque is over. Colour and grace fly to the wings. Elegance, in male attire, makes a last courtly bow. Personality, in distinguished garb, makes its final exit, and drabness and ugliness grinningly rehearsing their double turn, eagerly await their call to occupy the dreary stage.

Fashion is a pendulum controlled by perpetual motion ; and woman is an emotion controlled by the perpetual pendulum. But whereas woman has refined herself to a cultured fickleness with fashion, man has degenerated to a slave-like faithfulness.

It is amazing that man, having dressed for æons in splendid colours and with artistry in design, should continue to accept with a herd-like submission the drab garb of to-day.

Men's fashions, splendid as they had been before, rose, during the eighteenth century, to an apex of perfection, only to crash during the next century to a level of ugliness never before conceived in history. Like the fall of empires, the realm of men's dress decayed in its ruins.

During the ten years' reign of the dissolute George, the foundation was laid for some of the dress fashions of to-day. Pantaloons strapped under the boot were the origin of our trousers and our modern evening dress coat made its appearance. The old-fashioned full frock-coat and the glossy silk top-hat came in. Waistcoats, similar in length to ours, but with a deep opening, and made in buff or light neutral shades were worn. The dandy, in his desire for distinctiveness and tired of colours, adopted quieter shades. Blue coats were the vogue, and the colour of the waistcoat was selected to blend and not to contrast. The folding of the white stock around the collar was a work of art and man was judged by his linen, cleanliness coming before gorgeousness. A good figure was an asset, and those not so blessed, padded themselves.

George the Fourth must have studied his dress, since his second-hand wardrobe fetched £15,000. It is to his credit that he managed to attempt something, even though Thackeray did describe him so ironically: "But a bow and a grin. Take him to pieces and find—some clothes and then nothing."

Simplicity reigned with the women. White muslin, taffeta, and chintz for the morning, white-figured gauze over white satin for the evening ; cashmere shawls and coloured bonnets in the cottage style, tied demurely with ribbons under the chin, or leghorn hats trimmed with green foliage.

Simper on, sweet lady, and make the most of your allurements. Be generous to my lord when he is in his cups, because when he is sober he has a fine grace and a devastating manner. Eat with him, drink just a little with him, and for art's sake please be merry with him, for to-morrow you will both be dead to style.

You, sweet maid, will soon enter a period of horse-hair furniture and horsehair minds. It will be an era of bounty and the beast. You will manufacture a protuberance behind with your bustle, he will evolve one in front by his prosperity.

One leaves the Georgian era as one leaves a garden of flowers for a pathway of weeds. The Victorian era of ugliness is, thank God, only a phase in which woman etherealises her ailments instead of her allurements. After a lapse, with the Fifth George on the throne, her resurrection of fashion is complete, and she again displays her freedom in all its transparency. But man, timid, shrinking, struggling feebly with the chains of his ugly conventions in dress, is hardly yet brave enough to shake away the dust of his self-consciousness.

CHAPTER XXXVIII

THE REIGN OF THE DANDIES

The artist revels in the world of illusion—Carlyle's careless conception of the dandy—Ugliness breeds cruelty and destruction—Cinematic glance : Congreve fortunate in his Irish birth, Samuel Foote has the spirit to squander his fortune, George Augustus Selwyn, M.P., seldom sleeps or sits in Parliament, George Byron Brummel introduces the black evening dress with white waistcoat, Count Alfred D'Orsay, the last of the dandies.

I

It would be niggardly to leave the Georgian feast of fashion without paying tribute to the entertainers ; it would be as if the guest had so gorged himself that his leave-taking was a muttering of drunken incoherence.

The artist appreciates all work of art and refines himself by criticism ; he revels in his understanding of the world of illusion in which he lives. He is sateless.

Art in each of its specialised forms is the splendid allurement, and the artist in one sphere does not venture to condemn its exhibition in another. That is why one must dismiss Carlyle's careless, negative, and inartistic conception of the dandy. Carlyle's mind was typical of the dreary philosophy of the Victorians. He existed during eighty-one years of the nineteenth century and was privileged to look with unseeing eyes upon five early years of the eighteenth. His views in all things might be termed Cromwellian or Carsonian. Considering the period in which his " Sartor Resartus " was first published (in 1838), from which period man's dress became simply ludicrous, his philosophy may have had an influence. Though to be generous one should really accept the decadence that followed as a coincidence, the realisation of a bad dream, and not as a commentary on Carlyle.

It is absurd to conceive the dandy as a witness and living martyr to the eternal worth of clothes. The martyr suffers and parades defeat in suffering. The dandy enjoys and displays triumph in enjoyment. He does not live to dress, but uses dress to decorate the art of life. He is a compliment to woman in his endeavour to vie with her. His artistic masking is a delicate compliment to his ego.

If the dandy looks to the world to recognise his existence, even if only as a visual object reflecting rays of light, should we not be thankful for the relief he affords us from the eternal drabness, both physical and mental, which the majority of men exhibit ?

The dandy will come again into his own, and with him may return manners and culture, which are in a state of decay in these poverty-stricken and vulgarised times. He was practically eclipsed in the ugly and miserable and sordid responsibilities of the World War. Breed in ugliness, surround yourself in ugliness, clothe yourself in ugliness, think, scheme, and evolve in ugliness, and cruelty and destruction are the natural sequences.

The twentieth century must think differently, and the dandy when he appears again in some new disguise, must be welcomed as a symbol of a new clean thought. In the past he has always been noted for his valour and his fighting with clean weapons. Can you imagine the eighteenth century dandy fighting a duel with poisoned gas ?

He typifies individuality, and unless one is afflicted with the serf-mind, individualism is the only creed an honest intellect can accept.

Those who criticise and sneer at the dandiacal type do so in the exasperation of their envy. They exhibit their own affectation, inasmuch as they would love to don fine clothes themselves, but knowing they possess neither the figure nor the manner to carry them, they seek to attack the more fortunate with the weapon of ridicule. The only way that ugliness can evade observation is in the gloom of drab surroundings.

II

In the eighteenth century class distinction was clearly defined in dress. Each grade of society claimed its style of costume, and each craftsman or mechanic the uniform of his trade. Fine raiment was the hall-mark of the society beau. The foil to his magnificence was provided by clergymen, attorneys, and physicians, who dressed in black, but wore the distinguishing wigs of their professions. The costume of the sober citizen was also made in black, which was relieved by lace ruffles, brown stockings, and a full-bottomed wig.

All men, except those of the lower classes, shaved their heads and wore wigs. It was assumed that this was the only way a gentleman could keep clean, as the heads of their servants swarmed with vermin.

The affairs of the day were discussed in the popular coffee-houses. Every man who paid his penny was an eligible member, every rank and profession came in time to have its own particular house, in which a stranger would find no kindred soul. Later in the century many of these coffee-houses developed into fashionable and exclusive clubs. At Whites, Brooks, and the Cocoa-Tree, the gambling was tremendous. The bucks plunged with a spirit which would unnerve most sportsmen of to-day. At faro the lowest stake was £50. To win or lose £10,000 at a sitting was an ordinary occurrence, and as much as £100,000 was often known to have changed hands during an evening. On one occasion £180,000 depended upon the cut of a card.

Charles James Fox was a pre-Napoleonic gambler and before he was twenty-four cost his father £140,000.

It was the age of extravagance. Take a glance at the extent of the wardrobe of a typical man of fashion of the period.

He would possess at least six coats of coloured velvets and white satin, trimmed with gold and silver lace, with perhaps one made in a plainer fashion for use on mournful occasions. With these he would have the choice of perhaps a dozen long waistcoats, made in blue satin, gold brocade, green silk, white satin, scarlet, black silk with fringes, all laced and embroidered in coloured silks. His wardrobe also contained nine or ten pairs of breeches of velvet, satin, and cloth ; half a dozen three-cornered hats, silver laced scalloped, laced with gold *point d'Espagne*, some with gold binding, and some bound plain ; three dozen ruffled shirts and three dozen lace neck-cloths, and a like number of white silk, black silk, and fine cotton stockings ; cambric and silk handkerchiefs galore ; shoes adorned with gold and silver buckles set with diamonds ; silver-handled swords, silver-mounted pistols ; and as varied a choice in jewellery as his means would allow.

III

Let us take a cinematic glance at the men who held the eighteenth century stage of fashion. It can only be a parsimonious survey ; an indelicately hurried greeting to genius before a necessitous visit to Victorian vulgarity.

The early part of the century was graced by the presence of the most brilliant writer of comedy in English literature. William Congreve lived until 1728 and his plays will live whilst letter-press lasts. He was a master in joyfully cynical psychology, and an artist in supreme satiric philosophy. His cunning analysis of human nature in addition to his subtly iconoclastic dialogue, rank him in comedy beyond Shakespeare. He was the aristocrat of letters and a man of fashion. He knew how to live and preferred living to writing. To his credit stand five great plays. He understood the economy of genius, and was wise enough to use his art without allowing his art to use him.

Of course he was fortunate in having passed his childhood and youth in Ireland, and in being educated at Dublin University ; but then the gods always smile on the genius of wit, and are wise in their choice of a magnetic atmosphere.

During the last few years the Stage Society in London has produced Congreve's " The Way of the World," and the Phœnix Society " Love for Love." Both were splendid performances. Any one scene of either play contains more brilliant wit than the whole of the plays of the last century lumped together. To-day in genius we possess only the finely drawn, psychologically dramatic studies of John Galsworthy, and as a contemporary and sincere dramatist of the times it is logical to appreciate his discardure of the unfashionable weapon of wit.

After Congreve, in the mid-eighteenth century, came Samuel Foote, who was handicapped in the writing of his comedies by the knowledge that he would have to act in them himself.

The twenty-four plays he wrote were just amusing burlesques of the period, but he originated the Haymarket Theatre, and before doing so, possessed the spirit to squander his fortunes.

In his frock suit of green with silver lace, and bag wig, sword, bouquet and point lace ruffles, he was a figure of the town, and on occasions he would swagger in the coffee-houses in full dress or enjoy a promenade with the beaux in the parks.

Then came Richard Brinsley Sheridan, born in 1751 and living until nearly the end of the reign of George the Third. He depicted the manners and the fashions of the latter part of his century, and endeavoured in his methods to imitate the master mind and wit of Congreve. But Congreve's standard was infinitely beyond him, and attractive as is the superficial wit of Sheridan's " School for Scandal," in comparison with the innocuous wit of Shaw's " Heartbreak House," both are shattered when compared to the wickedly subtle and polished wit of " The Way of the World."

Goldsmith intervened in a mild manner midway in the century, but " She Stoops to Conquer " serves only to illustrate the personality of the modest Oliver with his simple humour and tea-cup comicality.

IV

Among the leaders of fashion in the middle of the Georgian era there shone George Augustus Selwyn, who amused himself in exclusive circles and was a Member of Parliament for forty years, though he seldom sat or slept there, and scarcely ever condescended to make a speech. But he fortunately enjoyed the privilege acquired by the few of nominating two members for Ludgershall, which enabled him to add about £9,000 to his banking account whenever there was an election. He had a considerable reputation as a wit, but it was built upon a somewhat slender foundation. Perhaps his aptest witticism was at the time when Charles Fox became enamoured of Mrs. (" Perdita ") Robinson. Selwyn remarked, " Who should the man of the people live with but the woman of the people."

George James Williams (" Gilly "), a bosom friend of Selwyn's, was a gay beau with fashionable and elastic principles. Owing to the fiscal policy of the time, smuggling developed into a fine art, and ministers of the Crown were naturally expert evaders of the Customs. Selwyn, when visiting the Continent, willingly assisted his friend to smuggle point lace ruffles and velvet suits into England, thus ' Gilly," having defrauded the King's revenue, was enabled to make a particularly elegant appearance at George the Third's birthday parties.

Later came William Beckford (" the Abbot of Fonthill "), a dandy who wrote some books that died long before he did. He was somewhat of a *poseur* but made an impressive figure when painted by Romney.

Then Lord Byron, a master in the art of dress and a boon companion of the dandies of his time, proving that genius finds no inspiration in the company of fools.

With the close of the century there appeared a new leader of fashion. George Bryan Brummell, for long the boon companion of the Prince Regent, was born in 1778. He revolutionised the prevailing style, directed new modes and originated tasteful and symmetrical designs, which, though not so picturesque and elaborate as many of those of past days, were at least his own, and from which many of our styles have been adapted. His influence was such that he could claim to make a fashion. After his reign his designs were so mutilated in the nineteenth century that they degenerated into ugly shapelessness, and became as senselessly untrue to their origin as an Anglicised version of a French comedy.

After a century of gorgeous colour it is natural that the artistic eye sought a temporary relief from profusion. Beau Brummell, who gained a reputation for unobtrusive elegance—which is the perfect expression of the art of dress—was accepted as a leader of fashion on a solid foundation. He dressed with perfect taste. He was conspicuous because he blended his colours so that they became illusively inconspicuous and stood in artistic relief from those who, with a lack of taste, crudely contrasted their colours. In his later days he would wear a blue coat with a velvet collar, black trousers and boots, a white neckcloth and an opera hat, with white gloves carried in his hand. He also introduced the black evening dress with white waistcoat. His neckcloth was perfected by innumerable experiments. He succeeded in giving it a form and an artistry which has long since disappeared. His linen was perfect, and to his credit, especially considering the days in which he lived, he was a rigid disciple of cleanliness.

Brummell carried his clothes with a supremely unconscious air. He possessed a fine manner and a thorough appreciation of his own dignity, which he refused to sacrifice after his unfortunate quarrel with his friend, the Prince Regent (George the Fourth).

After the final quarrel the Prince Regent was walking arm-in-arm with Lord Moira, and they happened to meet Brummell with Lord Alvanley. All four stopped and the Prince deliberately ignored Brummell, and, to make the cut apparent, talked only to Alvanley and passed on. As the Prince and Moira turned away, the Beau said with the bored air of a superior, who idly wishes to be informed, but in a tone loud enough to reach the Prince's ear, "Alvanley, who's your fat friend?"

Brummell was reckless, good-natured, good-humoured, and was blessed with a fine conceit. Like many other great characters when he got old he became a little mad. His last years were spent in France. In his later days, when living in poverty in Caen, he would arrange his poor sticks of furniture at dinner-time, light all the candles, and, opening the door, announce the imaginary guests. He would pretend to receive all the London celebrities who had formerly idolised him in the realms of fashion.

"His Highness the Prince Regent," "Lady Conyngham," "Lord Yarmouth," "Lady Jersey," "Her Grace Georgiana Duchess of Devonshire"—the famous names would ring out one by one.

Then, in a loud voice, the poor imbecile would announce, "George Bryan Brummell"—and collapse.

Beau Brummell died in the asylum at Caen in 1840.

Though he died an imbecile, he had lived with knowledge. And as if in sympathy, at the date of his death in 1840, dress again followed his fashion, and became imbecilic.

After Brummell's compulsory retirement from the field of fashion the next and last leader to appear was Count Alfred D'Orsay. He may be correctly described as "the last of the dandies." The handsome young Frenchman was born in 1801 and, coming to London when he was twenty-one, proved so attractive in fashionable circles that he was induced to spend most of his life there.

He did not possess the cool manner and ironic wit of Brummell, from whom his styles were adapted, but he carried his clothes with a grace, and the dazzling ardency of his personality created a considerable flutter and response amongst the women of his time. In the early days of George IV., D'Orsay presented a striking figure in his cream-coloured coat lined with velvet of the same hue, with a blue satin cravat, and jewelled breastpins, surmounting a blue velvet waist-coat and light coloured trousers. Later in life, in the early Victorian period, he would wear a fine blue coat with brass buttons, a buff waistcoat displaying his fine linen and neckcloth, tight trousers, a bell-topped silk hat and white or primrose gloves. Or perhaps he would appear in a study of subdued shades, with a dark brown coat and trousers, and a lighter shade brown velvet waistcoat and white cravat.

His inclinations were all towards the arts, and as an amateur he painted a portrait of the Duke of Wellington, which greatly pleased his subject and was exhibited in the National Portrait Gallery. He also sketched Carlyle, but whether the sketch was a bad one or not Carlyle certainly retorted in his " Sartor Resartus " with a worse sketch of dandies.

Carlyle wrote of him, " a dashing man, who might, some twenty years sooner born, have become one of Bonaparte's marshals, and *is*, alas—Count D'Orsay."

A stupid analysis, for had D'Orsay been one of Napoleon's marshals he would simply have been fuel or a stoker, and as either he would have shared Napoleon's extermination.

D'Orsay might have returned Carlyle's condolence, and written of him, " a dreary man, who might, some couple of centuries sooner born, have become one of Cromwell's ' cupbearers,' and is, alas—Thomas Carlyle."

He was exceptionally popular with almost all who mixed in the fashionable, literary, and Bohemian circles. His friend Disraeli apostrophised him as " the inimitable D'Orsay . . . who, with the universal genius of an Alcibiades, combined a brilliant wit and a heart of quick affection, and who, placed in a public position, would have displayed a courage, a judgment, and a commanding intelligence which would have ranked him with the leaders of mankind."

Disraeli was about the same age as D'Orsay and also posed as a dandy. But his effects in dress were bizarre. His extreme assurance inclined him to over-dress and overact his part. In his younger days he wore a black velvet coat ; purple trousers, with gold braid running down the outside seam ; long lace ruffles, reaching to the tips of his fingers ; white gloves with several brilliant rings outside them ; and he wore his hair in long black ringlets rippling over his shoulders. At Lady Blessington's receptions at Gore House, he would sometimes appear in a waist-coat splendidly embroidered with gorgeous gold flowers. He had a number of chains about his neck and was seldom seen without a black stick with a white cord and tassel. He is said to have walked along St. James's Street in boots with high red heels.

In contrast to the florid personality and promiscu-ously lavish attire of Disraeli, it is natural that D'Orsay stood in splendid relief.

The romance of Count D'Orsay's life is a fascina-ting story. At one of the many brilliant affairs following the coronation of George IV. he met the " most gorgeous Lady Blessington." With birds of paradise an affinity is inevitable.

Lady Blessington was a Tipperary girl, the daughter of Edmund Power. When D'Orsay came into her life she was a woman fully equipped in the arts of allurement. At the age of fifteen she had married a Captain Palmer, from whom she escaped as soon as possible. For five or six years she lived under the protection of the rich and amiable Captain Jenkins. Then desiring a change of protection she graced the house of the Earl of Blessington in Man-chester Square, and in 1818 Captain Palmer obliged her by falling out of an open window in the King's Bench Prison and breaking his neck. Thus at the age of twenty-six she was in a position to permit the sweet-natured Earl to make her his Countess.

At this time she met D'Orsay. Although eleven years older than him, she was still in the splendour of her youth, with the added attraction of considerable experience. She was the furnace, moulding men to her will. The difference in age was no matter. In her brilliance woman is of all ages and of no age.

Lord Blessington was charmingly simple. He was a winsome character, unconsciously warming his hands in other people's sunshine. The manners of both D'Orsay and the Countess were perfect, and Blessington took a wonderful liking to D'Orsay, which was perfectly understandable under the delicately disguised circumstances, but which, unfortunately, produced unique effects for the principal performers.

The Earl and Countess went on a tour of the Continent. D'Orsay was invited to join them. Two is boredom, three is fun ; at Genoa they joined Byron and the trio became a quartette. Then the generous-hearted Earl, who had been led to appreciate D'Orsay more and more, decided to marry his heiress daughter, Lady Harriet Gardner, to the Count. The situation assumed a dramatic intricacy, in which silent acquiescence was imperative.

Lady Harriet was only fifteen, and in those days young girls were ruled with a rod of iron and compelled to take the husbands assigned to them by their parents. Which is a further instance of the immorality of discipline and a disgusting offence against nature.

Any dissension on the part of the Countess or D'Orsay might have endangered disclosure. D'Orsay married Lady Harriet in 1827. Two years afterwards Lord Blessington died from an apoplectic stroke which, although history records as physical, might justifiably have been mental. The young Countess D'Orsay, proving a young woman of discernment, left her husband when she was nineteen and led her own romantic career in Paris. D'Orsay and Lady Blessington proceeded to make Gore House famous in London.

It was an amazing comedy. D'Orsay standing in masculine neutrality between the alluring maturity of the Countess and the provoking simplicity of the stepdaughter. Allurement won—by the length of a generation.

At Gore House Lady Blessington instituted the most popular *salon* of the period. Literature, art, and fashion were represented there. Thackeray, Dickens, Prince Louis Napoleon, Macready, Landon, Crabb Robinson, Foster, Samuel Rogers, Theodore Hook, Landseer, and Liszt were among her visitors. All the artists flocked to this *salon* of universal Truth, whilst discarding the unattractive temples of conventional lies.

Lady Blessington and Count D'Orsay entertained magnificently and both died in financial ruin, in which a fine philosophy is shown, the antithesis of the miserable miser. What are life and riches for but to spend, when one can only take spirits to heaven or hell?

Lady Blessington died in 1849 and Gore House was turned into a restaurant during the ghastly Great Exhibition of 1851. Later it was demolished and in its place the Albert Hall was erected, and the Albert Memorial leers on its site.

D'Orsay survived the woman he loved until 1852, when decay in all artistic things was manifest. Since then there has been no leader, and there is no one living who can claim the power to establish fashion. At present we are living in an age of mediocrity. There is no originality in dress, unless we accept Mr. Winston Churchill's comic headgear experiments —which at least have the merit of being less costly than his empiric exploits.

CHAPTER XXXIX

WILLIAM IV. (1830–1837)

*William pleases the people, though he is saturated in port wine,
horrifies his Ministers, shocks his flunkies, and maddens
his sister-in-law—Colour goes for a brief siesta, and suc-
cumbs to sleeping sickness in the Victorian era.*

THE absence of a legitimate heir to the throne had
long caused a naïve perturbation among the seven
middle-aged sons of George III.

The illegitimate lines were many and various, but
the descent of a crown is governed by a rigid
etiquette—an etiquette of which the Duke of Kent
was the more or less willing martyr.

The family negotiations which brought about the
sacrifice of the fifty-year-old Duke, with the bald
top to his head, his carefully dyed hair, and his
cherished mistress, on the altar of marriage for the
sake of providing an heir to the throne, is among
the purely comic passages in history.

And the Duke of Kent was not altogether willing.
True he needed the money, but, on the other hand,
he was perfectly happy and was become intensely
domesticated. Still, he had a sense of duty, and as
he told Creevey, " Although I trust I shall be at
all times ready to obey any call any country may
make upon me, God alone knows the sacrifice it
will be to me, whenever I shall think it my duty
to become a married man. It is now seven-and-
twenty years that Madame St. Laurent and I have
lived together ; we are of the same age and have been
in all climates and in all difficulties together, and you
may well imagine, Mr. Creevey, the pang it will
occasion me to part with her. I put it to your feelings—in the event of any separation between yourself and Mrs. Creevey."

But stern necessity compelled the awful step, and to make assurance doubly sure if possible, both the elderly Duke of Clarence and the elderly Duke of Kent put their heads in the matrimonial noose in the sacred cause of the legitimate succession.

The Duke of Kent begat Victoria and died.

The Duke of Clarence became William IV., and died childless.

Each was dissatisfied at the remuneration a grateful country voted for his services.

His accession to the throne well-nigh drove William the Fourth mad with excitement.

There was nothing of "the manner" about William, and he could hardly be expected to acquire it at the age of fifty-six.

A good-natured old eccentric, saturated in port wine and seafaring lore, he horrified his ministers, shocked his flunkies, maddened his sister-in-law the Duchess of Kent, and on the whole pleased his people.

Not only had the Crown ceased to interfere with the people but it amused them, and if the nation ever spared time from its work of reconstruction to think seriously of its bubbling old turkey-cock of a King, it smiled kindly and tolerantly.

After all, he did little harm, and he enjoyed being King immensely.

But while he was genuinely fond of little Victoria, he could not abide her mother, the Duchess of Kent, nor her uncle, the prim and somewhat sanctimonious Leopold of Belgium, who was later to figure so prominently as a would-be adviser of the young Queen.

For one thing, of course, Leopold drank only water.

"God damn it, sir!" expostulated the Royal William in disgust, "why don't you drink wine? I never allow anybody to drink water at my table."

Then there was a deadly feud with the Duchess of Kent over an attempt by that lady to seize an extra suite of apartments in Kensington Palace, and the old King, well primed, spoke his mind at a birthday banquet, while the Duchess raged in silence, and the little Princess openly wept, and the astonished guests eyed one another and thought deeply.

The most noteworthy deed the old King accomplished was in living until his successor reached her legal majority—a feat which he prayed publicly that he might succeed in, for he had at least the wit to perceive the perils attending the minority of a young girl.

He just, and only just, succeeded in what had become his dearest ambition, and died on the morning of June 20th, 1837.

In dress this short and alcoholic reign was significant as the extraordinary transition period. It was the day which saw the last of the dandies. The orgy of style was nearing its end. The mood was changing. Colour, exhausted by its long revelry, was accorded a brief siesta, but succumbed to sleeping sickness in the Victorian era.

CHAPTER XL

VICTORIA (1837–1901)

*Albert's virtues and vices—Suspicion that the goody-goody
age of Victoria is a delusion ; hard drinking, hard loving,
hard gambling, hard living — Fertile domesticity :
Royal cradles never cease to rock, hence Albert's appeal to
the lower classes—The upright John Brown—Victoria's
four phases ; the Girl-Queen, the Ideal Wife, the Widowed
Queen, the Mother of her People.*

THE Victorian era was, above all, an era of
individualism and of forceful personalities.

And from her childhood, the Queen herself was no
contemptible personality.

As her latest biographer records, her first request
to her mother after that memorable First Council was
a significant one. " Dear mamma, I hope you will
grant me the first request I make to you as Queen.
Let me be by myself for an hour." For an hour
she remained in solitude. Then she reappeared and
gave a significant order ; her bed was to be moved
out of her mother's room. It was the death knell of
the influence of the Duchess of Kent.

Until her marriage, the personality of this little
girl-queen—pink-cheeked, fair-haired, and strong-
willed—was dominant, and the public, delighted at
the contrast between the new occupant of the throne
and her dissolute old predecessors with their debts,
their mistresses, and their public scandals, whole-
heartedly gave her their affection.

It is true, there were occasional storms.

The unfortunate scandal over Lady Flora Hastings,
who on a medical examination proved innocent of
the charge made against her, turned an important
section of high society against the Throne, and the
young Queen's refusal to part with the Ladies of
the Bedchamber on a change of Government alienated

I

an important political section. The Queen was
" cut " and was publicly hissed, but the clouds passed
and Albert arrived on the scene.

Albert—with his " exquisite nose," his " delicate
moustache and slight, but very slight whiskers," his
" beautiful figure," broad in the shoulders and a
fine waist—came and was seen and conquered, and
for the years of her married life the history of
Victoria is largely the history of the development of
Albert.

And Albert did develop. In the end he was
something far more important than a figure for an
Albert Memorial.

Cold, pedantic, outwardly unsympathetic, without
that element of " panache " which is so desirable a
possession of a prince or politician—these were his
principal and worst faults. In addition, he did not
understand women, with the all-important exception
of Victoria.

Conscientious, hard-working, intelligent and honest,
with a genuine desire for statesmanship—these were
his virtues, and he made the most of them.

But to those of a different temperament, he must
at times have been very trying, and his eldest son
had a very different temperament. When on his
seventeenth birthday the future Edward VII. received
from his parents a lengthy memorandum of advice
as to his future conduct in life, he burst into hopeless
tears. Albert the Good was surely too good.

Victoria's long reign of peace, broken only by
what we should now look upon as small, detached,
and remote wars, was favourable to the growth of
personality and to the fostering of individualism and
individual effort.

Smile as the *fin de siècle* neo-Georgian may at what
he or she may choose to call the antiquated early
Victorian age, it was an age of singular freedom and
originality in most things except dress.

Never before had woman been a greater political
force ; for though she was voteless she had a voice.
In the political houses the hostesses entertained,

planned, schemed, and intrigued, and the power behind more than one political throne was essentially feminine.

Ministers wrote confidentially to great ladies, knowing full well that their confidences would be placed before the royal eye ; the Prime Minister himself corresponded daily—one might say hourly, when one remembers the volume of Disraeli's letters to Lady Bradford and Lady Chesterfield—with his dearest female friends on the highest matters of State. A great lady's smile or frown made or marred the social aspirant's prospects, and at the head of the whole social system was the great lady who wrote to her dear Uncle Leopold :

" Albert grows daily fonder and fonder of politics and business and is so wonderfully fit for both— such perspicacity and such courage—and I grow daily to dislike them both more and more. We women are not made for governing—and if we are good women, we must dislike these masculine occupations ; but there are times which force one to take interest in them *mal gré bon gré* and I do, of course, intensely. I must now conclude to dress for the opening of Parliament."

This proves that a great lady may be a great unconscious humorist, for before very long the same royal letter writer was to rate Lord Palmerston like a naughty schoolboy, to let Mr. Gladstone know very plainly what " the Queen's " wishes were, and to cause even that wily old courtier, Disraeli, to wipe perspiration from his brow.

After the failure of Lord Chelmsford in the Zulu War the Queen in indignant italics pressed Lord Beaconsfield to receive the general at Hughenden, but the old man steadily refused. He realised that he had hurt the Queen's feelings, and wrote humorously to Salisbury : " My greatest trouble is from my having refused to receive Lord Chelmsford at Hughenden. I am quite in disgrace, and may have to follow Andrassy's example. If so, you will know the truth, and that the cause is not the Afghan War, but only Mrs. Masham's petticoat."

Amusing instances of the female domination in the pre-vote days abound in Victorian records.

The Czar Alexander, on a visit to England after the marriage of his daughter to the Duke of Edinburgh, proposed to stay on for a couple of days beyond the date fixed by the Queen for her usual visit to Balmoral, and the Queen refused to modify her plans. Ministers were in a panic, the Court was well-nigh in hysterics, Lord Derby implored Beaconsfield's help, and it took all that favourite minister's powers of persuasion to avert the danger of an insult to Russia.

" My head is still on my shoulders," wrote Disraeli to Lady Bradford, who was ever his political and social confidante. " The great lady has postponed her departure ! Everybody has failed, even the Prince of Wales ; but she averted her head from me —at least I fancied so—at the drawing-room to-day, and I have no doubt I am not in favour. I can't help it. Salisbury says I have saved an Afghan war, and Derby compliments me on my unrivalled triumph."

And then the Queen :

" . . . It is for Mr. Disraeli's sake and as a return for his great kindness that she will stop till the 20th. . . . The Queen thinks Lord Derby and Lord Salisbury have little knowledge of what is the etiquette between Sovereigns."

Over the Russian and Turkish trouble in 1878 Disraeli had considerable scope for the exercise of his unrivalled tact in answering the great lady's letters. The Queen writes :

" She feels she cannot, as she said before, remain the Sovereign of a country that is letting itself down to kiss the feet of the great barbarians, the retarders of all liberty and civilisation that exists. Her son feels more strongly than herself even. . . .

Be firm, and rally your party round you. The Queen
means to speak very strongly to Count Beust. It can
do no harm ; it may do good. Oh, if the Queen were
a man, she would go and give those Russians, whose
word one cannot believe, such a beating ! We shall
never be friends again till we have it out."

But in all intercourse with women there are
gleams of sunshine as well as gusts of storm. Here
is such a gleam.

Writing to Lady Bradford the Prime Minister
proceeds :

" . . . Osborne was lovely. . . . The Faery sent
for me the instant I arrived. I can only describe my
reception by telling you that I really thought she
was going to embrace me. She was wreathed with
smiles, and as she tattled, glided about the room
like a bird. She told me it was ' all owing to your
courage and tact,' and then she said ' To think of
your having the gout all the time ! How you must
have suffered ! And you ought not to stand now.
You shall have a chair ! ' Only think of that ! I
remember that *feu*. Lord Derby, after one of his
severe illnesses, had an audience of Her Majesty, and
he mentioned it to me, as a proof of the Queen's
favour, that Her Majesty had remarked to him how
sorry she was she could not ask him to be seated !
The etiquette was so severe. I remembered all this
as she spoke, so I humbly declined the privilege, saying I was quite well, but would avail myself of her
gracious kindness if I ever had another attack."

Over the assumption of the title of Empress of
India there was more trouble, but the strong-minded
lady who, short and portly as she was, " tattled "
and " glided " about the room like a bird had
her way. In Disraeli's view, the moment was
inopportune, but the Faery would brook no delay,
and not only had the leaders of the Opposition not
been communicated with over this matter affecting

the dignity of the Crown, but even the Prince of Wales, who was abroad, had been left in ignorance.

Naturally, the Opposition leaders were annoyed, and the Prince of Wales was spurred to write to Disraeli from Seville :

" As the Queen's eldest son, I think I have some right to feel annoyed that . . . the announcement of the addition to the Queen's title should have been read by me in the newspapers instead of having received some intimation on the subject from the Prime Minister."

Later, the Queen admitted through Ponsonby that " she blamed herself for not having written to the Prince about the Titles Bill," adding, however, " that she certainly thought she had done so."

The modern relationship between Minister and Sovereign has been largely influenced by the precedents established by Disraeli and Queen Victoria, and the Disraelian view cannot be better set forth than in the word of Mr. Buckle.

" Disraeli saw in the Sovereign not merely the Chief Magistrate of a self-governing nation—a magistrate sprung from a German stock which it had suited the Whigs to put upon the throne of England, but the heir to the historical monarchy of Alfred, of William the Conqueror, of the great Henries and Edwards, of Elizabeth, of the Stuarts, and of the wrong-headed, but sturdy and national George III. He realised that it was the Sovereign who, owing to historical and personal causes, was the chief unifying influence, not merely in the nation at home, but even more, in an empire of extraordinary diversity and extent. He recognised, moreover, in the actual sovereign, whom it was his privilege to serve, one who had by the seventies a larger mastery of State affairs, domestic or foreign, than any conceivable minister, one, therefore, of whose judgment and experience the fullest possible use should be made in the government of the country."

Yet such is the eternal paradox of the eternal feminine that the Queen, whose very whims perturbed great ministers, on her attention being directed to the Woman's Rights movement in 1870, wrote in hot haste to Mr. Martin :

" The Queen is most anxious to enlist everyone who can speak or write to join in checking this mad, wicked folly of Woman's Rights, with all its attendant sorrows, on which her poor feeble sex is bent, forgetting every sense of womanly feeling and propriety. Lady ———— ought to get a *good whipping*. It is a subject upon which the Queen is so furious that she cannot contain herself. God created men and women differently—then let them remain each in their own position. . . . Woman would become the most hateful, heartless, and disgusting of human beings were she allowed to unsex herself, and where would be the protection which man was intended to give to the weaker sex ? "

Yet twenty years before that august member of " the poor feeble sex " had written to Lord John Russell after one of Lord Palmerston's outbursts :

" With reference to the conversation about Lord Palmerston which the Queen had with Lord John Russell the other day, on Lord Palmerston's disavowal that he ever intended any disrespect to her by the various neglects of which she has had so long and so often to complain, she thinks it right, *in order to prevent any mistake for the future*, shortly to explain, *what it is she expects from her Foreign Secretary*. She requires :

" (1) That he will distinctly state what he proposes in a given case, that the Queen may know as distinctly to what she has given her Royal sanction.

" (2) Having *once given her* sanction to a measure that it be not arbitrarily altered or modified by the Minister ; such an act she must consider as failing in sincerity towards the crown, and justly to be visited by the exercise of her Constitutional right of dismissing that minister. She expects to be kept informed of what passes between her and the Foreign Ministers before important despatches are taken, based upon that intercourse ; to receive the Foreign Despatches in good time, and to have the drafts for her approval sent to her in sufficient time to make herself acquainted with their contents before they must be sent off. The Queen thinks it best that Lord John Russell should show this letter to Lord Palmerston.''

Which is not a bad effort at political castigation for a member of the " poor feeble sex."

The Victorian woman's clothes may have been shapeless, and the Victorian woman may have been voteless, but in the imperishable slang of the day, " she got there, just the same."

It is the present mode to sneer at the Victorian era—to regard it as an epoch of primitive and plain simplicity, of the homely and domestic virtues of suppressed women and smug men.

But as the facts emerge, as the intimate documents concerning Victoria herself emerge, we begin to perceive the reality.

It is true that poor Albert—" the German lad," as the street songs of the day labelled him—went through his phases of unpopularity, but the cradles of Windsor, of Buckingham Palace, and of Balmoral never ceased rocking, and fertile domesticity had a potential appeal to the lower middle-classes.

Then came a curious and prolonged phase, the phase of " The Widowed Queen," and for years the ideal of the recluse impressed the nation.

But there were stories.

In political circles stories began to be told of a very autocratic recluse ; in the background of Scotland or of Windsor there was a very potent and a very important personality in the shape of a stout little person in black who sat for hours with her despatch boxes, writing, reading, dominating ; ministers were sent for, to stand for hours in the

presence listening to her views ; letters in the royal
hand were continually passing to potentates ; complicated political affairs such as royal marriages and
alliances were regulated from a mysterious and
arbitrary background. But to the Capital City and
to her people at large the Queen became a myth.

There was grumbling, because it began to dawn
upon even the lightly-taxed folk of that day that she
was an expensive myth.

Of what use the costly apparel of State, the cream
horses, the gilded coaches, the walking footmen, the
Life Guards' band in gold, the Crown and the sceptre
and orb, if they were never seen ?

There was a jealousy of the Highland home ; of
the upright John Brown—that stalwart, whisky-
drinking Scot, upon whose arm the Queen was wont
to lean in public ; a resentment against a secluded
life which, decent and even admirable in a newly-
made widow, seemed superfluous in the case of a
mature, healthy, and extremely capable woman of
affairs, whose influence was felt, not only in every
department of State, but in many aspects of the life
of the day.

So, grudgingly, reluctantly, largely at the instance
of the wonderful Jew Disraeli, Victoria came to town
at rare intervals.

It was something. The cream stallions had their
manes and tails arranged for processions to West-
minster ; the gilt carriages were repolished, the State
uniforms were refurbished, the Life Guards shone
resplendent in scarlet and gold, and as the great
swaying coach bore her in resentful state upon her
State occasions, Victoria entered by degrees upon yet
another phase, that of " The Mother of her People."

There was one more phase to come. On her death
she became " Victoria the Good " ; and amid semi-
hysterical scenes of grief she made her last journey
through her capital—and then came the reaction.

The age of Victoria the Good began to be
denounced as the age of goody-goody, and the strange
delusion has persisted.

The neo-Georgian jazz-club flapper, revelling in the freedom of her legs and sipping her " club-cup " at midnight, turns up her carelessly powdered nose in scorn at the bare mention of Victorianism.

And then, as the jazz-frenzy slowly evaporates in an excess of non-stimulating liquors, the neo-Georgian maiden, if she is very neo-Georgian indeed, hies her on to some elaborately surreptitious " little place, where they play, you know," and in an atmosphere of depreciated paper money and heavily diluted stimulants has her " little game."

In the hard-drinking, hard-living, hard-loving, hard-gambling Victorian sixties, Panton Street, Jermyn Street, and the purlieus of the Haymarket were lavish in " hells " ; red gold and golden wine flowed in showers from night to dawn ; there was little " club-cup " drunk in such resorts as Mott's and Kate Hamilton's ; and the Raleigh Club could tell what high play meant.

Never have there been later hours, never harder living, heavier gambling than in those quaint Victorian days.

Lord Chaplin is still alive, but with all his experiences he would be hard put to it to back another Hermit to win £100,000 over another Derby—and get paid.

The Hastings era alone is a revelation of the domesticities of Victorianism—with its racing, its gallantries, its cock-fighting, its fighting men with the " raw 'uns," its deep drinking and heavy play.

It was an age of individualism *in excelsis*, and the most amazing individual of all was the stout, arrogant, dowdy, shrewd, clear-sighted, commercial, and intensely self-centred little figure in black, who dominated the whole strange medley with her personality ; who imposed her lack of fashion upon the female " smart-set " of the period, and last, but far from least, who imposed the colossal myth of " Victorian respectability and dullness " upon succeeding generations.

CHAPTER XLI

THE VICTORIAN MAN

Mad little overcoats, sloppy greatcoats, ill-fitting frock-coats,
comic morning coats; children clothed like freaks—Add
to the merriment: carbuncular bowler hats, bell-bottom
trousers, and Dundreary whiskers—The author's sincere
sympathy to the women who spent their maturity in the
Victorian era.

THE pageant is over. From the illusive dreams of
costumed unreality, we awake to a grey dawn of
merciless materialism.

Industrialism is in its lusty infancy; it has not yet
arrived at the age when it can control its crudities,
and its pukings obliterate the arts. That it may grow
into a forceful manhood, its appetite is appeased by
the consumption of culture, style, manners, grace, and
all the confections of beauty. For its religion it is
led to worship at the altar of utility; for its diversion
it dons a mask of hypocrisy; for its warmth a garb
of smugness; for its shelter a canopy of cant. And
thriving on its prosperity its plebeianism becomes a
universal doctrine.

With the mechanical stultification of the arts, the
forms of expression were revolutionised. The pose
of sensual piety was varied by pious sensuality, and
both emotions were practised in hypocritical attitudes.
The machinery of industry was insatiable in its
demands on humanity. The population increased
and multiplied with amazing rapidity. Fecundity
was subtly suggested as the fashion and the abnormal
demands were met by a stimulated supply.

It is natural that the physical clothes became
characteristic only of the spirit of the age. In all
sense of dress they were characterless in style,
stagnant in all ideas, save those which were ludicrous,

and typical only of the drabness of the times. The only joy to be extracted in recording impressions is that one is following a funeral of necessity.

With the development of the industrial era thought and its expression in costume became sombre and narrow, and taste in all things execrable. In the wild rush to cater for utility, all sense of symmetry and style was lost. Woman's dress became a grotesque lie in its absurdity and man's a devastating truth in its ugliness. Women have survived and escaped completely from the nineteenth century bondage, but men are still enduring an inheritance of negative fashions and dull and dreary colours.

In the early days of the reign the styles were passable ; men wore tight-fitting trousers, which they strapped under the instep, a civilian fashion which has revived for a short period in the twentieth century. The silk hat was imperative and its vogue has continued until the present day, but whereas then its use was general for all sorts of occasions, even to being the correct but uncomfortable head-gear for the sport of cricket, now it is relegated to the dullness of ceremonial duties.

On a sudden, style degenerated. Ugliness came creeping in and symmetry vanished. A wave of wilfulness to destroy the wrap of cultured illusion with which the leaders of the eighteenth century had adorned their bodies swept over the country. A grim determination to negative all that was beautiful in clothes was fostered by the maggot of jealousy of past artistic glories. No new leader sprang up to stem the tide, which in its ebb wrecked all that had lived before. And in the succeeding chaos crudity ran amok.

Mad little overcoats appeared cut short above the knee, with an indecorous little slit at the back, fastened with three unnecessary buttons. Shapeless trousers with horrible large checks, several inches wide, and bold bad bows of idiotic length ! Sloppy great-coats, fastened with elephantine discs ! The frock-coat lengthened and became very ill-fitting, the sleeves being long and generally covering awkward hands. The comic little morning coat came in with its apologetic tails. From first to last the shapes of all garments were vile.

Grotesque as was the appearance of the Victorian parent, he was not content until he had perpetrated his monstrosities on his offspring. He committed the unforgivable crime of dressing his children like freakish old men and comic old women.

In such a wild medley no one individual can be held responsible ; it would therefore be unfair to accuse Albert of Memorial fame of being a leader of any fashion.

Between 1860 and 1870 the styles became more horrible than any conceived in history. As a concession to the much-needed gaiety of the nation, it became the great age for whiskers. The Dundreary pattern added to the merriment. The lapels of the coats were niggardly and narrow, little bowler hats like black carbuncles were perched on the head, and the legs were encased in a couple of loose bags made in materials of execrable design, finished perhaps an inch or so too short. Then some inventive genius introduced bell-bottom trousers to disguise the ungainly feet, and the masher, striving to make some impression, donned a tight little lounge jacket, cut so short that it stood out in a feeble flounce and exposed most of his seat.

In the eighties the evening suit was the best garment worn, and the type worn to-day is an improved adaptation, but the entire effect was often spoilt by an ugly low polo collar, which gave the men a hang-dog look. Utility was probably again responsible, for waltzing was vigorous and perspiration prevalent. In manner men were stiff-looking fools, and starch was their only stand-by.

Towards the end of the century the frock-coat recovered a certain symmetry, and a few of the younger bloods may be thanked for the revival of shape. But the lounge suit remained the hopeless " sack," by which name it was called, until well into the present century when it acquired a character and distinction of its own.

The men of to-day have not yet revived beauty, but they have rid themselves of the beastliness of the dress of the nineteenth century.

It is a healthy asset to possess a virile scorn for sentimentality as the refuge of the weak and the prison of the strong. So the critic must be free from bondage, even when he attacks the sex from which he derives most entertainment. Fairness, however, compels one to offer, not sentimentality, but a true sympathy to our mothers who were condemned to spend their maturity in the later Victorian era. Those of us whose experience consists of a mere vague recollection of adolescent days, disturbed by an orgy of pompous, bustling men, and affected and bustled women, are fortunate in our generation.

CHAPTER XLII

THE VICTORIAN WOMAN

*The author is astonished that this generation is begotten of
the Victorian—Wide crinolines enter—Age of production
and utility—Woman's fashion is maternity; crinoline
and optimism—First appearance of woman's underclothing; some remarks thereon — Bustles, leg-of-mutton
sleeves, bolstered posteriors—Grim story about an
inflated, palpitating bust.*

IF we are morbidly inclined and disposed to picture
the peculiar atmosphere of this ugly era, we are
assisted by the circumstance that we live to-day in an
age of insignificant autobiographies, the most be-
trumpeted of which might be called "Feminine
Inanities of a Political Appendage."

From one personal testimony, although uncor-
roborated, it appears that women contrived to be
fascinating, even in those days. There were giddy
episodes, exhibiting quite an exasperating exuberance.
Marriage proposals were prolific, which is more than
ever strange. But more wonderful than all, they considered themselves beautiful, though candour compels
one to state that, viewed as pictures, they most
certainly did not look it. And it is already proved
by the mess of the world they have left us as a legacy,
that the men were fools.

Yet from these Victorians our generation was
begat. It is astonishing! It might almost be
acclaimed as their vindication!

Women's apparel was certainly worse than that of
prehistoric times. In the early Victorian era they
wore their bodices so tight that they accentuated
nature's developments; their poke bonnets assumed
a timid aggressiveness, and lest their assumption of
simplicity might pass unnoticed they had pattens on

their feet, so that the noisy clattering would not fail to attract attention to their pretty ankles.

Their full skirts were first slightly hooped, then the hoop became huge in competition with the prosperous rotundity of the men. As the men grew pompous the hoops of the women sympathetically developed into crinolines, and the vogue continued for more than forty years.

The poke bonnet evidently failed to appeal to the big bugs of the day, and consequently shrank until it became little bigger than a big insect, which afforded no protection to the false hair of its wearer. With this speck of a bonnet woman bravely ventured abroad in a shapeless little coat with an ugly, sloppy skirt.

Then in the sixties art took the knock-out and retired to the undressing-room. Very wide crinolines came in. It was the age of production and utility, and with women the fashion of modernity was maternity. It was in every way a prolific period, in which every woman did her bit, and her disguise not only successfully concealed her condition, but suggested in its design an optimism more exuberant than exhilarating.

Like the men of the day she was so busily engaged in production that she lost all sense of art, and expressed herself only in crudities. The maidens, passing the compliment, wore their hair in ringlets or streaming loose and enlivened attraction, but the matron, in sympathy with the man's Dundreary whiskers, wore huge plaits of false hair which hung from the back of her neck in a chignon, a netted excrescence longer than her head.

Her skirts became terrific, more voluminous than any recorded, but she had no conception of balance ; with it she wore comic little hats and ugly little boots with striped stockings showing above.

It was an age in which the Robeys were the dandies, and the Nellie Wallaces the belles.

Despite the handicaps of the prevailing modes, the lady of fashion made a slight attempt at allurement.

In contrasting economy to her generous skirt her evening gown was cut very low in the neck, and her shoulders were completely uncovered. She was very tight-laced, and wasp-waisted, wore very high heels, and cultivated a fashionable " Grecian bend."

Beneath her crinoline, which stood six inches from the ground, peeped the frilled hem of her long drawers, boldly inviting public inspection. This must have been a disclosure of desperation, indicative of the times, for lovers of lingerie prefer a more delicate discovery and resent all public exhibitions. The first Victorian illustrations of this plural garment are, however, historically interesting. It is the record of a first appearance which in its attenuated shape-lessness endured an ugly infancy. The garment must be conceded the dignity of invention, for prior to its existence its place was occupied by nothing. Since these crude days it has developed in subtlety, has long since ceased to be a lengthy exposition, and short as the inverted growth of the skirt has hygieni-cally become, the more intimate garment in its variety of designs and transparent adornments has acquired the delicacy of becoming shorter still.

To the credit of the age of which we are the cleanly survivors, although their vast consumption of port bequeathed to them an unfortunate legacy of uric acid, they certainly did make some spasmodic experi-ments in the virtuous use of water. It is a disgusting statement of fact, but for centuries the world had stunk considerably. There were few baths in private houses until the mid-Victorian era. We, who would feel like lepers without our vigorous daily scrub, might pause for one moment to imagine the unhealthy world of fashion as it then existed. Epidemics of every description were rampant.

Sea-bathing came into fashion with the ladies as an exciting sport on the end of a rope. But it was conducted with becoming modesty, and the pro-prieties were observed in a manner which must have brought joy or disappointment to the Borough Councillors of the day when pursuing their tours of prurient inspection. Lest their forms might be seen emerging from their machines a great hood was fixed from the door to the bottom of the steps so that bathers could, if they desired, take immediate refuge in the waves, and expose only an untousled head. Since their bathing costumes were made with capes and flounces which completely covered them from tip to toe and would have afforded adequate protection for an expedition to the Arctic regions, it is difficult to appreciate the affected coyness of their entrance.

The æsthetic vogue in the seventies did a little to revive a semblance of style in woman's dress, but freakishness had gained too strong a force to be controlled for long. The low-necked gown with its ambition for a nineteen inch waist, slightly sprung from the hips and becoming tight again at the knees and finishing in a thin train, was a garment possessing a suggestion of line. But the long trained gown worn in the street, presumably only for the excuse of holding up the skirt when crossing the road, was simply an insanitary refuse collector. During the æsthetic period ladies were so extremely sensitive that they wore chamois leather underclothing.

Then some satirical genius invented for woman a most horrible contrivance aptly called a bustle. It was a padded article placed under the skirt below the back of her waist, in order to give an exaggerated importance to that part of the anatomy. At first it was quite small, but growing bolder it swelled rapidly until it stuck out twelve inches beyond its resting place. On fat women the effect was ludicrous. Dresses were frilled and gathered and had small puffed sleeves. Then the idiotic leg-of-mutton sleeve returned ; followed by flounces in a variety of designs, some hanging from bolstered posteriors as if they belonged to no one. Such were the garments in which budding Lenglens played unstrenuous lawn tennis.

Later, in the eighties, with crinolines proudly projecting at the back like pea-hens, the little poke bonnet came back, under which women simpered demurely at the sallies of side-whiskered wits.

Throughout it was an era of peace and plenty and physical protuberance. With the unprecedented commercial prosperity one might excuse the inclination of the men to become swollen-headed and even pardon blatant exhibitions in the fatness of their stomachs, but the artificial excrescences of woman are beyond understanding. Whether she envied man's obesity or sought to inspire him by a similar affectation, it is certain that she cultivated a fashion for fatness in parts. She was versatile in her distributions. About 1886, not content with natural blessings, she sought to make herself more buxom by the assistance of a false bust inflated with air. So ingenious was this contrivance that it could actually be made to palpitate, and life was one long flutter of perpetual emotions. A tragedy occurred when a love-sick swain, thrilled by ostensible charms, sought to pin a flower on his lady's breast. In his agitation he pricked too deeply and the whole bust burst. Thus at the first pin-prick did love's young dream collapse.

Until the end of the nineteenth century, until the end of the Victorian era, styles continued to expose their hideousness. A new force of progress, welcome despite its grotesque disguise, was sweeping through the world, and if art in dress was temporarily narcotised, it has since proclaimed in woman its deathlessness. Through the centuries of English history woman, with her marvellous subtlety of response, has recorded in her dress every conceivable emotion and had expressed the spirit of each age. For centuries her instinct to respond had led her to imitate men's fashions in adaptation, thus passing him the compliment of flattery. When the gorgeousness of men's apparel subsided under the stress of world-wide commercialism, she was thrust upon invention and passed through the inevitable fantasy of infantile crudity. From adapted fantasy she degenerated to original farce. And from the comic costumes of her Victorian masquerade, the curtain is raised to-day on a wonderful transformation.

She has developed in her newly-won freedom the charm of personality. Individuality has become the note of style. The woman of account is no longer a slave to the details of fashion ; she is the arbiter of her own. It is a glorious and symbolic emancipation of vast significance—it is like the freedom of artistic Ireland.

In compliment to women throughout this historical survey a delicate irritation has been purposely simulated—an irritation which is a sign of delicate appreciation. That this acknowledgment may be more complete, here is a splendid tribute. The modern woman is more artistic in her dress than ever ; she has evolved a magnificent illusion, alluringly translucent to the philosopher, and mystifyingly transparent to the observer.

In her triumph she has achieved union of utility with grace, of originality with beauty, and she has wisely conceded to art the freedom to flirt with allurement for the ultimate production of a wonderful disguise.

It is the splendour of to-day that counts. Saying farewell to history is merely sniffing one's nostrils at a past that has decayed. Tradition is the manacle of thought. To-day is the wonderful present, to-morrow an amazing adventure.

CHAPTER XLIII

EDWARD VII. (1901–1910)

*Personality succeeds personality—Woman discards Victorianism
—Style is developed—Edward's stimulating influence on
dress—A half-hearted compliment.*

On the death of Queen Victoria a personality
succeeded a personality.

The Victorian era was that of dominating personalities, and it says much for the inherent strength
of character of King Edward VII. that he survived
the dominations of childhood, youth, manhood, and
middle-age, and emerged strong, self-reliant, and
dominant.

As a lad of seventeen he burst into tears as he read
his parents' counsel of perfection, but he had the wit
to recognise stark impossibility when it met him.
There was a parental visit to Oxford, but in spite of
all, Bertie contrived to live his own life within limits
and to develop his inclinations in his own way.

Beaconsfield was a shrewd judge of youth and the
possibilities of youth, and he demonstrated his
acumen of the social gifts and political promise of the
future King in writing of him to his intimates as
" Prince Hal."

In the Disraeli letters are two concerning a visit of
the Prince to Hughenden, which are in amusing
contrast.

To the Queen the artful old observer writes :

" The royal visit to Hughenden, he hopes he may
say, was not altogether unsuccessful. A Prince who
really has seen everything and knows everybody is a
guest one might despair of interesting and amusing

even for a passing hour. . . . The conversation was grave as well as gay ; and His Royal Highness, Lord Beaconsfield can say with the utmost truth, maintained his part with felicity—even distinction. His Royal Highness had that opportunity of speaking alone with Lord Salisbury, and also with Lord Beaconsfield, and at more social moments Lord Rosslyn and Mr. Osborne expressed and elicited many a flashing phrase."

To Lady Bradford the old man is more explicit :

" The visit has, all say, been a great success. . . . He praised the house, praised his dinner, praised the pictures, praised everything ; was himself most agreeable in conversation, said some good things and told more. When I found out that both Rosslyn and B.O. had been his companions at Cumberland Lodge, I was afraid they must have exhausted all their resources ; but I was wrong. Success inspired them, and the dinner was like a pantomime, where there are two clowns, and both capital ones. We played at whist in the evening—his own choice. I had hoped to have induced them to play nap, which would have left me alone, for I don't understand that mystery. But he would not have it, and insisted on playing with B.O. against Salisbury and myself at whist. He beat us, which does not displease him. . . . They returned from their barouche drive in a snowstorm in high spirits ; his companions, Monty, and the two clowns ; B.O. affecting seriousness and a sense of hardship, his Grace, the Lord Commissioner, on the other hand, rollicking."

From the lad who burst into tears at the parental counsel of perfection, who marched past with his company in Phœnix Park and " did not look so very small," a strong and wise personality developed—a personality, however, over-shadowed and dominated for many years by another wonderful personality. Even as a man of fifty, when he arrived late for dinner at Osborne, owing to the then German Emperor having refused to call off a becalmed race between their yachts, he was observed standing behind a pillar, wiping the sweat from his forehead, nerving himself to go up to the Queen, who received him with a stiff nod.

And in spite of this influence and surroundings he had made for himself an established position in society and affairs before he ascended to the throne. At Cowes his position was embalmed in the following paragraph :

" The Prince appears, and a flutter ensues, as the pretty ladies edge insensibly towards him for the coveted notice. He disappears, and the flutter ends in a comparison of frocks and success in notice."

In the Prince a new social force had slowly and irresistibly arisen ; there was again the arbiter of fashion, of manners ; and " the Prince's set," " the Marlborough House set "—controlled the modes for dinners, for parties, and for dress. Moreover his personality permeated more serious circles than the worlds of amusement, of sport, and of clothes.

Statesmen found that there was another personality to be reckoned with ; a worldly-wise and kindly personality, one, should the need arise, possessed of the old dominance, but willing to be guided and inspired by the desire to do well for his country. What higher praise can be given to any ruler ?

So when Edward VII. was crowned at Westminster he ascended the throne a made monarch—made after a long and arduous apprenticeship.

The dress of the reign of the popular Edward is like the reign of William IV., a remarkable transitory period. Woman discarded all traces of Victorianism in her apparel, and from then has continued to develop her style, until to-day she has mastered every trick of graceful form. King Edward's regard for formality in dress had a stimulating effect on the fashions, and from the time of his reign until now the styles, though timid and subdued, have persistently improved.

Judged on the standard of history men's dress to-day is negative and dull, but judged in comparison with the Victorian era it is elegance indeed. Which in reality is the slightest compliment one can concede.

BOOK III

SARTOR MODERNUS

CHAPTER I

THE MODERN LOOKING-GLASS

*The author pleads for a world fit for artists to live in and
deplores the gloom of man's clothes—Silly evening dress ;
ironic twin tails—Tyranny of starch—Prediction of revolt
against death and drabness for life and colour.*

THIS young twentieth century of ours has made
great strides in progress. It has developed science
and machinery, cultivated hygiene and applied
utility to all things. These are the great material
advancements. But if its will is to develop science
and machinery for slaughter, hygiene for the fostering of finer flesh and blood for human sacrifice, and
utility for the usage of fools as fodder, then progress
has failed. If the will is to lead science to direct
its discoveries to life instead of death, hygiene to
apply its culture to joy, and utility to seek the aid
of art instead of artfulness, then we might make a
world fit for artists to breathe in.

If the world will learn to use these great forces
for constructive purposes, our civilisation will survive ; if they are designed and used for destruction
they must inevitably lead to a catastrophic end.

Pursuing this thought ; if material forces are applied
to construction, but remain independent of art, then we
shall be condemned to an efficient but a mechanical,
colourless, and sexless existence. It is only by art
that these forces can be refined. Art is the saviour.
But it is well to remember that art is peculiarly
sensitive and must be carefully wooed. The renaissance of a deceived civilisation lies in the daring
union of artistic culture with cold materialism.
Without the splendid illusion we become frozen
hermaphrodites.

That is the philosophy that must be applied to

the political, social, and intellectual senses, and to their corresponding illustration in dress.

In surveying modern dress one feels a curious aversion—a desire to evade the crudity of criticism. It savours of a vivisection of unavailing fashion.

In their styles to-day men have conceded nearly everything to utility, and in doing so have abandoned flirtation with art. With this negation, dress has merely attained a cleanliness masked in drab stupidity.

It is inartistic and undistinguished. Its mournfulness is exhibited in the average crowd. The picturesque clowns of the past are replaced by the red-nosed comedians.

Only in the evening is there any semblance of an affectation of style, and then just because the imposed black and white of the men act as fine foils to the colours of the women. In design, men's evening coats are silly and unsymmetrical, the mere legacy of a Georgian artist's nausea. The shape and cut are meaningless, the thin twin tails ironic. To its credit the white vest is good, it has a sharply pointed humour, with its colour emblematic of purity of motive.

The whole costume could easily be improved upon. A few years back the late Mr. H. B. Irving wore an original evening suit in which the lines were symmetrically studied. There were no absurd cuts at ugly angles. The fronts from the waist to the knee were cut away in a line which balanced that of the lapel, and in unison turned back to show the satin facing. The effect was strikingly graceful.

The morning coat is good in its simple lines as a body-fitting garment, but its limited usage illustrates a timid revolt against formality. The frock-coat is a cumbersome relic with many unpleasant associations of the past. The starched collar is ridiculous and uncomfortable, and is condemned by throat specialists. For day wearing during the last few years it has been replaced by the infinitely more sensible and artistic silk collar, and the introduction of a new and softer form of evening neck-wear is inevitable in the future. There is no necessity for men to symbolise the stiffness of their conventions by the starchiness of their neck-bands. An escape from the tyranny of starch, in the form of the unbending collar and the aggressive boiled shirt, is imperative.

Now the silk hat has a style of its own. Its qualities are of a feminine character, inasmuch as it demands delicate handling and it is easily ruffled. The bowler hat is beastly, a black carbuncular relic of Billy Coke.

On the other hand the lounge suit has improved beyond original design in the nineteenth century and is now the almost universal utility dress for men. One is compelled to concede that its popularity lies in the success of its protective utility; it can be donned in less than a minute. No masculine leg could be adequately clothed in less time than the fixing of the trousers, and even braces are un-necessary if the waist is properly fitted. Turned-up bottoms are designed to avoid the mud. The jacket can be accepted now that it has arrived at the definition of the figure. In its present shape it has developed on its freedom from formality to the use of formality. It is worn by all classes, and is thus the most democratic costume in the history of the world.

The dinner suit, a fairly presentable though undistinguished garment, is really a lounge suit masquerading with the dignity of silk facings. Comfort dominates again, but it is absurd that it should always be made in black.

Golf suits and sporting suits are naturally con-trolled in design by utility, but offer possibilities in colour, and it is here that the revival of colour in men's dress may take place.

There is more originality and variety in the design of overcoats than in any other garment. Just prior to 1914 there was a considerable prospect of development, but the war smashed all progress. One good evening overcoat was introduced, shaped closely to the figure, with facings of silk and fastened by one link at the waist. Another was of a similar shape, but sleeveless and with a short half-cape, reaching in the front from the shoulders to the hips.

In the hunting-field only is man afforded an opportunity to look his best, and hunting pink remains the one modern expression of his emotion in colour ; unless, of course, we exclude the natural and conscienceless exhilaration he displays in the exuberance of his silken dressing-gowns and pyjamas.

Man's culture in dress to-day lies in his undergarments. His pants are cut by expert craftsmen to fit like hose, and are tightly laced from the centre of the waist at the back to support his figure. Next to the skin, silk is the only material to wear. Linen is cold, cotton is coarse, and wool is irritating to the flesh and the spirit.

Beyond these few intimate excursions, the twentieth century chiefly exhibits in men's dress an entire lack of individuality. There is practically no expression of character. The Britisher is still conservative and conventionally self-conscious. The painter of pictures and the painter of houses, the aristocrat and the artisan are indistinguishable in the general design of their day suits. Style is therefore dependent upon microscopic subtleties.

This is a period of negative fashions with stagnate styles—a condition which is understandable, considering the poverty-stricken condition of the world. But after every great war there has followed a revolution in fashion, in manners, conventions, and in the more vital influences of politics and philosophy. Every era has expressed itself in costume and it is inevitable that this twentieth century, which will probably record the most wonderful material and artistic progress in history, will symbolise itself in dress. Utility and hygiene will continue to dictate material design, but art will be enjoined to create the illusion in colour.

Yet at the mere suggestion of the renaissance of

colour, one can almost hear the discordant but amusing shrieks of the timid fools in their herd-like dismay. In their self-conscious fear they picture themselves with the eyes of the multitude scanning their decorated ugliness. Only consciously ugly people fear the power of beauty, knowing that beauty, in its autocratic contempt, invariably despises them.

We shall break away from this atmosphere of blackness in which we are but smuts disfiguring the landscape. There is no picture in history so gloomy as man's dress. Look at the portraits in the Royal Academy.

There was farce and there was comicality in the absurdities of the Victorian era ; and to-day there is scarcely any relief from the eternal drabness. The vision is one of human black beetles soiling the pavements of the streets. The same spirit that regards as vice all attempts at revelry, cries out that any man who clothes himself in colours is an effeminate fool.

We have not succeeded in escaping from the Victorian tradition, the apotheosis of which was exposed in the Great Exhibition. Ugliness is not masculine nor are style and taste decadence. The commercial era of the nineteenth century vulgarised clothes, and men are still accepting a vulgar tradition. Tradition is a handicap imposed by ghouls. The world must discard it, or progress decays.

When the revolt comes, as it will come some time during this century, against death and drabness, we shall see a different world of life and colour. If the ugly conventions of our purblind ancestors persist then we deserve our dreary fate.

The herd will always choose the garb which illustrates its mind, but the true rulers must choose a cloak in which to symbolise their thought. The artist, understanding the subtleties of every disguise, has the power to clothe his mind in wondrous tints, and lives in a world eternally beautiful.

CHAPTER II

WHITHER MEN MAY WANDER

*The Great Dress Tradition—Man's venture into colours—
Unrecorded dress history of two months—Purple and
gold in London streets—Ugliness is not morality nor
shapelessness chastity—Vision of man clad in beautiful
colours.*

BLACK as the outlook may appear at the moment let
us assume with an altruistic optimism that we are
on the threshold of a great revival of learning, wit,
art, beauty, and joy. To maintain the equipoise of
civilisation such a revival is necessary and overdue.
We have only to will it and the transformation will
take place.

It is time we had done with dead imagery and
decayed tradition. We must cast aside the rotten
principles and iniquitous precepts imposed by
knaves and fools. We must think afresh and for
ourselves.

In the revival of the arts, there will be a natural
expression in costume.

But first we have the remnants of a horrible
legacy to make away with—a legacy which fettered
our limbs, stultified our minds, warped our characters, poisoned our intellects, and ruined our sunny
natures—the Great Dress Tradition bequeathed to
us by our Victorian ancestors.

It is, perhaps, hardly possible now to imagine the
state of civilisation in which an emerald green
crinoline, a lurid shawl, a poke-bonnet, and an
elastic-sided boot were accounted beauty's perfect
setting ; when massive whiskers, endless chains, and
shapeless rags, tortured into a faint semblance of
clothing, were the only Romeo wear.

Worse still, our egregious ancestors, under whose

yoke we have groaned for precious generations and whose influence is still faintly pervading the atmosphere, in some inexplicable manner always contrived to tangle up the lesser moralities with ugly clothes. Ugliness breathed virtue, they were wont to assert, so on with pads, bustles, improvers, and whiskers— and hide, oh hide, the sinful human form ! And yet they do not seem to have been wholly successful. Does not one of their classical bards complain in deathless verse :

> " Clothes make the man ; yes ! to a large extent
> This world is still deceived by ornament."

And small blame to the world, when ornament for male and female comprised stout horsehair pads.

Small wonder that the Victorian sun set in a welter of hypocritical immorality and humbug.

Clothes are necessary, not—as our earlier Victorians seemed to have imagined—for the sole purpose of swaddling the human form in an unrecognisable bundle, of hiding every possible likeness to the Godhead, of concealing not only sex but humanity, of destroying every possible form of self-satisfaction, but for the purposes of protection against the climate and for the perfectly legitimate purpose of personal decoration.

The will to change has already manifested itself. Just prior to the outbreak of the World Insanity in 1914, there was a revolution against the dreary Victorian conventions, which bound man to drabs and greys ; and man, whose only sacrifice to colour was a tie, a sock, or a suit of pyjamas, was awakening from his stupor.

Woman had clothed herself as a tulip, and man, surveying the animal creation wherein the male invariably lords it in the most splendid robe, began to think, and, after thinking to assert his right to colour.

" Why," he asked, " should the gorgeous golden cock pheasant outshine the demure hen, the glittering

K

peacock shame his spouse into her proper station, the magnificent tiger outblare his tender tigress, and why should man slink behind his mate in dirty drab and undistinguished, offensive neutrality ? ''

It was not the nature of things, nor according to the book of life.

In the eighteenth century, when the equality of the sexes in manners made antagonism more interesting, the beaux outshone the belles and the dandies paced stately through their world safely in the consciousness that they filled a picture not unworthily. But there came that appalling Victorian reaction with men and women vying one another in shapeless caricatures.

Woman revolted.

But man had become a timid, sartorial beast. A few nervous excursions into waistcoats, which usually ended in the mildest of greys or fawns ; a tie or two chosen with uncultivated taste, but indicating a hope that somewhere in the world there was such a thing as sunshine and colour ; scarcely seen coloured hosiery which were a faint expression of a belief in the future : these were the limits of man's courage in adventure.

But such ventures were not unproductive. The crudeness of his immature passion could be stimulated by refinement. And since art in dress is dependent upon materialism—as every woman knows—the leading British woollen manufacturers, then in the zenith of prosperity, called in the arts of artisans and succeeded in producing many wonderful materials in cleverly subdued blendings of rich and subtle colour.

This is history, hitherto unrecorded only in the ledgers of the manufacturers. It marked the beginning of a revolution in men's dress. It was a period of emancipation and it lasted—two months. Nothing but an act of God or the devil could have quelled it. It was artistic and commercial—an invincible combination.

Men of fashion, without realising it, were actually walking the dirty pavements of London Town clothed in purple and gold.

The man of taste found an opportunity for individualism which pleased him.

To be able to call for a mixture of russet brown and peacock blue, indigo and purple, or pheasant and violet, and to be conscious that there would be nothing in the finished garment to make horses shy or passers-by stare made an unconscious appeal to his artistic sense.

Then war! In a flash the ironic gods doomed men to the muddy uniformity of khaki and a world of drab and mud.

But the recurrence of this symptom is automatic with the world's recovering to normality. Whether in ten or twenty years does not matter. It is inevitable.

During those short two months—a period of holiday before the world's cancer claimed as victims the flower of the boyhood of all the European nations—man made discoveries in the art of dressing life.

He had discovered that fashions and, as he learned later, humanity, had stagnated under Hanoverian and Coburg influences.

In the dressing for life, he found that he could exchange darkness for light and feel unashamed, and therefore godlike, and that colour in dress is pleasant to gaze upon.

Man is a sensitive animal. He is easily upset by the crack of the whip, which woman, being untamed, emotionally enjoys. So the tradition-hampered man, when he is again led to discover himself, will not immediately dare on his own initiative to adopt a new mask and blossom forth like the lilac or the rhododendron.

Being timid, he will require a discreet guiding. He must be nursed and whistled to follow a stronger will. He must be fed, little by little, on arrogance, And after awhile he may be encouraged to bear himself bravely in other shades than black or grey, and feeling and looking better for the change he may decorate the world for us and give us the privilege of smiling in our nakedly unashamed approval.

This at least is certain in the ordinary process of evolution. Man, having acclaimed the revolt and struggled to cut himself free from a decadent tradition, will never return to the rules and regulations of the Victorian conventions of dullness and horror which he was casting off with joyous relief.

There was nothing admirable in them.

Ugliness is not morality ; shapelessness is not always chastity—and even when it is, there is no virtue in the chastity of necessity. Lack of self-respect does not necessarily indicate uprightness, nor does contempt for appearance denote the master-mind.

Now that the old orders have changed, the old Bastilles have toppled in dishonoured ruin, the old absurd tyrannies have been flung from their pinch-beck thrones ; now that men, with awakened vision, with new ideas and untrammelled minds, are seeking to construct a new future, do not let us clog our bodies with an environment which stifled us for too long.

We may not go back to the rainbow shades and wonderful stuffs of the bucks and dandies—do what we will, we live in utilitarian days—but whatever comes we shall never revert to the hideous hues and shapelessness of the Victorian era.

But whatever problems the immediate future presents, men must never lose the vantage they have gained over the ghouls of ugliness and drabness ; nor forget that colour and beauty have their utility in a utilitarian age.

After which dictum the philosopher is inclined to divest himself of all trappings, and in the complete freedom of a marble bath ruminate on the extravagances and futilities of all personal adornments, and welcome any poetical interruption which is capable of stimulating the naked impotence of material philosophy.

CHAPTER III

HAIL ! WOMAN FULL OF GRACE

Discourse upon woman's splendid adornment—Dress the ever-apparent symbol of personality—Art allied with hygiene—Shy, self-conscious glance at the modern woman.

JUST as civilisations decay in one region and achieve re-birth in another, and cultures become exhausted in one sphere and are transferred to another, so are certain of the arts consumed or temporarily neglected through satiety and then re-created and annexed afresh. Men in the past conquered the field of fashion, grew careless, and found the spoils annexed by women. Woman is an instinctive adapter, and keenly perceptive of values. She has disarmed man, and commandeered his weapons for herself.

Until the end of the Georgian era men reigned supreme in dress. Then came the long Victorian revolution against all expression of art in dress and in the succeeding chaos humanity was submerged in ugliness. The indomitable spirit of woman enabled her to survive.

In the twentieth century woman awakened to the realisation that before her lay a world that could be dominated by a gesture. And the world of fashion which she now rules is a world of more powerful illusion than the drab-coated dullard conceives. In fact, the drab coat is symbolic of the drab mind, to which conception of any kind is almost impossible. Beyond his servitude as provider and his periodical summons as fertiliser, in the modern world man has no value. After which disturbing confession, one is compelled to proclaim that if man aspires to the distinction of creation he must foster the arts.

All things are symbolic of good or evil, of ugliness

or beauty, of stupidity or subtlety, of impotence or virility. Dress is the ever-apparent symbol of personality.

After the Victorian debacle man's spirit for experiment was broken, so he clung to the fibrous weed of materialism. Woman, thirsting for the emotion of adventure, carelessly drifted with the torrents into safety, and casting aside her bedrenched garments, left herself free to seduce art to clothe her afresh.

To-day she appears beautiful, even though the comment is clothed in an eternal platitude.

To the student it is fascinating to watch her steady progress of emancipation. In observation it is the privilege of the artist to use the material illustration—a privilege denied the materialist who is incapable of using art. Therefore in the argument of art, no apology is needed for crudity; which is a mere concession in explanation of the sentiments to follow.

Until the nineteenth century man used the right of the provider to spend more money on his personal adornment than he allowed his mistress. In the Georgian period he expended at least five times more on his own clothes than he allowed his wife to expend on hers. To-day the position is not only reversed, but in the case of the majority of society women the proportion of difference is a minimum of ten to one in favour of the woman ; an eloquent testimony of her supremacy. In upper suburbia the proportion is about five to one, with spasmodic increases, controlled by occasional extravagant outbursts, affected perhaps by hectic love affairs.

It is in no spirit of resentment that one criticises. Here is the usage of man's material productivity by woman in the art of allurement. It is a splendid circulation that defeats stagnation. If man has lost the art of dress, woman by rescuing it is entitled to pose as the saviour. And having vanquished him in the artistic struggle she does not hesitate to impose an indemnity to the full extent of his capacity.

It is natural that having gained her triumph she should remain fully armed and jealously guard her territory, and any concession she may make to man will be frugal and will not affect her revenue. She is content for her subjects to remain as black-masked foils to her own magnificence. Adorned in plumes man would be more difficult to hold captive.

But her autocracy is one to be appreciated and accepted, since her power is used in artistic decoration. And is man not privileged to view the picture for the cost of which he has paid ?

We have viewed woman in passing through the centuries, mistress always of the art of disguise. Let us pass a shy, self-conscious glance at her to-day. Not with the narrowed eyes of the analyst, but with the merest fleeting vision of the impressionist.

She is nearer to the superlative in dress than ever before. She has studied grace, caressed art, considered hygiene, and employed utility. That she will develop still further in the culture of beauty is inevitable.

All this she has achieved from the decayed ruins of the nineteenth century. It is a wonderful triumph, and in her progress she has left man struggling in the mire.

A few years ago she donned more Victorian absurdities in the form of outer clothes and underclothes than were conducive to her health. She became enervated by the overweight. She courted quantity in material and neglected art in design.

To-day she is beautiful because her adornment is controlled in outline by nature. Her gowns are designed to define and not to distort her figure. Each line and curve and limb is studied. Her gown is a mere sheath ; in the evening her complete apparel is so light that it could be tossed in the air and carried to the clouds on a summer breeze. There are hungry dogs about who leeringly condemn this delicate aspiration to the illusion of the ethereal, but their growlings are the rage of the unappeased beast.

Ugliness craves for beauty and, enraged by a

scornful reception, viciously attacks it. But ugliness
fails inasmuch as it cannot conceive delicacy. There
is an immensity of difference between the artistic gaze
and the pornographic stare. Pruriency must be put
in its place and taught to realise that art is beyond
vulgar censure.

In her dress woman is autocratic and pays
no regard to the opinions of the coarsened herd.
Such a weakness would be a reflection on her art.
It is because of this disregard that the artist can
acclaim her as the most delicately disguised creature
of all the ages. Which is a dangerous compliment ;
truth being always devastating.

She displays her form ! Why not ? Is not her
form beautiful ? If her gowns are diaphanous,
should the artist turn away his eyes from the crowning allurement of nature ? Is the human form beautiful or is it ugly ? That is a significant question ! In
the abandonment of her disclosure lies woman's
challenge. It is a decree for physical valuation, but
beyond this she affords personality the opportunity
to triumph.

Her gown is slipped over the head and donned in
the twinkling of an appreciative eye. Comfort has
been studied and grace has been attained. The neck
is invitingly open and the arms are splendidly free.
The waist is defined and the skirt is cut short enough
to display beyond conjecture the elegance of her legs.
High necks, trains, fastenings at the back, and all
superfluous buttonings have been thrown on the Victorian dust heap. Beneath her gown a pair of knickers
of the finest silk or *crêpe de Chine*, delicately abbre-
viated and chosen from a dozen different designs and
florally decorated in a hundred different ways ; a silken
vest or camisole ; no corsets at all, or, if any, a tiny
pair so intimately elastic that they escape observance ;
a pair of silk stockings to match her dainty dancing
shoes. The *ensemble* is a triumph of diaphonic
lightness, beneath which is concealed a thousand
moods and purposes.

But if she has arrived at the irreducible minimum

of garments, the infinite variety of her changes is staggering.

For her sports her loose woollen jumpers and skirts are tinted with each colour of the rainbow. And her regard for attraction is no handicap to her efficiency, for in nearly all sports she has become brilliantly expert. Compare the clean, virile, slim-built beauty of to-day with the obese or anæmic woman of the last century, who, taking little exercise, found pleasure in the discussion of her consequent ailments and made a fashion of newly invented diseases.

The Victorian woman wore far too many clothes. Beneath her skirt were three petticoats—one of flannel, one of heavy *moiré*, and one of rustling silk. Then a pair of lawn drawers—one bequeaths the appellation to the era—and next the skin an encasement of woollen combinations, the body part of which was compressed by long and strong whale-boned corsets, vice-like in their ferocious grip, and imprinting an unattractive tattoo mark on the rebellious flesh. It is little wonder that the woman was often sick and ailing, and it is certain that she was always sore. She enervated her body, and reflected her enervation in her mind.

The modern woman has allied art with hygiene, and produced healthy attraction. It is the age of health. Physically and mentally, woman is stronger than ever before. It is a splendid and significant sign with boundless future possibilities. Artistically she has fearlessly created a personal standard of beauty. In her fashions she has symbolised the culture of the body. A pretty face is no longer a sufficing claim to acceptance. The form is no longer hidden or condemned to monstrous exaggerations. The ankle is a more important feature than the nose. Pedicure is as essential as manicure. It is the progress from a slothful effeminacy to a virile self-regard.

Woman no longer poses as the weak, dependent creature. She is daily asserting her power in every field. During the twentieth century it is certain with her newly won freedom, that she will develop far beyond our present conception of her. It will be interesting later on to observe the usage of her powers ; though the observation may be from the clouds and one's perspective gained from a monoplane. But to-day one meets her with a complimentary hail, offers one's hand with the assurance of acceptance, and one is glad to dance through life with her in unison.

And when the music ceases, one passes on—to dreams.

CHAPTER IV

THE FUTURISTIC VISION

The purpose of the book—The balance sheets of Governments
—Who is responsible for the war myth?—Fighting
politicians should fight—Wars do not benefit the people
—No reason why nations should be in debt—Inefficient
administrators should be impeached—World's greatest
man—New spirit of commerce—Coming of the race for
the enjoyment of life.

IF we could dream our way through life we should
arrive at the artistic millennium. We could then exist
without clothes and dispense with their allurements
and their irritations. But to merit the privilege of
dreams we must pay the price in physical exhaustion.
The culture of the spirit is an aristocratic art ;
humanity demands material feeding. And there is a
drought in manna, which no longer falls from the
clouds. Therefore, one must philosophise materially
before one earns the freedom to dream.

In this costumed philosophy, careering through the
ages to modern illusion, men and women have been
shown in their transparent disguises.

The penetrative few may have discerned the
symbolism and the purpose contained in the study.
In both there is a tear and a smile. Dress is symbolic
and sexual. It masks for destruction and creation.

Yet in the philosophy there is a new thought,
beyond the decorating of the body and beyond the
undressing of history. The thought, which is the
underlying purpose of the work, is the consideration
and the valuation of all that has happened in the
past. The past has been adequately dressed, but the
garment has covered a cancerous body. So, with a
resentful seriousness, it is impossible to evade the
responsibility of reviewing the effects. In so doing

it will be necessary to burn the infected garment of tradition.

Tradition has no value. It is negative, retrospective, retrogressive ; the cult of the dead illusions. Artistically, it is a handicap to origination.

This meteoric review of English history, which is merely a reflection of the type of thought governing all other nations, is a critical analysis of effects, with a healthy disregard for patriotic sentimentalism. The presentation attempts reality and truth.

The past is dead. The toast is to the future.

We can achieve nothing if we are manacled to yesterday. If we would build afresh, we must accept iconoclasm. If a structure is faulty it must be razed to the ground before an erection of security can be designed.

It is only by our refusal to accept the traditional principles of the past that we can hope to evolve new and constructive thought.

Study the bygone Governments of Europe ; make out a balance-sheet of their achievements for humanity. On the credit side is one small sheet which is practically blank, showing the asset of goodwill mortgaged to the hilt. On the debit side is a vast sheaf of documents on which is written the miseries of the world.

The power placed in the hands of rulers has been invariably used for the subjection of the people, for the restriction of their personal liberties, and for the exaction of the fruits of their toil on an estimate carefully calculated to the limit of endurance. Each small concession of liberty or relief has only been obtained by the revolt of public opinion when the limit of endurance has been passed.

In war-time methods of government become simplified. Rule then becomes open intimidation. The subject is frankly regarded as a serf and deprived of all his liberty ; new laws and restrictions are ruthlessly improvised, criticism is denounced as treason, money is squandered with shameful prodigality by the ever increasing army of administrators, taxation is extortion, and the country is eventually left with the twin millstones of debt and bureaucracy, between which succeeding generations may be successfully crushed—to the infinite profit of bureaucracy.

There is no originality in this system. As it exists to-day, so has it existed, in different degrees and values, throughout the ages and throughout the countries of Europe. The principles of the conduct of war seldom vary.

Civilisation has now arrived at a stage when new and constructive leaders are imperative to its salvation. These leaders must discard the traditional acceptance of war as an unavoidable evil and no longer tolerate its negative and destructive principles. They must determine upon the declaration of a policy of universal peace and boldly insist upon a rigid adherence to this policy. They need have no fear of support, for the peoples of all nations of the world will be behind them.

It is stupid mediævalism to advance the argument so frequently expressed that " there must be wars." Intelligence demands logical reason and justification.

Man is not instinctively warlike ; it is doubtful whether he was, even in his primitive state, except for the safeguarding and provision of his physical welfare. Therefore, since man as an individual—whether he be English, Irish, French, German, Russian, American, or Japanese—is not instinctively inclined to kill his fellow-being, who is responsible for fostering the war myth ? The responsibility rests with the various government cliques, and must be accepted by them.

We must concede to the individual the right to his own opinions. If the reason for war is the warlike views of the members of a government clique, they are entitled to those views. But in justice to themselves they should be afforded the opportunity of personal demonstration, and not be deprived by administrative duties of the privilege of displaying their physical valour. The member of each Parliament and the minister of each State should be elected with a peace-abiding deputy who, in time of war, can carry on affairs at home, while the fighting politician takes his rightful place in the forefront of battle.

A critical study of the history of wars is an illuminating education. To arrive at judgment the study must be made without regard for the transparent decoration of glory with which historians, in their insular patriotism, are inclined to paint the picture. It is necessary to study the cause of each war and the effect. Apply this analysis to any war and the discovery is that the cause is always painfully flimsy and the effect tragically futile.

Wars have benefited no people and no empire. They have thwarted progress, killed prosperity, and degraded civilisation. Military victory has no value, for military victory is ephemeral, and the balance of power is a perennial will-of-the-wisp, ever shedding the germs of destruction.

War has been the plague of the world, and it has been deliberately imposed by the few to gratify their misguided megalomania or their material brigandage.

The doctrine of war has always been disguised in the subtle garb of defensive preparation ; and the mask of security, when torn aside, displays the grinning teeth of aggression.

If man accepts war as inevitable and displays his weakness he deserves serfdom. If he wills it to cease a new world is within his grasp. If he achieves this by his spirit it will be better for his individual development than learning it by economic pressure.

When international problems are solved by the negation of wars—which will automatically happen before the end of the twentieth century whether there is another and greater world-war or not—it will be necessary to evolve a new system of internal government. *Wars will cease because—although the world does not appear to be awake to the fact as yet—the involved system of our comparatively new commercialised civilisation has already proved the impossibility of its survival if a war policy is adhered to.*

The simple lesson economists have learnt is that

war does not pay, and that it leads to commercial and financial collapse.

In this prognostication that wars will cease there is no suggestion of sentimentalism or trimming of illusive idealism ; it is cold, hard logic. War, and its inspiration, *will cease from sheer necessity*. Our modern civilisation will not collapse, because it possesses an instinctive power of resistance, and the policy of destruction will be discarded from a world-wide realisation of its futility.

With this discovery man will arrive at a stage of advanced simplicity, which he will demand to be applied to internal government.

Peoples must accept a form of government for the administration of accepted laws and orders. But the few simple laws that are necessary must not restrict individual liberty or national or international development. And the administration can be run generously at an infinitesimal minimum, instead of, as now, at a paralysing maximum.

The current problem with which Britain is faced is a National Debt which has arisen through parasitical extravagance to a figure which has no longer any meaning. The figure is neither conceivable nor realisable. In the endeavour to realise the noughts, the nation is in danger of becoming naught. This is the problem of every power. If the millstone of debt is attached to the feet of Europe—and Europe is still the nucleus of the civilised world—of what use is it clinging to straws ? The burden should be cut loose and the peoples be left free to swim.

The various governments have wrapped up their war finances in an illusion of noughts as an offset, perhaps, to the reality of millions of crosses. During the war they squandered on credit. On borrowed capital Britain alone spent the equivalent of forty years of pre-war revenue. But credit when clothing a figure beyond realisation becomes a myth ; at a breath its garment is blown away and nothing remains.

To maintain this illusive thing called credit, the whole world—not two or three nations—must stand together and agree to accept it as a reality on a practical basis. Unless this is agreed to in the near future, the modern civilisation of finance may crumple.

There is no evading the problem.

Drastic measures are necessary. National finance should be conducted in precisely the same way as business finance. If a business is handicapped by huge debts it cannot prosper until those debts are redeemed, depreciated, or cancelled.

Identical as the principles of national finance and business finance should be, there is at present a fundamental difference in the methods of control; a business is compelled to exercise efficiency and economy or financial supplies automatically cease, whilst a government, practising neither, annexes the power to draw upon the entire resources of the nation to pursue a negative policy of prodigal extravagance, with an utter disregard for the liabilities or for consequences.

What is the position to-day?

The British national debt is ten times greater than ever before, and the interest on the debt alone is nearly double that of the entire pre-war revenue. There will be no progress for the nation until this crushing debt is liquidated. It would be wise to realise this fact at once and to seek the best means of financial reconstruction.

There is another important factor to be considered. In the present complicated and perilous condition of the finances of the European governments, there is sufficient motive for a dozen new wars.

The present disastrous position must be faced with determination, and the realities and impossibilities must be coldly estimated. With firm handling there is the possibility of redemption, and the road to the recovery of national and international prosperity will then be in sight.

Man should view with supreme contempt the miserable achievements of the past, and determine finally to free himself from the legacies of blood and hate imposed upon him.

Procrastination is the perennial fashion of all incompetent rulers; but the day for procrastination is past. The blatant lie that the war was for posterity has now contemptibly resolved itself into the shelving of the liabilities on to the shoulders of posterity.

It is possible, however, that posterity may repudiate this unfortunate inheritance and claim the right to escape.

But for the debts of the various governments of the world, prosperity would now be universal. These debts should be liquidated. A mutually agreed cancellation of Allied loans should be the first step. Then it would be possible for all countries to agree internally to liquidate their entire national debts within twenty years by writing them down five per cent each year during that period, and paying a proportionately decreasing interest. This would avoid immediate financial chaos and give the necessary time for individual and national reconstruction. Drastic as the suggestion may appear, it is infinitely better than the prospect of the producers of the world being faced with the crushing burden of a perpetual income tax of from six shillings to sixteen shillings in the pound.

The inevitable result of excessive taxation is the paralysis of all commercial development and the consequent creation of national poverty and widespread unemployment.

There is no justifiable reason why a nation should ever be in debt, and the producers are to blame for their apathy in not controlling governmental finance.

When the nations become free from debts, the electors of each country should demand that the administration be controlled with rigid economy. The administrators are the non-producing class, and their expenditure has first to be earned by the producers. Bureaucracy is essentially non-productive and parasitical, and should therefore be reduced to an irreducible minimum. If bureaucracy is permitted to grow to a bureaucratic maximum, national insolvency is automatic.

Governments should be compelled to balance their

accounts year by year, and if they prove the efficiency by a credit balance they should be accorded the fruits of further office. If, by their administration, they show a debit balance, they should be held liable to impeachment.

With the liquidation of national debts, which are the evidence of scandalous and inefficient administration in the past, it should be possible to run any country on a maximum income tax of sixpence in the pound. This suggests a material millennium, but it is a practical possibility.

In government, commerce no longer requires intricate laws and devitalising restrictions. The greater the freedom, the greater the trade and the universal prosperity. All that commerce requires from government is an administration which will undertake to flush the drains of the country and regulate its traffic. It requires no interference or imposed subjection of workers, which under the label of discipline crushes the will to productivity.

The development of civilisation has been stupidly thwarted for centuries by the futile insularity and fear of the rulers. The time has arrived for a new orientation. In the past, governments have ruled by the retrogressive principles of restriction and obstruction.

The amazing fact of history is that when politics stagnate, commerce and prosperity progress.

It is healthy to regard all that has passed with a virile scorn, so that one may be free to arrive at a constructive opinion.

Despite the perilous position in which the world appears to be to-day, in the broader vision it is merely a passing phase. Commerce and industry, internal and international, are in their infancy. The evolution of the steam-engine was only a century ago, and machinery has revolutionised progress. The present condition of commerce is due to war. Commerce may be likened to an industrial Phœnix, which, having consumed itself in a world conflagration, is already arising from its ashes—a new and greater force to control the world.

The twentieth century will witness the greatest era of commercial development that civilisation is capable of imagining. Nothing can retard it, not even the puny and limited iniquities of attempted government. It is the scientific age—handicapped perhaps for a decade by the ruthless annihilation of one generation of splendid creators, but soon to be replaced by another. Science is bound to revolt from its application to destruction and thirst to apply itself to construction.

Commerce will rule as the supreme material force and as the only means by which the populations can be adequately and generously provided for.

There is no danger from the sordid level of the doctrine of Socialism, which would merely entail an impoverished chaos. Who but the clod desires a level ? Those who possess intellect seek to climb the heights. Socialism is the negation of individual advancement. The world has suffered sufficiently from a surfeit of vulgarity, and anxiously awaits a new progressive culture.

The development of commerce is essential to the modern needs of the world. The arts are even now dependent upon it, and it was mere evidence of a snobbish senility for one of our cynical playwrights publicly to deride commerce, whilst he displayed an acute, commercial regard for his royalties and was excessively annoyed when the longitude of his witticism was reflected in a heart-breaking brevity of run.

The world will soon welcome not only new leaders but new valuations. It will be merely amused by affectations and will judge by effects. Therefore the only value to be discovered, in an analytical study of the " great ones " of the past, is the illuminating record of their pitiable achievements.

In our judgment of men coldness is a virtue, in our appreciation of women coldness is a vice.

Stripped of the lying historical glamour surrounding their memories, what legacy of value have the so-called great men of the past left us ? Excluding the artists and the scientists, who allowed their genius to be misapplied, they have left us simply nothing.

Who, then, is there living to-day ? There are a few fine artists, lazily enjoying life, and cynically refusing to interfere with the scheme ; but beyond these few, what man of outstanding force can be accepted ? There exists one man who may challenge comparison on his achievements. If the writer were asked to name the greatest material bene-factor in the history of the world he would distend his nostrils at the mention of Napoleon and all of his type, and acclaim the living man in Henry Ford. Ford has done more for the world than all the military conquerors of two thousand years. His tens of thousands of employees are the highest paid of mechanics. He enables them to live in comfort and by his organising genius he has established the most wonderful production of modern times. One symbolic gesture he made which certainly astonished the world. Realising the futility of armaments and loathing the sordid materialistic spirit of war, he offered to buy the French Fleet. It was a gesture of significance.

The spirit of Henry Ford is the forerunner of the new spirit of progress and commerce, and it will inevitably lead the material world. It hoists the banner of Production and prophetically calls for the surrender of the lying colours of Destruction. In paying this material tribute to Ford, it does not follow that one concedes to him any acceptance what-ever of his philosophy, influence, or intellectuality in other spheres.

Despite the existing chaos of Europe the world is plunging ahead.

Progress surmounts all obstacles, and the decadent old minds soon find their graves. The material advancement of commerce during this twentieth century is certain. In the phenomenal development which will take place when the force of the new generation exhibits itself, art, in its modern subtlety and contemptuous of antics, will ally itself with progress and decorate commercial materialism.

Woman, in her newly-acquired freedom, will proclaim her force in a new and potent guise. She will cultivate and inspire original arts, and in their usage she will stimulate a fresh illusion.

The dominoes of the masquerade of politics will be torn aside in the near future and the ugly form revealed, but illusion will persist throughout all time in the alluring form of woman, with her more cleverly designed and eternal masquerade.

This is the first century in the history of the world during which we have learnt to fly. The few men and women who have discovered how to soar aloft, both physically and mentally, must show the way to live and enjoy.

Then, in a while, the fearless laughter of the wise will enlighten the Stygian minds of the fools, and in the race for the enjoyment of life the devil will be welcome to the hindermost.

INDEX

CREATION

THE THOUGHT

All the most beautiful things in life are inarticulate.

The most wonderful books remain unwritten. The most wonderful plays remain unspoken. The most wonderful dreams remain uncaptured.

What is the reason for this delicate silence ?

Should the true artist waste the golden hours of life on the writing of a word, whilst in possession of the youth which enables him to love and to live ? Should the energy of the fine emotions be prostituted to a pen, whilst the arms are yearning to capture some real creation ?

*   *   *   *

A NOTE

Mr. H. Dennis Bradley is as daring and searching in this book as he was in " The Eternal Masquerade." Since the publication of that notable work he seems to have found in the world many more images, which he makes haste to break ; and such is his hurry that he has no time for frothy eloquence or fanciful thoughts, or foolish jests : he says what he has to say baldly and with no regard for the squeamish. Nor does he speak in allegories or riddles. The allegory is the veil with which images are covered, and the riddles he has already unravelled and he is sure that his answers are correct : why should he pause to explain this or expound that ?

Maybe he sat for years in his room near the sky, his eyes, like God's, on the street below ; and the voice of God came to him, firing him with the command : " Tell the House of Israel of their sins, and the House of Jacob of their transgressions."

This he does and with amazing courage and impudence—the courage and impudence that are conceived in belief. No prophet has bade people turn from their naughty ways with more scorn than that which Dennis Bradley lashes cant, humbug, and civilisation, and no Solomon has spoken more profoundly about woman. His worst enemy is the politician, who, he declares, is the seed of unhappiness. Unique in his day, he does not fight with his enemy's weapon, for all such battles end with compromise ; that is why he compels one to read him ; that is why he triumphs ; that is why his work is rare in our literature.

Bradley hates more than he loves, and again like Solomon, he seeks his loves among the roses and his enemies among the thorns. " I want to live wonderfully," he says somewhere in this book. But there are so many things that stop him from doing so : theatre managers, actors and comedians and play-goers, starch, bad hotels, politicians and their parties. He deplores the low wage of genius and the high price of the worthless. He calls for new measures and manners and he knows how to reach them if the politicians

A NOTE

of Europe would go to sleep. Truly he sits in judgment, but his judgments are never loose or ill-conceived, not even when he strips a beautiful woman.

Here is surely a man of letters, but his place in literature is difficult to define. His observations are as unlike any living writer as are those of Horatio Bottomley and Mr. D. Lloyd George unlike Mr. Asquith and Mr. Ramsay MacDonald.

Speaking of him in " Papers from Lilliput," Mr. J. B. Priestley says : " If Mr. Bradley is not at heart a man of letters, then I do not know the breed. . . . Being an original, Mr. Dennis Bradley cannot be fitted into any of our little pigeon-holes ; he is not easily labelled."

An amazing and an entrancing work !

Caradoc Evans

of Europe would go to sleep. Truly he sits in judgment, but his judgments are never loose or ill-conceived, not even when he strips a beautiful woman.

Here is surely a man of letters, but his place in literature is difficult to define. His observations are as unlike any living writer as are those of Horatio Bottomley and Mr. D. Lloyd George unlike Mr. Asquith and Mr. Ramsay MacDonald.

Speaking of him in "Papers from Lilliput," Mr. J. B. Priestley says: " If Mr. Bradley is not at heart a man of letters, then I do not know the breed. . . . Being an original, Mr. Dennis Bradley cannot be fitted into any of our little pigeon-holes ; he is not easily labelled."

An amazing and an entrancing work !

CARADOC EVANS

CONTENTS

CONTENTS